Seductive Mirage

Seductive Mirage

An Exploration of the Work
of Sigmund Freud

Allen Esterson

Open Court

Chicago and La Salle, Illinois

OPEN COURT and the above logo are registered in the U.S.
Patent and Trademark Office.

Printed and bound in the United States of America.

Library of Congress Cataloging-in-Publication Data

Esterson, Allen, 1936–
    Seductive mirage : an exploration of the work of Sigmund
Freud / by Allen Esterson.
       p.   cm.
    Includes bibliographical references and index.
    ISBN 0-8126-9230-6. — ISBN 0-8126-9231-4 (pbk.)
    1. Freud, Sigmund, 1856–1939. 2. Psychoanalysis—History.
    3. Seduction—Psychological aspects—History.   I. Title.
BF109.F74E78   1993
150.19′52′092—dc20   93–994
                                                  CIP

Contents

✧ ✧ ✧ ✧ ✧ ✧ ✧ ✧ ✧ ✧ ✧

Acknowledgements

A number of scholars were kind enough to comment on papers I sent to them based on material in this book. Of these Paul Roazen and Edward Erwin were particularly generous in giving their valuable time to correspondence arising from their responses, and Richard Stevens undertook to read through a late draft of the whole book. I am especially grateful to Peter Swales not only for sending me most of the papers he has written in relation to Sigmund Freud but also for apprising me of numerous articles and newspaper clippings concerning items about which I would otherwise have remained in ignorance. Special mention must be made of Frank Cioffi, who kindly read through and commented on some papers based on chapters in the book and gave invaluable advice in regard to the final draft. My thanks are also due to Lystra Riches for meticulously reading through and commenting on the very first draft of the book and for miscellaneous advice on the finer points of grammar. Finally, my thanks go to Yvonne Gee for generously volunteering to assist with the laborious task of proof-reading.

I am grateful to David Ramsay Steele and Edward Roberts at Open Court for their contributions to the final product. Naturally, any errors of fact or other deficiencies in this book are entirely my own responsibility.

Grateful acknowledgement is made to the following for permission to reprint previously published material:

Sigmund Freud Copyrights, The Institute of Psycho-Analysis and the Hogarth Press: excerpts from *The Standard Edition of the Complete Psychological Works of Sigmund Freud,* translated and edited by James Strachey.

Allen and Unwin (Unwin Hyman and HarperCollins): excerpts from *The Interpretation of Dreams, Part 1,* by Sigmund Freud, translated and edited by James Strachey.

W. W. Norton and Company, Inc. : excerpts from: *The Psychopathology of Everyday Life* by Sigmund Freud. Translated by Alan Tyson. Edited by James Strachey. Editorial matter Copyright © 1965, 1960 by James Strachey. Translation Copyright © 1960 by Alan Tyson. (USA and Canada); *Beyond the Pleasure Principle* by Sigmund Freud. Translated and Edited by James Strachey. Copy-

Introduction

To mention the name of Sigmund Freud is at once to conjure up a host of associations. He is widely regarded as a giant of twentieth-century thought who has made a unique contribution to our understanding of ourselves and society, exerting an inestimable influence on the arts and humanities as well as on psychotherapy and its related disciplines. The controversies which have always surrounded his theories have scarcely diminished his perceived stature; fifty years after his death his significance is thought by many to be on a par with that of Charles Darwin. What this book sets out to do is to lay before the reader evidence that this view of the value of Freud's contribution is profoundly mistaken. Far from his having significantly extended our knowledge, there are substantial grounds for maintaining that the body of alleged findings that forms the basis for his theories is largely an artefact of the analytic procedure which he invented and which he mistakenly believed to be a means of deriving reliable information about the hidden workings of the mind. This view of his work is, of course, not new; from the beginning of psychoanalysis many critics have argued in similar terms without appreciably diminishing Freud's influence. However, in recent years, thanks to the researches of a number of scholars, material has been accumulating which throws a fresh light on the early history of psychoanalysis and enables a clearer idea of its development to be formulated. The works of Henri Ellenberger [1970] and Frank Sulloway [1979] in particular are rich sources of factual information which provide much of the bedrock upon which a re-evaluation of Freud's life and work can be founded; and more recently Malcolm Macmillan [1991] has published a painstakingly scholarly and remarkably wide-ranging historically-based critique of Freud's theoretical framework which will remain an invaluable sourcebook for many years to come. This present work, though by no means a comprehensive overview of the whole of his vast output, is intended to be a contribution to the reassessment currently under way.

While Freud's theories have always been subjected to trenchant criticism, this is not the case with respect to his personal reputation. Largely on the basis of the impression conveyed in his own writings and in those of his first biographer, Ernest Jones, the received view of Freud's character, with very few dissenters, has always been that he was a man of absolute integrity. Ellenberger and Sulloway have now documented evidence that Freud's accounts of the early history of psychoanalysis are often gross distortions, and at times the complete opposite of the truth, but for the most part these aberrations seem to have been treated as little more than unfortunate lapses of memory. A different view is taken by Frederick Crews, who observes that the field of Freud biography, with few exceptions, "has been dominated by writers who follow Ernest Jones in taking Freud's scientific greatness and healing power as given, and who therefore swallow virtually everything that Freud himself asserted about his empirical scruples and his heroic originality. Yet when one looks at the record without such presuppositions, a very different picture begins to take shape". On the basis of that record, augmented by recent scholarship, he concludes that "Freud's greatest creation was not a scientific discovery but a seductive work of art, namely, the story he devised about a mythic Sigismund who had returned from the frightening psychic underworld with precious gifts for human-kind". Noting the words of Frank Cioffi concerning the difficulty commentators have in endeavouring "to stand upright in the presence of the Freud legend", Crews asserts that the latter's "psychoanalytic career was both launched and maintained by systematic mendacity", and urges that "it is time . . . to understand the necessary relation between Freud's cavalier ethics and the scientific failings of his movement". [Crews 1986 : 44, 100–02]

Of course there are many who vigorously dispute views such as these, and the impugning of Freud's honesty is, to say the least, highly contentious. In the following pages evidence will be presented that provides support for Crews's assertion that Freud did not always maintain the highest ethical standards, but the question of his probity, while not unimportant, is essentially peripheral to the main argument. More significant than his lapses in this regard is his propensity for self-deception. This is especially so with respect to the events pertaining to the infantile seduction theory, an episode, it is universally agreed, whose consequences had a crucial effect on the development of psychoanalysis. What will be demonstrated in chapter 2 is that the claims made in the original seduction theory papers were based, for the most part, on preconceived inference rather than direct clinical observation; that Freud could only have convinced himself of the clinical justification for these claims by a considerable degree of self-deception; and that subsequently, as his explanations of the supposed clinical material evolved with his changing theoretical postulates, his story could only be maintained by dishonest manoeuvres and blatantly false statements. Further-more, as the development of his ideas is traced in succeeding chapters it will be shown that the misrepresentation of tendentious analytic inference as clinical fact became standard practice and that this feature of his research procedure undermines most of his theoretical claims.

That a single theme on these lines informs much of the critique in the forthcoming pages no doubt leaves the book open to the charge that it is insufficiently comprehensive, and certainly the view of Freud and his theories which emerges in the course of this enquiry is predominantly negative. However, while it cannot be claimed that every aspect of his wide-ranging writings is invalidated by the crucial flaw in his investigative procedure, the case presented in this book suffices of itself to invite the conclusion that his perceived stature rests on a remarkably insubstantial basis.

We shall open that case with a brief sketch of Freud's early professional life, directing particular attention to those aspects of it which pertain to the all-important seduction theory that was to set him on the path to worldwide fame.

CHAPTER ONE

Prelude

Sigmund Freud was born in 1856, the first of eight children (one of whom died in infancy). His father, who already had two grown-up sons by a previous marriage, was some twenty years older than his mother, for whom Sigmund seems to have been the especial favourite from among her offspring. Regarded from the beginning as being marked out for success, he gave early signs that he would live up to expectations and was consistently top in his class at secondary school. He enrolled in the Medical Department at the University of Vienna in 1873, studying a wide variety of subjects before taking his medical degree eight years later. In 1881 he was appointed Demonstrator in the Institute of Physiology, where he had already been working for some time. However, the following year he became engaged to Martha Bernays and sought a post promising greater financial remuneration so that he might as soon as possible be in a position to marry his fiancée (an ambition not achieved until 1886). To this end he entered the Vienna General Hospital as a clinical assistant, working in several departments before moving to the Department of Nervous Diseases in 1884.

Around this time, impatient to make his reputation, he began an investigation of the therapeutic properties of the then little-known alkaloid cocaine after reading a German Army doctor's report of its power to enhance endurance. In the event, this project, which gave rise to a number of papers between 1884 and 1887, failed to live up to his high hopes, though it subsequently played a significant role in the development of his view of the physiological basis of neuroses.

Freud's conviction that he would one day be famous is displayed in a remarkable letter he wrote to his fiancée in April 1885, in which he informed her that he had destroyed all his notes of the previous fourteen years, as well as letters and scientific manuscripts. The reason, he explained, was that he wanted to frustrate his future biographers, and he was already looking forward to seeing them go astray. [Clark 1980: 63] In the meantime he achieved his more limited aim of acquiring a prestigious university lectureship (in Neuropathology), but before taking up the post he was awarded a travel scholarship which enabled him, at the age of 29, to go to Paris in 1885 to study at the Salpêtrière hospital for nervous

1

diseases, under the supervision of the celebrated Jean-Martin Charcot. It was there that his interest in hysteria (an illness presenting
somatic symptoms having no apparent organic cause) was aroused.
Charcot worked with patients subject to convulsions, and later
investigated hysterical paralyses, demonstrating that non-organic
paralyses could be induced with the use of hypnosis. However, this
aspect of his work fell into disrepute after his death in 1893,
especially when it became clear that he was the victim of deliberate
deception by some of his patients.

Charcot's demonstrations at the Salpêtrière made a great impression on Freud, and following his return from Paris he utilised
the opportunity afforded by the opening of his own private practice
in Vienna in the spring of 1886 to pursue his interest in hysteria and
hypnosis. Though he published a number of well-received papers
on neuroanatomical topics in the next few years, it was to the subject of neurotic disorders that he increasingly turned his mind. The
future course of his ideas in this regard was crucially influenced by
his friendship with Josef Breuer, a gifted and highly respected physician many years his senior, with whom he had become acquainted
several years earlier.

Anna O. and *Studies on Hysteria*

Between 1880 and 1882 Breuer had devoted extensive periods of
time to treating a patient (later referred to as "Anna O.") for a
remarkable variety of severe symptoms, including hallucinations,
speech disturbances, intermittent paralyses, and visual problems.
During the various stages of her complex illness the patient experienced two different states of consciousness, and was subject to
extended periods of spontaneous somnambulism. Breuer found
that in the latter state she would, with encouragement, narrate
imaginative stories, after which her condition temporarily improved. Following the death of her father, whom she had been
nursing when her first symptoms appeared, her condition deteriorated, and she suffered distressing hallucinatory and anxiety
states. Breuer observed that she obtained some relief from these
symptoms if she could be persuaded to talk about her hallucinations during her auto-hypnoses. This process she described as her
"talking cure" or "chimney-sweeping". (At this stage she spoke in
English, as she had lost the ability to communicate in her own
language.) A chance occurrence led to the final stage of the
treatment. The patient started to talk about the incident which

marked the onset of one particular symptom which had recently developed (a considerable difficulty in swallowing), and following the verbal utterance the symptom disappeared. After a considerable expenditure of time and effort, Breuer eventually discovered that if she was induced to recall in reverse chronological order each past occurrence of specific symptoms until she reached the first occasion on which they had occurred, he was able to achieve remission of most of them the same way. A description of the case and of his procedure was provided by Breuer in *Studies on Hysteria,* which he published jointly with Freud in 1895.[1] [S.E. 2: 21–47]

The verbal reports he received from Breuer in regard to this case were eventually to have a considerable influence on Freud's therapeutic procedure when he came to deal with patients of his own some years later. However, in his first years of private practice as a neurologist he tended to use traditional methods of treatment, such as electrotherapy, massage, and hydrotherapy, soon augmented by hypnosis. The use of direct hypnotic suggestion to remove symptoms was pioneered by Bernheim, whose demonstrations at Nancy were studied firsthand by Freud in 1889. (He also translated two of Bernheim's books into German.) Within a short time Delboeuf, Janet, and Freud each took Bernheim's procedure a stage further by first inducing patients to recall the precipitating cause of a symptom or state of distress before using hypnotic suggestion to erase it.

As he reports in *Studies on Hysteria,* during the early 1890s Freud began to seek means of locating symptom-inducing memories which would enable him to discard the use of hypnosis. When he had difficulty in inducing hypnosis in particular patients, he resorted to a method he derived from Bernheim. He started off by asking patients if they remembered what had originally occasioned the symptom in question. If they were unable to recall anything specific, he would insist they did know, and tell them to lie down,

---

[1]Although the impression is given in *Studies* that the case demonstrated a successful treatment of hysteria, Ellenberger has traced Breuer's original case notes and documents pertaining to Anna O.'s subsequent experience in a sanatorium, which show that the patient was by no means cured of her illness under Breuer's treatment. [Ellenberger: 1972] Moreover, it is not known with any degree of certainty what the precise nature of the illness was, albeit it was diagnosed as hysteria.

Malcolm Macmillan has drawn attention to the fact that although it appears from the report in *Studies* that Anna O.'s remission of symptoms occurred following emotionally expressive recall of past events, this does not find support in the original case notes. In the latter are to be found descriptions of *verbal* utterance; the stress on emotional expression or discharge was retrospectively added.

close their eyes, and concentrate. When stronger means were necessary, he exerted a pressure on the forehead, having previously
assured the patients that this would induce the occurrence of a
picture or idea, and asked them what came to their mind. In this
way he was able to set in motion a chain of associations which he
hoped would lead to the pathogenic idea he was searching for, or,
as generally was the case, at least point to the direction for further
investigation. He believed that the associations generated by this
procedure were strictly internally determined and therefore uninfluenced by his own ideas and expectations. Hence it could safely
be inferred that appropriate incidents or ideas which emerged as a
result of the procedure played a significant role in the formation of
the symptom under investigation.

From the patients' communications Freud strove to infer the
event or situation which was responsible for the genesis of the
symptoms, and from his analysis of the patients' associations to
construct coherent narratives to explain the subsequent course of
the illness. In the process he might well have had to propose (and
even insist on) the existence of conjectured unconscious ideas or
motives to fill in "lacunas" in the patients' accounts. By 1895 his
therapeutic technique had also increasingly turned to actively
encouraging the patients to talk about the relevant events or
circumstances with the aim of getting them to "abreact" the
"excitation" which had accumulated.[2]

Because of the efforts he had to exert when using the pressure
technique, particularly in regard to the necessity for insistence, it
seemed to Freud that he had to overcome a "psychical force" in the
patient which was opposed to the supposed pathogenic ideas becoming conscious. He went on to postulate that this same psychical
force had played a part in the generating of the hysterical symptom
and had at the time prevented the pathogenic idea from becoming
conscious. On this view, the patient's ego was defending itself

---

[2]It is not always clear whether abreaction *necessarily* involves expression with
affect. In the last of the cases reported in *Studies,* that of "Elizabeth von R.",
Freud explains that, having discovered to his satisfaction the main unconscious
idea which caused the patient's symptoms, he wanted her to abreact it. He goes on
to recount how the final stage of her treatment involved her going over with him
verbally all her recollections of events possibly related to the idea. But though he
writes that "this process of abreaction certainly did her much good" [S.E. 2: 158],
nowhere in the account is there the least indication of emotional expression or
discharge by the patient (in contrast to an earlier case, in regard to which his
description of a verbal utterance involving abreaction includes violent agitation
with accompanying affect).

against a distressing idea, and Freud writes that he already had definite opinions on the nature of such ideas.

From the theoretical section that he contributed to *Studies* we learn that Breuer believed that hysterical symptoms may derive from unconscious ideas, the latter frequently originating from distressing events, sometimes occurring in childhood. Such psychical traumas might be sexual in nature, but he did not regard this as necessarily so in all cases. However, Freud, later described by Breuer as "a man given to absolute and exclusive formulations", became convinced that adverse sexual experiences lay at the root of *all* cases of hysterical illness, and of neurasthenia and obsessional neurosis as well. This conviction laid the basis for much of his future theorising.

The Fliess Correspondence and Emma Eckstein

The evolution of Freud's theoretical ideas during the 1890s can be traced through the prolific correspondence he engaged in with Wilhelm Fliess, a Berlin nose and throat specialist whom he had met in 1887.[3] Fliess became his closest friend and confidant, soon displacing Breuer in this regard. Freud's letters to Fliess bear witness to the immense amount of time and energy he devoted to the task of unravelling the causes of the neuroses. Throughout the period of their friendship, before they became estranged at the end of the decade, the two men exchanged ideas, Fliess himself being a fertile source of hypotheses in his own right. Though few of these have stood the test of time, Freud held a very high opinion of his abilities, and, as Sulloway has demonstrated, was considerably influenced by his theories. One of Fliess's postulates that Freud was later to utilise extensively is that of universal bisexuality. Another which he endorsed for a period involved a supposed relation between the nose and a number of physical disorders. Though no longer of interest, this latter idea played a crucial role in a case of Freud's which is worth examining in some detail because of the way

---

[3]In the 1930s Freud attempted to retrieve his letters to Fliess with a view to destroying them, as he had done with many of his documents on at least two previous occasions. A disciple, Princess Marie Bonaparte, had bought them from a Berlin bookseller, and Freud attempted to acquire them from her. In a letter dated 3rd January 1937 he told her: "I don't want any of them to become known to so-called posterity." [Schur 1972: 487] Fortunately she resisted his appeals. Fliess's letters to Freud have not survived, presumably because Freud destroyed them.

it illustrates his use of another concept which he had come to espouse, that of symptoms having a meaning (an idea utilised extensively in *Studies on Hysteria*). The patient in question was Emma Eckstein, a young woman whom Freud started treating in 1894. The exact nature of her complaints is not known, but it seems they included stomach ailments and menstrual problems.

Fliess believed that he had discovered that a wide variety of symptoms, including disturbances of sexual function, were related to a specific spot in the nose,[4] and he treated such cases of "nasal reflex neurosis" by the application of cocaine to nasal mucous membranes and by surgical procedures on the turbinate bone. Freud reported to Fliess, in a letter dated 30 May 1893, that he found the nasal reflex neurosis to be one of the commonest disorders, and he made reference to the same syndrome in relation to the "Dora" case of 1900: "It is well known that gastric pains occur especially often in those who masturbate. According to a personal communication made to me by Wilhelm Fliess, it is precisely gastralgias of this character which can be interrupted by an application of cocaine to the 'gastric spot' discovered by him in the nose, and which can be cured by the cauterisation of the same spot."[5] [S.E. 7: 78] He had presumably made a similar diagnosis in the case of Emma Eckstein, for following a consultation with Fliess it was agreed that the latter should perform an operation on her nose in February 1895.

The course of her post-operative condition over the following months is recorded in Freud's letters to Fliess. In March she suffered several severe haemorrhages, coming close to death on two occasions, and Freud had to enlist the urgent assistance of several consultants. One of these discovered that half a metre of gauze had been left in the cavity resulting from the operation, and a second operation had to be performed to repair the damage caused by the first. The patient continued in a serious condition until the end of April. [Masson 1985: 115–16, 120–21, 122, 125, 128, 130]

---

[4]In 1897 Fliess published a monograph on "The Relationship between the Nose and the Female Sexual Organs".

[5]E. M. Thornton has pointed out that "the application of cocaine to mucous membranes, such as those inside the nose, results in extremely speedy absorption. Entering the bloodstream the drug reaches the brain rapidly and practically unchanged. The effects Fliess attributed to reflex action were thus, in reality, those of the action of cocaine on the brain. The dramatic amelioration of the pains of such conditions as dysmenorrhoea [painful menstruation] or migraine by nasal applications of cocaine resulted from the action of the drug on specific brain centres and had no connection with the nose itself." [Thornton 1983: 161]

Freud continued to treat Eckstein for almost two more years, but her name is not mentioned again in his letters for some considerable time. Then in April 1896 he informed Fliess that he had arrived at "a completely surprising explanation of Eckstein's haemorrhages—which will give you much pleasure": "I shall be able to prove to you that you were right, that her episodes of bleeding were hysterical, were occasioned by *longing,* and probably occurred at the sexually relevant times (the woman, out of resistance, has not yet supplied me with the dates)." (This presumably relates to Fliess's theory that symptoms of the nasal reflex neuroses and other disorders including nasal bleeding manifest a periodicity corresponding to that of the female sexual cycle.) In his next letter (4 May) he reiterates that "she bled out of *longing*", and explains that "she described a scene from the age of fifteen, in which she suddenly began to bleed from the nose when she had the wish to be treated by a certain young doctor who was present (and who also appeared in the dream)". When she saw how affected Freud had been at the time of her second major haemorrhage (reported 8 May 1895), "she experienced this as the realisation of an old wish to be loved in her illness, and in spite of the danger during the succeeding hours she felt happy as never before". Then, in the sanatorium to which she had been taken, "because of an unconscious wish to entice [Freud] to go there . . . she renewed the bleedings, as an unfailing means of rearousing [his] affection". He gives more information on 4 June: "Her story is becoming even clearer; there is no doubt that her haemorrhages were due to wishes; she has had several similar incidents, among them actual simulations, in her childhood." [181, 183, 186, 191–92]

It is clear that in his anxiety to exonerate his friend of the responsibility for nearly causing Eckstein's death, notwithstanding the botched (and unnecessary) operation, Freud had come to believe that her haemorrhages were hysterical. He attempts to support this conclusion by asserting that "she bled spontaneously three times and each bleeding lasted for four days, which must mean something". But since the wound was packed to stop the bleeding after each haemorrhage, it is difficult to see how he could possibly have ascertained that each one lasted four days. [117, 121, 124] Equally doubtful is his assertion concerning her state of mind after the second major haemorrhage, which followed the removal of the gauze that had been left in the cavity. At the time he had written that she had "turned white, her eyes bulged, and she had no pulse", and that afterwards she was "unrecognisable". [117] This seems unlikely to have been a prelude to a feeling of supreme happiness over the succeeding hours. It would also be of interest to know on what grounds he could confidently claim that she had simulated bleeding episodes in her childhood.

There are several points of interest regarding Freud's analysis of this case. The first is that it would seem to be an illustration of his predilection towards "absolute and exclusive" formulations, in this instance with respect to the notion that symptoms have a meaning. Increasingly he tended to utilise this idea in the extreme form that *all* somatic symptoms have a meaning. This is exemplified by the interpretation of migraine attacks he gave to Fliess in 1899: Hysterical headaches rest on an analogy in phantasy which equates the top with the bottom end of the body (hair in both places— cheeks and buttocks—lips and labia—mouth=vagina), so that an attack of migraine can be used to represent a forcible defloration, while nevertheless the whole ailment also represents a situation of wish-fulfilment.'[6] [340]

The second point of note is that having arrived at what he regards as a satisfactory interpretation, he proceeds to fashion the clinical material in such a way that it provides support for his thesis. One is left wondering whether something of the kind may have occurred in regard to any of the cases he describes in *Studies on Hysteria* for which we do not have any background information to enable us to assess his analyses. In fact Macmillan has pointed out that Freud's expectations were becoming a significant factor in his reconstructions of the events he considered to underlie the symptoms of some of the patients whose illnesses are described in that publication. In particular, in the case of "Elizabeth von R." Macmillan observes that "it is very evident that Freud used [his] assumptions to create a *plausible* account of the development of her symptoms rather than to re-create a *real* history, a plausibility achieved in part by disregarding observations conflicting with the assumptions. It is also evident in that case that he preferred the plausible reconstruction to the observable or ascertainable facts." In short, he was showing "a rather ominous preference for the plausible but theoretically neat over the factually uncomfortable".[7] [Macmillan 1991: 116–18]

From the perspective of subsequent developments, the final

---

[6]Another example comes in a letter he wrote to his colleague Karl Abraham in 1908 with regard to the convulsive fits of a young epileptic: "I observed one of his attacks myself, and it was uncommonly instructive, as it represented an act of coitus, or rather his rage at an act of coitus observed by him (obviously his parents'). His spitting is sperm-ejaculation." [Abraham and Freud 1965: 15]

[7]There is an odd discrepancy in Freud's reporting of this case. In a brief note

point is perhaps of particular interest. Freud's physician, Max Schur, has written a commentary on the Emma Eckstein episode in his paper "Some Additional 'Day Residues' of 'The Specimen Dream of Psychoanalysis'". With regard to the incident the patient describes from the age of fifteen in the letter of 4 May, he translates Freud's words as "She had [the image of] a scene . . .", which implies that it may have been something less than a definite memory. He notes that in two later letters alluding to Eckstein in which there are references to "scenes", Freud "clearly describes what he later called phantasies" (i.e., unconscious ideas), and adds that "this holds true for Emma's 'scenes'". [Schur 1966: 81, 83n] This interpretation of Freud's words, together with the unexplained reference to "the dream" in the 4 May letter, suggests that what he was describing may well have been at least partly his *reconstruction* of an event, made on the basis of the analytic technique he had already developed at that time. (As we shall see, "phantasies" in his later writings were almost invariably reconstructed in this manner.) This is of particular relevance as we move on to consider the momentous events occurring contemporaneously with the latter part of Eckstein's treatment.

---

about a patient clearly identified as Elizabeth von R. in a paper published in 1894, he refers to an episode involving "a young man who had made a slight erotic impression" on the girl. However, when the same episode is discussed in *Studies,* he writes of the "hopes" the girl attached to her relationship with the young man, that she "was firmly determined to wait for him", and of the "blissful frame of mind" she experienced in his company. (The patient was treated during 1892–93.) [S.E. 3: 48. S.E. 2: 145, 146]

CHAPTER TWO

The Infantile Seduction Theory

The story of how Freud's early clinical experience led him almost inadvertently to a discovery which was to revolutionise the development of psychoanalysis is well known and has been repeated, with slight variations, on a great many occasions. It runs as follows.

During the 1890s, when Freud was energetically searching for an explanation of the causes of the neuroses, many of his patients reported that they had been sexually abused in early childhood. Freud became convinced that in eliciting the accounts of infantile assaults he had indeed found what he was seeking, and announced the fact in a number of papers. However, he eventually came to realise that he had been deceived, and that in most cases the assaults had not actually occurred. This led to the revolutionary discovery that the events in question had been phantasised by his patients, and from this he developed the theory of infantile phantasies which became one of the cornerstones of classical psychoanalytic theory.[1]

The extent to which this version of events has become almost universally accepted can be seen from a random selection of accounts given by various commentators. According to Christopher Lasch, "Psychoanalysis came into being when Freud began to understand that his patients could not have been sexually assaulted by their parents with the frequency they reported; that is, when he began to understand these reports as a recurring fantasy." [Lasch (1984) 1985: 213n] Likewise, Marie Jahoda tells us that "Freud came to realise that what his patients had reported to him were memories not of actual events but of phantasies and early wishes". [Jahoda 1977: 28] More specifically, Juliet Mitchell writes that "Freud was stunned to hear women patients over and over again recount how, in their childhood, their fathers had seduced them", but he came to recognise that "the whole thing was a phantasy". [Mitchell (1974) 1975: 9] Similarly, in his 1988 biography Peter Gay states that "for a time [Freud] continued to accept as true his patients' lurid recitals" [of childhood seductions] until he realized

---

[1]The spelling "phantasy" will be used exclusively to denote an unconscious idea or image, as hypothesised by Freud. When the word "fantasy" is used it will be in the normal everyday sense of a *conscious* imaginative process.

that they had been "a collection of fairy tales [which] his patients had first told him". [Gay 1988: 94, 96]

Almost all writers on the subject have reported this episode in similar terms, for this is how Freud himself recounted it, as can be seen from the following quotations:

> One was readily inclined to accept as true . . . the statements made by patients in which they ascribed their symptoms to passive sexual experiences in the first years of childhood—to put it bluntly, to seduction. (*On the History of the Psychoanalytic Movement*, 1914) [S.E. 14:17]
>
> Under the influence of the technical procedure which I used at that time, the majority of my patients reproduced from their childhood scenes in which they were sexually seduced by some grown-up person. With female patients the part of the seducer was almost always assigned to their father. (*An Autobiographical Study*, 1925) [S.E. 20: 33–34]
>
> In the period in which the main interest was directed to discovering infantile sexual traumas, almost all my women patients told me that they had been seduced by their father. I was driven to recognise in the end that these reports were untrue and so came to understand that hysterical symptoms are derived from phantasies. . . . (*New Introductory Lectures*, 1933) [S.E. 22: 120]

However, in spite of the almost unanimous acceptance of this version of events, there are good grounds for believing it to be false.[2] In documenting the evidence in support of this assertion, we shall show that the propagation of the legend served two purposes for its originator. It enabled him to metamorphose clinical claims, which in their original form were open to serious doubts, in such a way that most of the objections were rendered irrelevant, and at the same time it provided clinical evidence for his theories of unconscious phantasies and the Oedipus complex.

---

[2]When Jeffrey Masson created a stir by arguing, in his book *The Assault on Truth* (1984), that Freud showed a failure of nerve by revising his claims and asserting that patients' reports of childhood seductions were mostly unconscious phantasies, of the reviewers, only Frank Cioffi appears to have pointed out that the supposed factual basis on which the controversy was played out was suspect. Cioffi had first challenged the accuracy of the traditional version of events in 1974 in a BBC radio talk entitled "Was Freud a Liar?", but his thesis was almost universally rejected or ignored. Since then Robert Steele [1982], E.M. Thornton [1983], and, in considerably more detail, Jean Schimek [1987] have published accounts at variance with the received view. Morton Schatzman [1992] notes that Isolde Vetter has also challenged the traditional account. The following pages, though written completely independently, cover much the same factual ground as Schimek, but go considerably further in revealing the full extent of Freud's self-deception and disingenuousness, and in exposing the degree to which his unsound procedures remained an inherent part of subsequent psychoanalytic practice.

In his *Five Lectures on Psychoanalysis*, delivered in the United
States in 1909, Freud claims that at the time of the joint publication
by himself and Breuer of *Studies on Hysteria* in 1895 he had neither
adopted nor postulated the view that "erotic disturbances" were
foremost among the causes of neurotic illness, and that he only
became converted to it when his experiences became more numerous and penetrated into the subject more deeply. [S.E. 11: 40] However, it is clear both from the book itself and from his correspondence with his friend Wilhelm Fliess prior to this time that this
statement is untrue.[3] By the early 1890s he had already gone beyond
Breuer's position that sexual factors play a role in many neurotic
illnesses. In a draft paper dated 8th February 1893, he postulated
that neurasthenia is always a sexual neurosis, and stated that he had
already argued in favour of a similar view with regard to hysteria.
From the correspondence with Fliess around this period it is
apparent that Freud was becoming increasingly convinced that his
postulate that adverse sexual experiences were a root cause of
neuroses was a fundamental discovery, and one which could make
his reputation. In the spring of 1893, with reference to a paper being
prepared by Fliess, he averred that to fail to mention the sexual
aetiology of the neuroses would be like "tearing the most beautiful
leaf out of the wreath". He urged his friend to "announce the
forthcoming investigations, describe the anticipated result as that
which it really is, as something new, show people the key that
unlocks everything, the aetiological formula". Achieving the anticipated result was not always easy, for as he tells Fliess in a letter of
7th February 1894 in relation to one of his cases, the connection
between obsessional neurosis and sexuality would have been overlooked by someone "who had not searched for it as single-mindedly
as I did". And on 21st May 1894 he wrote: "I have the distinct
feeling that I have touched upon one of the great secrets of nature."
[Masson 1985: 39–40, 45–46, 66, 74]

It was out of this quest that there came three remarkable papers
in early 1896. In these, Freud claims that in the course of his clinical
practice he had made the fundamental discovery (which he described as a "source of the Nile" in neuropathology) that the cause
of hysteria and obsessional neurosis lay in perverse sexual experiences undergone by his patients in early childhood.[4] This notion

---

[3]As early as 1888 he had written an article for an encyclopaedia in which he had
put forward the view that sexual factors play a part in all neuroses. [S.E. 1: 51] The
probable source of this preconception will be mentioned in the next chapter.

[4]Freud distinguished between the psychoneuroses (such as hysteria and obses-

came to be known as the infantile seduction theory, and in the
papers in which it was presented Freud refers for the first time to his
new technique of psychoanalysis, by means of which he claimed to
be able to uncover repressed memories of early traumatic experiences. Utilising this technique, he had discovered that the patients had
all been seduced, or otherwise sexually abused, in infancy and that
these experiences lay at the root of their later neurotic symptoms.
The events in question are described as either "a brutal assault
committed by an adult" or "a seduction less rapid and less repul-
sive, but reaching the same conclusion". The more serious experiences were "positively revolting", and included "all the abuses known
to debauched and impotent persons, among whom the buccal
cavity and the rectum are misused for sexual purposes", for "people
who have no hesitation in satisfying their sexual desires upon
children cannot be expected to jib at finer shades in the methods of
obtaining that satisfaction". [S.E. 3: 151, 203, 152, 164, 214]

Who were responsible for these perverse acts? In regard to the
cases of hysteria Freud divides the culprits into three groups, the
first consisting of adult strangers, the second of adults in charge of
the child, such as a nursery maid, governess or tutor, or a close
relative, and the third of boys who had engaged in sexual relations
with slightly younger sisters.[5] [164, 208] In the latter cases the
relationship may have continued for several years. The age at which
the precocious sexual experience occurred was most commonly
from the third to the fifth year, or even earlier in one or two cases.
[152, 165] However, the patients could only be brought to recall the
experiences with great difficulty, and under extreme pressure from
the physician. [152, 165, 212] Moreover, Freud makes no attempt in
these papers to give precise details of his new technique, and since
his conclusions were controversial they were received with considerable scepticism. When one of the papers ("The Aetiology of Hysteria") was delivered as a lecture to the Vienna Society of Psychiatry and Neurology in April 1896 it was given, as recounted by Freud
himself, "an icy reception by the asses. . . . And this after one has
demonstrated to them the solution of a more than thousand-year-
old problem. . . ." [Masson 1985: 184]

In view of Freud's indignation at the response to his ideas, it
comes as something of a surprise to find that only eighteen months

---

sional neurosis) and the actual neuroses (neurasthenia and anxiety neurosis),
believing the former to originate from early sexual experiences and the latter from
current sexual practices.

[5]The considerably fewer cases of obsessional neurosis are dealt with separately
in all three papers and without any categorising of the seducers.

later he is confiding to Fliess that he no longer believes in his theory of the origins of neurosis. Among the reasons given in a letter dated 21st September 1897 are: that he had been unable to bring a single analysis to a successful conclusion; that partial successes could be explained in other ways; and that it was improbable that there could be such widespread perversions against children, as would have to be the case in view of the high frequency of hysterical illness. [Masson 1985: 264–65]

In this same letter is a hint of the theory which is to replace the one being discarded and to play a crucial role in the further development of psychoanalysis. In the context of his perception that in regard to the unconscious "one cannot distinguish between truth and fiction which has been cathected with affect", Freud suggests, as a possible solution to his problem, that "the sexual phantasy invariably seizes upon the theme of the parents". This relates to his theoretical surmises concerning unconscious phantasies, which he subsequently postulated to underlie somatic symptoms, a notion he was to utilise extensively in the "Dora" case history, written in 1901. The reference to parents is a precursor to the theory of the Oedipus complex, the first exposition of which occurs in *The Interpretation of Dreams*, completed in 1899.

In essence, the Oedipus theory is that in infancy boys harbour unconscious sexual wishes towards their mother and develop hostile impulses against their father, while girls adopt an analogous attitude. Freud insisted that his ideas were not to be taken as symbolic; a child's first sexual choice is an "incestuous one". [S.E. 4: 263n; 16: 335]

Although he was not to state it explicitly for some considerable time, the Oedipus theory eventually replaced that of infantile seduction as a means of explaining his early clinical results. Yet though utilised for this purpose, the later theory does not actually account for the clinical results claimed by Freud in his papers of 1896, for while Oedipal sexual impulses might just conceivably induce infantile phantasies of parental seduction, there is nothing in the theory to explain why the phantasised culprits should have been strangers, servants, teachers, governesses, or elder brothers, as reported in the early papers.[6]

---

[6]In the first two seduction theory papers, adult close relatives were not mentioned at all. In "Further Remarks on the Neuro-Psychoses of Defence" Freud writes: "Foremost among those guilty of abuses . . . are nursemaids, governesses and domestic servants . . .; teachers, moreover, figure with regrettable frequency. In seven out of these thirteen cases, however, it turned out that blameless children were the assailants." [S.E. 3: 164]

Freud deals with this difficulty in the easiest possible way—he simply ignores it. What he does instead is to produce explanations which incorporate his notion of unconscious phantasies: "If hysterical subjects trace back their symptoms to traumas that are fictitious, then the new fact which emerges is precisely that they create such scenes in *phantasy*" in order to "cover up the auto-erotic activity of the first years of childhood. . . ." [S.E. 14: 17,18] And eventually: "It was only later that I was able to recognise in this phantasy of being seduced by the father the expression of the typical Oedipus complex in women." [S.E. 22: 120]

In none of the retrospective accounts does he mention the more brutal sexual assaults or the variety of assailants, both of which were emphasised in the papers of 1896. But apart from the difficulty in reconciling the reports in the latter with the versions he was to give later, there are other reasons for approaching Freud's claims with some scepticism. The seduction theory was first announced in "Further Remarks on the Neuro-Psychoses of Defence" and "Heredity and the Aetiology of the Neuroses", both papers being sent off on 5th February 1896. (The second of these was written for publication in a French journal.) It was also presented again in a lecture ("The Aetiology of Hysteria") given on 21st April. In the two earlier papers, in relation to hysteria, Freud refers to his analyses of all thirteen cases he has been treating, while in the third he reports he is basing his conclusions on eighteen cases of hysteria. [S.E. 3:152, 162–63, 199, 207] In addition, he reports his results for all six of his cases of obsessional neurosis. [155, 168] With every single one of these patients, he states, he has demonstrated the occurrence in their early childhood (mostly below the age of five) of a traumatic sexual experience. [152, 165] He also reports that the precocious sexual events were traced with extreme difficulty against "an enormous resistance". [153] This being so, it seems remarkable that he should be able to claim one hundred percent success with his current patients using what he himself describes as a laborious and difficult new procedure. [220]

In "The Aetiology of Hysteria", Freud himself raises the question as to whether it is possible "that the physician forces such scenes upon his docile patients, alleging they are memories". [204] In his response he asserts that all doubts would be removed when a complete presentation of the analytic technique and its results was made available. In fact at one stage in the lecture he rhetorically asks his audience whether he should put before them the actual material he had obtained from his analyses, or whether he should "first" try to meet the many objections to his claims. [203] In the event he chooses the latter course, and notwithstanding the implication of his use of the word "first" he never, either then or subsequently, produced this material.

The Contemporary Reports

Did most of Freud's patients in this period report that they had been sexually abused in early childhood, as the legend has it, or is there a rather different story to tell, with a very different conclusion?

The answer to this question can be found in Freud's own writings, and we shall start with the seduction theory papers themselves. For instance, from "The Aetiology of Hysteria" we learn that "before they come for analysis the patients know nothing about these scenes" and "are indignant as a rule if we warn them that such scenes are going to emerge. Only the strongest compulsion of the treatment can induce them to embark on a reproduction of them." The patients insist "they have no feelings of remembering the scenes" and assure Freud "emphatically of their unbelief". [204] In fact, as he tells us in "Further Remarks on the Neuro-Psychoses of Defence", the "traces [of these childhood traumas] are never present in conscious memory, only in the symptoms of the illness". [166] Then, in "Heredity and the Aetiology of the Neuroses", we are told that "these patients never repeat these stories spontaneously. . . . One only succeeds in awakening the psychical trace of a precocious sexual event under the most energetic pressure of the analytic procedure, and against an enormous resistance." [153] A few lines later he adds cryptically: "Conviction will follow in the end, if one is not influenced by the patients' behaviour, provided that one can follow in detail the report of a psychoanalysis of a case of hysteria." Insofar as any sense can be made of this, it would appear to be the first instance of Freud's insistence that acceptance of his technique of analysis is a prerequisite for conviction.

The most explicit presentation of Freud's forceful approach at that time (in this instance in relation to the "actual" neuroses) is found in "Sexuality in the Aetiology of the Neuroses" (1898), where he writes: "Having diagnosed a case of neurasthenic neurosis with certainty and having classified its symptoms correctly, we are in a position to translate the symptomatology into aetiology; and we may then boldly demand confirmation of our suspicions from the patient. We must not be led astray by initial denials. If we keep firmly to what we have inferred we shall in the end conquer every resistance by emphasising the unshakeable nature of our convictions." [S.E. 3: 269]

Equally revealing are his words in *Studies on Hysteria*, where he
writes, "We need not be afraid, therefore, of telling the patient what
we think his next connection of thought is going to be". At one
point he refers to having "laboriously forced some piece of knowledge" on patients. He also tells us that "even when everything is
finished and the patients have been overborne by the force of logic
and have been convinced by the therapeutic effect accompanying
the emergence of precisely these ideas—when, I say, the patients
themselves accept the fact that they thought this or that, they often
add: 'But I can't *remember* having thought it'." And even more
revealingly, with reference to "the things that we have to insist upon
to the patient", he writes; "The principal point is that I should guess
the secret and tell it to the patient straight out." [S.E. 2: 295, 299,
300, 281]

The above quotations give a rather different picture from the
one usually described, in which the patients supposedly recount
lurid stories of sexual abuse to a surprised physician.[7] Indications
that the sexual scenes were indeed proposed by Freud himself are to
be found in his later writings in contexts in which the significance of
his words is easily missed. In *The Interpretation of Dreams* (1900),
in a reference to a dream which occurred in 1895, he writes: "It was
my view at that time . . . that my task was fulfilled when I had
informed a patient of the hidden meaning of his symptoms." [S.E.
4: 108] Then, in his paper "On Psychotherapy" (1904), he explains
that the psychoanalytic method involves "*persuading* [the patient]
to accept, by virtue of a better understanding, something that up to
now . . . he has rejected (repressed). . . ." [S.E. 7: 266] Again, in the
paper on "Hysterical Phantasies" (1908), he writes: "The technique
of psychoanalysis enables us in the first place to *infer* from the
symptoms what [the] unconscious phantasies are and then to make
them conscious to the patient." [S.E. 9: 162] And from *Beyond the
Pleasure Principle* (1920): "At first the analysing physician could do
no more than discover the unconscious material that was concealed
from the patient, put it together and, at the right moment,
communicate it to him." [S.E. 18: 18; emphases added in all cases.]

The matter is put virtually beyond doubt by his introductory
comments in "The Aetiology of Hysteria", where he refers to the

---

[7]This is not to deny that a few of Freud's patients may have reported genuine
instances of sexual abuse in childhood, though not necessarily in infancy. As we
shall see later, there is evidence of only *one* such case during the relevant period.
(Contrary to the view expressed by some commentators, the current concern with
childhood sexual abuse has no bearing on the question at issue, as should be
apparent by the end of this chapter.)

patients' own ideas in regard to the origins of their neurotic illness and goes on to say that "it would be a good thing to have a second method of arriving at the aetiology of hysteria, one in which we should feel less dependent on the assertions of the patients themselves".[8] By way of analogy he instances how a dermatologist "is able to recognise a sore as luetic from the character of its margins, of the crust on it and of its shape, without being misled by the protestations of his patient, who denies any source of infection for it", and how "a forensic physician can arrive at the cause of an injury, even if he has to do without any information from the injured person". He continues: "In hysteria, too, there exists a similar possibility of penetrating from the symptoms to a knowledge of their causes." [S.E. 3: 191–92] The words quoted here indicate clearly that what he describes as "the method which we have to employ for this purpose" (namely, pyschoanalysis) achieves its aim without extracting *direct* information from the patient. Now since he is here explaining the nature of the technique by means of which he has arrived at his clinical validation of the infantile seduction theory, the clear implication of his words is that *the patients did not themselves report sexual experiences from infancy*—these were *inferences* made by Freud himself on the basis of a theoretical postulate. This receives further confirmation from his colleague and biographer Ernest Jones, who writes: "But up to the spring of 1897 he still held firmly to his conviction of the reality of these childhood traumas, so strong was Charcot's teaching on traumatic experiences and so surely did *the analysis of the patients' associations* reproduce them." [Jones 1953: 292; emphasis added.][9]

It is noteworthy that it was not until 1925, nearly thirty years after the events in question, that Freud first publicly reported that most of his early female patients had accused their father of having seduced them, though he had referred to those events several times

---

[8]The patients' assertions referred to here are in regard to those "harmful influences" to which they themselves initially (and mistakenly) attribute their falling ill.

[9]Another piece of evidence comes from Leopold Löwenfeld, who published the following in 1899: "By chance, one of the patients on whom Freud used the analytic method came under my observation. The patient told me with certainty that the infantile sexual scene *which analysis had apparently uncovered* was pure phantasy and had never really happened to him." [Masson 1985: 413n; emphasis added.] Now had the patient *reported* the sexual scene to Freud he would have been quoted as saying something like "which came into his consciousness" or "which he thought he had recalled" in place of the italicised words. It is clear from the words actually used that the "sexual scene" was revealed by means of the "analytic method"—in other words, it was a product of analytic inference.

prior to this time. Freud's editor and translator, James Strachey, suggests that the failure to implicate fathers in the original papers was due to discretion on Freud's part, and he points to the mention of fathers in the letter to Fliess of 21st September 1897 in support of this. There Freud gives as one of the reasons why he no longer believes in the seduction theory, "then the surprise that in all cases, the *father*, not excluding my own, had to be accused of being perverse" if he were to be able to maintain his theory. [Masson 1985: 264] However, it seems that he is not saying that in all cases the father *had been* accused, but is referring to a consequence of his latest theoretical developments rather than to his clinical results. His expression of surprise points to this, for why should he only now be experiencing surprise about clinical results obtained for the most part over eighteen months before? Further, in a letter to Fliess earlier that same year (11th January), in one of the rare instances when he specifies a particular case, he writes that he has traced the "seducer" to the *uncle* of a male patient, and he gives the tabulated heredity clearly distinguishing father from uncle. [222] This is not consistent with an interpretation of the letter of 21st September as saying that in all cases he had found that fathers were accused. Again, on 11th February 1897 he states that his own father was "one of these perverts", responsible for what he calls the hysterias of his brother and several of his younger sisters. [230–31] Clearly he has not *analysed* his siblings; the assertion arises out of his latest theoretical speculations.[10] (In fact he exonerates his father in a letter of 3rd–4th October 1897.)

Strachey cites two cases referred to in *Studies on Hysteria* where Freud later added footnotes in which he admitted that he had substituted uncles for fathers. [S.E. 2: 134n, 170n] But in the same year (1924), he also added footnotes, one specifically on his seduction theory "error" [S.E. 3: 168], to the 1896 papers prior to reprinting, and it would have been the natural thing to have added a similar footnote concerning discretion had he omitted fathers for this reason. Moreover, there would have been no reason for such discretion for, unlike the cases in *Studies*, no personal details of any patient were given in the papers in question. Again, the way in which

---

[10]In a letter of 24 January 1897 Freud speculates in regard to hysteria that fathers are involved on the basis of personality characteristics of adult hysterics. A few months later (May 31st) he reports a dream which he interprets as fulfilling his wish to catch a father as the originator of neurosis, a comment that scarcely accords with the idea that fathers had consistently been implicated by his patients prior to that time. There is also a reference to his "speculations" concerning the involvement of fathers in a letter dated 22nd June 1897.

Freud clearly distinguishes the different categories of supposed assailants conflicts with Strachey's suggestion, for he would hardly have gone into this kind of detail to hide the fact that they were generally the fathers. In any case, the clear indications that the supposed seductions were for the most part Freud's own inferred reconstructions renders the question of discretion irrelevant.

The Retrospective Accounts

It is instructive to trace in Freud's later writings all the references to the clinical experiences he described in the papers of 1896. The first occurs in an abstract of "The Aetiology of Hysteria" in a privately printed list of his writings prepared in May 1897 for an application for a professorship, where Freud states that those responsible for the infantile seductions are as a rule to be looked for among the patient's nearest relatives. [S.E. 3: 254] Now while this tends to accord with the current stage of his *theoretical* speculations, it is not an accurate summary of his findings as presented in the seduction papers themselves. In the paper in question close relatives were one group among many, and in the first of the 1896 papers, "Further Remarks on the Neuro-Psychoses of Defence", adult close relatives were not mentioned at all. [S.E. 3: 208, 164]

The first published reference occurs in *Three Essays on the Theory of Sexuality* (1905), where Freud writes that he "cannot admit" that he "exaggerated the frequency or importance" of the influence of infantile seductions. [S.E. 7: 190] However, in "My Views on the Part Played by Sexuality in the Aetiology of the Neuroses" (1906) the story is somewhat different. His material "happened by chance to include a disproportionately large number of cases in which sexual seduction by an adult or by older children played the chief part in the history of the patient's childhood", and he "thus over-estimated the frequency of such events", a statement which actually contradicts the first one. Though he adds that "in other respects [these events] were not open to doubt", he goes on to say that he has "learned to explain a number of phantasies of seduction as attempts at fending off memories of the subject's *own* sexual activity (infantile masturbation)".[11] [S.E. 7: 274]

---

[11]Freud seems here to be deliberately evading the embarrassing task of unequivocally retracting his self-proclaimed "source of the Nile" discovery of 1896, for how could the supposed sexual seductions not be open to doubt when in the next breath he intimates that in some cases they were actually phantasies?

In this same paper Freud writes that at the earlier period he had
been "unable to distinguish with certainty between falsifications
made by hysterics in their memories of childhood and traces of real
events" [S.E. 7: 274], but there are equivocations and contrivances
in the paper which make it something less than a frank admission of
error. In particular, with reference to "the form taken by the
theory" presented in the papers of 1895 and 1896 he states: "The
theory culminated in this thesis: if the *vita sexualis* is normal, there
can be no neurosis." [274] Now this can only be regarded as deliberately misleading, for it is manifestly *not* what was postulated so
emphatically in the 1896 papers. (In "The Aetiology of Hysteria" he
states explicitly that he is putting forward "the thesis that at the bottom of every case of hysteria there are *one or more occurrences of
premature sexual experience*". [S.E. 3: 203; emphasis in original.])
His false statement enables him to blur the distinction between the
old and new views, so that he can go on to say, "even today I do not
consider these assertions incorrect", and to intimate that the change
had involved only a need for a correction of "insufficiencies" and
"misunderstandings" in his previous position. [S.E. 7: 274]

Freud did eventually make a public retraction of the infantile
seduction theory without equivocation in his article *On the History
of the Psychoanalytic Movement* (1914), where he writes that "this
aetiology broke down under the weight of its own improbability
and contradiction in definitely ascertainable circumstances".[12]
Though he explains that he was misled by his failure to realise that
"the statements made by patients" were actually descriptions of
scenes created in phantasy he does not yet relate them to his
Oedipus theory: "these phantasies were intended to cover up the
auto-erotic activity of the first years of childhood, to embellish it
and raise it to a higher plane." [S.E. 14: 17–18]

After a gap of ten years he added to one of the original seduction
theory papers the footnote already mentioned in which he refers

---

[12]Although admitting to "a mistaken idea which had to be overcome", Freud
nevertheless plays down his error by disingenuously presenting it as resulting from
a situation in which "one has been deceived in one's expectations" by "hysterical
patients [who] trace back their symptoms to traumas that are fictitious".

Equally questionable is his claim of disproof in "definitely ascertainable
circumstances". Apart from the difficulty in imagining precisely what form the
latter might take, had such existed he could hardly have failed to mention the fact
and given relevant details when he dealt with the issue in the 1906 paper (and to
have reported the information to Fliess at the time). One is left with the suspicion
that the reason he did not is that he had only just invented the notion when he
wrote this sentence in his *History*.

again to his failure to distinguish between his patients' "phantasies about their childhood years and their real recollections". [S.E. 3: 168n] A detailed explanation, including an innovation, came in the following year in *An Autobiographical Study* (1925), where he writes of his early clinical experiences: "Under the influence of the technical procedure which I used at that time, the majority of my patients reproduced from their childhood scenes in which they were sexually seduced by some grown-up person. With female patients the part of the seducer was almost always assigned to their father." When he came to realise that "these scenes of seduction had never taken place", he was able to draw the "right" conclusion that "neurotic symptoms were not related directly to actual events but to wishful phantasies". [S.E. 20: 33–34] However, there is no reference to patients reporting such scenes at any time after that early period, and the clear implication is that they only reproduced them "under the influence of the technical procedure" he was then using. Had there been reports of similar occurrences subsequently, it would have been natural for him to state so in that context.[13]

A more general reference to infantile seductions occurs in the paper "Female Sexuality" (1931), where he is now able to report "the very common phantasy which makes the mother or nurse into a seducer". A few pages later he reiterates that "girls regularly accuse their mother of seducing them", though it still remains true that "in phantasies of later years, the father . . . regularly appears as the sexual seducer". [S.E. 21: 232, 238]

This time we do not have to wait long for Freud to broach the subject again. In his *New Introductory Lectures on Psychoanalysis* (completed in 1932), referring to "the period in which the main interest was directed to discovering infantile sexual traumas", he recalls that "almost all my women patients told me they had been seduced by their father", and that in the end he "was driven to

---

[13]In the same passage Freud disarmingly presents to the reader an image of himself as a rather naive therapist who was easily deceived by his patients' "stories": "If the reader feels inclined to shake his head at my credulity, I cannot altogether blame him; though I may plead that this was at a time when I was intentionally keeping my critical faculty in abeyance so as to preserve an unprejudiced and receptive attitude towards the many novelties which were coming to my notice every day." However, it is the innocent reader who is being deceived. The seduction theory error arose for the opposite reason to the one that Freud gives: it was because he was so utterly convinced of the validity of his theory that he foisted the supposed infantile sexual experiences on his patients. (To Fliess he wrote on 13th February 1896: "I am so certain that both of us have got hold of a beautiful piece of objective truth.")

recognise" that these reports were phantasies. [S.E. 22: 120] However, there is an apparent inconsistency between these last two accounts, for in the earlier paper the father "regularly" appears as the sexual seducer, whereas in the later one it is only with reference to his early period as a therapist that he writes about women patients having told him that they had been seduced by their father. The discrepancy arises from the fact that in the first case he had in mind "phantasies" he himself inferred using his analytic technique, while with respect to his early patients he had to maintain his story that they had actually reported their supposed phantasies to him—a story in which he may have come to believe by that time. (It should be noted, however, that he added footnotes to the 1896 papers in 1924, so he could hardly fail to be aware that he was giving a rather different account in 1925 in his *Autobiographical Study*. It is surely no coincidence that this is the only one of the post–seduction theory accounts which comes close to the truth, in that he admits the possibility, before rejecting it, that he may have "perhaps forced" the seduction scenes on his patients. [S.E. 20: 34])

As we have seen, in both the *Autobiographical Study* and the *New Introductory Lectures* Freud claims that in the period of the seduction theory most of his female patients implicated their fathers in childhood seductions, and he specifically refers to this as "an interesting *episode* in the history of analytic research". [S.E. 20: 120; emphasis added.] The implication of his words can only be that after this period the majority of his female patients *did not* report such seductions. But if the phantasies are projections of Oedipal yearnings, why were they not recounted by his later female patients in the course of depth analysis in the same numbers as before?

It is important to be clear that this is not just a challenge to the Oedipal phantasy theory. The problem is not resolved by assuming that Freud was mistaken in at least this part of his theory. *Whatever* the nature of the alleged reports, whether they were genuine, or phantasies, or any combination of the two, the same question must be posed: If he had indeed been the recipient of frequent reports of paternal seductions, why should such cease as soon as he abandoned the seduction theory? There would seem to be no plausible explanation of this anomaly, other than that most of his seduction theory patients did not in fact disclose instances of paternal abuse, as he later claimed.

Reviewing the various accounts quoted above, it is clear that the inconsistencies form a pattern which relates to the current stage of Freud's theories. In the original version, in the papers of 1896, there were a variety of people involved in the sexual abuse of his patients. At that stage, to satisfy the infantile seduction theory, it was only necessary that such abuses had occurred in infancy. The realisation that the seduction theory was untenable resulted in the sometimes "revolting" sexual assaults being toned down to unspecific "phantasies of seduction", which were postulated as having the purpose of covering up memories of infantile masturbation. Finally, following the belated application of the theory of the Oedipus complex to females came the accounts of how most of his early female patients had reported seductions by their fathers.

As we shall see, the discrepancies in Freud's accounts arose from his need, firstly, to safeguard his reconstructive techniques when he realised he could not maintain the seduction theory, and, later, to ensure consistency between his Oedipus theory and his reports of the early clinical findings. This necessitated appropriate emendations of the latter on the lines noted above. In short, the accounts of the early clinical experiences in question, which are of crucial importance in the history of psychoanalysis, exhibit tendentious retrospective changes such that they can only be regarded as suspect.

Elucidation of the True Story

We are now in a position to attempt to elucidate the true facts of the matter. A clue lies in a certain ambiguity in the language of the papers of 1896, where Freud frequently refers to patients "reproducing" the childhood events rather than recalling them. What he meant by this is indicated in the section called "The Psychotherapy of Hysteria" in *Studies on Hysteria*, where he describes the pressure technique which he was utilising at that time. The patient was informed that Freud would apply pressure to his forehead, and that while the pressure lasted he would recall either a picture or an idea. The content of the picture or idea may well have been suggested by Freud himself, as he informs us on more than one occasion, or even have been "laboriously forced" onto a patient. [S.E. 2: 299] Freud looks to the "facial expression" for an indication of the validity of his surmises, specifically the "tension and signs of emotion with which [the patient] tries to disavow the emerging recollection". [S.E. 2: 281] This description is not unlike that given in "The Aetiology of Hysteria", where he writes that when the patients "are recalling these infantile experiences they suffer under the most violent sensations". [S.E. 3: 204] It seems probable that Freud took signs of distress when he was, in his own words, boldly demanding confirmation of his suspicions, as evidence of their truth. No doubt his patients *did* exhibit some distress when their forceful therapist

insisted that some distasteful sexual experience had happened to
them in infancy. And, quite possibly, given that Freud presented
himself to them as "an elucidator, . . . a teacher, . . . a father
confessor who gives absolution" (*Studies on Hysteria*) [S.E. 2: 282],
they may have come to "accept the fact that they thought this or
that" even though they could not *remember* having thought it".
[300] Given also that he had "come to regard the participation of
sexual motive forces as an indispensable premiss" [S.E. 3: 200], one
can begin to understand how it was that he convinced himself that
his patients' reactions to his promptings were tantamount to proof
that his ideas were correct.

Freud claims as the climax of his procedure's "achievement in
the way of reproductive thinking" that it results in the emergence of
thoughts which the patient "never *remembers*, though he admits
that the context calls for them inexorably". [S.E. 2: 272] Clearly the
inferred infantile sexual scenes of 1895–96 are examples of unconscious thoughts which the patient does not remember, but which, as
Freud tells us, are "indispensable supplements to the associative
and logical framework of the neurosis". [S.E. 3: 205] It is evident,
however, that such "thoughts" derive from Freud's expectations
rather than from the patient's forgotten experiences.[14]

He first announced his theory that a prepubertal sexual experience was a precondition for hysteria and obsessional neurosis in a
letter to Fliess dated 8 October 1895, and on 15th October he
described it as "the great clinical secret".[15] The following day he
wrote that he was almost certain that with it he had "solved the
riddles of hysteria and obsessional neurosis". Two weeks later (2nd
November) he reported that one of his cases gave him "what [he]

---

[14]Macmillan has shown that Freud's seemingly naive conviction expressed in
Studies that he could not *force* his expectations onto his patients however much he
insisted on them resulted from his belief that every response emerging in the analytic context was strictly determined by *internal* psychical events. [Macmillan 1991:
109–114]

[15]The question arises why Freud should have become so convinced that it was a
sexual trauma in early childhood which was "the solution to the aetiological problem" of hysteria and obsessional neurosis. In "Heredity and the Aetiology of the
Neuroses" he explains: "It is precisely because the subject is in his infancy that the
precocious sexual excitation produces little or no effect at the time; but its psychical trace is preserved. Later, when at puberty the reactions of the sexual organs
have developed to a level incommensurable with their infantile condition, it comes
about in one way or another that this unconscious psychical trace is awakened.
Thanks to the change due to puberty, the memory will display a power which was
completely lacking from the event itself. *The memory will operate as though it were
a contemporary event.*" [S.E. 3: 154]

expected (sexual shock—that is infantile abuse in male hysteria!)", and that his confidence in the validity of his "psychological constructions" had been strengthened.[16] [Masson 1985: 141, 144, 145, 149] It is clear that it was his over-enthusiastic espousal of his theory which led directly to his supposedly finding over a period of a few months that every single one of his patients under analysis had had some kind of traumatic sexual experience in early childhood. The doubtful means by which he confirmed to his own satisfaction that such events had occurred are indicated above; nevertheless, there seems little doubt that he was absolutely convinced that his technique was enabling him to obtain confirmations of his "source of the Nile" discovery.

However, whatever his degree of conviction, the presentation of his case in the 1896 papers was not as scrupulous as it might have been. He writes of the patients "reproducing" or "recalling to consciousness" the sexual scenes, and in the same context also refers to "these stories" and "the statements" of his patients. [S.E. 3: 204, 153, 206] In his references to "memories" no attempt is made to distinguish clearly between events genuinely recalled and infantile scenes which he had inferred by means of his analytic technique. It is difficult not to conclude that his failure to make this distinction, and his use of such an ambiguous expression as "analytic confessions" [153], stems from an intention to obscure the fact that the infantile "seductions" were his own reconstructions and by no means as categorically demonstrated as he insisted.

It has frequently been observed that in the letter to Fliess in which Freud first voices his disbelief in the seduction theory, he writes that he is far from depressed, in spite of having to relinquish his "expectation of eternal fame". On the contrary, he emphasises that he is "in an opposite state". [Masson 1985: 265–66] It may well be that his failure to be depressed by the turn of events was indicative of a growing realisation that what he was giving up was in reality little more than an unproven speculation which had failed to live up to his high expectations. His elation no doubt stemmed from the intellectual excitement of pursuing the new speculations

---

[16]This is the only case of infantile sexual abuse he reported to his confidant Wilhelm Fliess in the relevant period prior to October 1895, up to the writing of the first seduction theory papers—and even this is not without ambiguity, as he refers to the "working through of the disputed material". (Jones writes that in a letter of 30 May 1893 there is a mention of early seductions, but in the letter in question Freud is discussing specifically cases of juvenile neurasthenia without indications of masturbation, for which he suggests among "unproven surmises" the possibility of abuse in the prepubertal period.)

he was by then engaged in, which were eventually to lead to a new
theory by means of which he was able to rescue (albeit with the aid
of a sleight of hand) his dubious clinical material.

It would seem that in the course of his speculative explorations
he had made a connection between the sexual trauma theory, his
more recent ideas relating somatic symptoms to unconscious phantasies, and his growing recognition of the central role of parents. No
doubt it began to dawn on him that his phantasy theory would
enable him to discard the seduction theory, about which he was
beginning to have some misgivings, and which he must have been
uneasily aware he had been able to confirm only after he had
resorted to excessive means to fashion evidence of infantile seductions from his patients. But with the advent of the phantasy theory
he sought to derive the contents of unconscious ideas exclusively by
means of his analytic technique, with the result that he was less
dependent on the explicit statements or emotional responses of his
patients. An additional benefit of discarding his former theory was
that he would no longer need to concern himself with objections to
it which he had failed to rebut entirely convincingly.[17] More significant in the long run was that he had alighted on a notion which,
in combination with the analytic technique, very largely took his
clinical evidence out of the realms where it could be subjected to
conventional empirical validation, for he insisted that only those
who had undergone a rigorous psychoanalytic training were in a
position to recognise and interpret the unconscious processes he
postulated. In other words, only those who accepted the validity of
his analytic technique could decide whether the products of that
technique were genuine. The tendentious application of this technique, essentially one of *interpretation* and *reconstruction*, ensured
that henceforth his clinical data would conform to his theories.[18]

Ramifications

A consideration of all the evidence, then, points to the conclusion
that Freud's early patients, in general, did *not* recount stories of

---

[17]Though, as Cioffi has pointed out, there are objections to the new theory
which Freud never addresses. Why should the belief that she had been sexually
abused by her father be less distressing to a patient than memories of infantile masturbation or of incestuous desires? And since that phantasies of seduction were as
unconscious as the genuine memories, what was the point of subjecting the latter to
distortion in the first place?

infantile seductions, these stories were actually analytic reconstructions which he foisted on them.[19] This explains why it is that after the abandonment of the infantile seduction theory there is a dearth of reports of *current* patients recalling sexual abuse in infancy, for by audaciously proposing that the occurrences which he himself had inferred were actually unconscious phantasies, he had no need in future to maintain that he gained this information explicitly from the patients, for his technique of interpretation (especially of dreams) was versatile enough to enable him to find evidence for all manner of infantile sexual experiences.

On a number of occasions Freud referred to the "error" he had made at the beginning of psychoanalysis, this being that he had espoused the seduction theory because he had mistakenly believed the reports of his patients. This account is misleading in two ways. The espousal of the seduction theory preceded the clinical material adduced to justify it; and he did not naively believe the infantile seduction reports, since in actuality they were his own reconstructions. In reality the essential error lay in the fact that he continued to retain his faith in the analytic technique of reconstruction by means of which he had inferred the scenes which had been utilised to corroborate an erroneous theory. As Cioffi observes, Freud was faced with the dilemma of how to jettison the seduction theory in which he had lost faith, without at the same time conceding that the sexual episodes claimed as clinical findings were an artefact of his reconstructive technique and thereby conceding the unreliability of the latter. He resolved it ingeniously by affirming the authenticity of the reconstructions while denying their historicity. By this means he was able not only to salvage his claim to have

---

[18]In relation to this question of the fashioning of clinical findings to accord with preconceived notions it is apposite to note that in the 1896 seduction theory papers Freud claimed that his clinical results also corroborated his more specific theory (first announced to Fliess in October 1895) associating hysteria with exclusively *passive* infantile sexual experiences and obsessional neurosis with *active* (pleasurable) experiences. [S.E. 3: 155, 163, 168–69, 219–220, 253] However, in his 1906 paper "Sexuality in the Aetiology of the Neuroses" he writes that after the relinquishing of the seduction theory he "was obliged to abandon this view entirely". [S.E. 7: 275] Now of course the theory of infantile unconscious phantasies (in its initial formulation having the purpose of covering up autoerotic activity) was no longer consonant with this specific differential aetiology, which no doubt accounts for the fact that Freud suddenly ceased to find clinical corroboration for the latter.

[19]Freud's statements in the seduction theory papers that the patients had no feeling of remembering the infantile sexual scenes leaves open the possibility that *all* the supposed infantile seductions may have been reconstructions.

solved the problem of the aetiology of neuroses, but to go on from there to construct the whole edifice of psychoanalysis.[20]

On several occasions Freud utilised the seduction theory episode to justify his positing of unconscious phantasies, a notion which plays a crucial role in psychoanalytic theory. In a passage in *Introductory Lectures on Psychoanalysis* relating to symptom formation, he writes that the "discovery" that the sexual "scenes from infancy" are not true in the majority of cases "is calculated more than any other to discredit either analysis, which has led to this result, or the patients, on whose statements the analysis and our whole understanding of the neuroses are founded", and in the course of exonerating analysis he subsequently elaborates on the latter part of this sentence by alluding to the patients' "invented stories". [S.E. 16:367–68] But this passage is characteristically both obfuscatory and disingenuous since the supposed "stories" are actually his own analytically inferred reconstructions. However, the dissembling has a very important function, for it serves to make plausible his claim that his imaginative interpretations and constructions represent phenomena occurring in the minds of his patients. Without this direct link with the latter, the post-seduction theory analytic reconstructions of infantile sexual life stand exposed for what they are: unsubstantiated and often highly improbable conjectures which are not amenable to empirical corroboration. In the words of Cioffi: "[Freud's] grounds for assigning his patients a history of polymorphous, perverse and incestuous phantasising were as dubious as his grounds for assigning them histories of infantile seductions had been." [Cioffi 1988: 69]

It is not without significance that Freud's edict that no one untrained in his technique for delving into the unconscious was entitled to challenge his findings was announced right from its inception. [S.E. 3: 164, 220, 282] In endeavouring in this way to protect his developing system at its most vulnerable point he was, in effect, affirming his commitment to the same flawed analytic technique by means of which he had derived the erroneous confirmations of the ill-fated seduction theory. But choosing this way of resolving his dilemma when he realised his "source of the Nile" claim was not sustainable did not mean that he could entirely

---

[20]As Clark Glymour notes, Freud failed to take the "scientifically honourable" course of action and face up to "the evidence that the methods on which all of his work relied were in fact unreliable". [Glymour 1983: 70] The reason he did not do so is suggested by his words in his *History*: "Perhaps I persevered only because I no longer had any choice and could not then begin again at anything else." [S.E. 14: 17]

escape from the consequences of his failure to confront the central issue, for, as we have seen, it gave rise to discrepancies which no amount of glossing over could conceal.

It is difficult to escape the conclusion that both self-deception and dishonesty play a role in this story, though at times it is scarcely possible to distinguish one from the other. In view of this, there remains to be considered how it happened that in spite of the inconsistencies in Freud's accounts of the seduction theory episode the legend remained unchallenged for so long and is still widely regarded as historical fact. It is important to appreciate first the extraordinary persuasiveness of Freud's presentation, and specifically the brilliant means by which obfuscation in the earlier versions blurs the distinction between unproblematic factual statements and psychoanalytic inference in such a way that readers are misled into mistaking the latter for the former. This enabled the subtle change from the earlier ambiguity to the later assertions to be almost seamless. It was natural that the final accounts were accepted; while the interpretations of a researcher may legitimately be challenged, only in exceptional circumstances are purportedly factual reports put in question. This point has especial force in the light of Freud's reputation for integrity, assiduously fostered in his own writings. Moreover, as he tells the story it is in part against himself; he somewhat shamefacedly confesses to the error of having naively believed the "stories" of childhood seductions ("If the reader feels inclined to shake his head at my credulity, I cannot altogether blame him.") Finally, the portrayal of the episode as one in which a seminal discovery arose out of initial error has been recounted so often that it has become almost unthinkable that it be false. However, there can be little doubt that the legend *is* false. The repercussions arising from this will be explored in the next chapter and beyond.

CHAPTER THREE

Unconscious Phantasies
and the Dora Analysis

The implications of the fact that the clinical evidence adduced by Freud, on the basis of his analytic technique, to substantiate the seduction theory (and subsequently the unconscious phantasy theory) was for the most part spurious extend considerably beyond the doubts it raises about his clinical judgement or his probity. In her book *Freud and His Father* Marianne Krüll writes that "Without exception Freud's biographers agree with him that the renunciation of the seduction theory was his great achievement, facilitating the discovery of the Oedipus complex, of infantile sexuality, and hence of psychoanalysis." [Krüll 1987: 2] Anthony Storr agrees that "Freud's realisation of the importance of phantasy" arising from the demise of the seduction theory "is a cornerstone in the construction of psychoanalytic theory", and adds: "On this basis rest Freud's theories of infantile sexuality and libidinal development, and also his view of dreams." [Storr 1989: 19] That the abandonment of the seduction theory and its replacement by theories involving unconscious phantasies opened the way for his analytic technique to provide him with his findings relating to childhood sexuality was affirmed by Freud himself on a number of occasions. In his *Autobiographical Study* (1925) he tells us that he had arrived at the seduction scenes "by a technical method which [he] considered correct"; when he realised his mistake he "was able to draw the right conclusions from [his] discovery: namely that the neurotic symptoms were not related directly to actual events but to wishful phantasies. . . ." Once "the mistake had been cleared up, the path to the study of the sexual life of children lay open". [S.E. 20: 34] That by "the study of" he means the utilisation of the analytic technique of reconstruction is clear from elsewhere in his writings. For instance, in his *History of the Psychoanalytic Movement* (1914) he writes: "In the beginning, my statements about infantile sexuality were founded almost exclusively on the findings of analysis in adults which led back into the past", [S.E. 14: 18] and his article "Psychoanalytic Procedure" (1904) confirms that by "analysis" he means the technique by which "the unconscious material may be reconstructed from the associations" by the physician. [S.E. 7: 252]

In the 1906 paper in which he intimates his renunciation of the seduction theory by stating that he had "learned to explain a number of phantasies of seduction as attempts at fending off memories of the subject's *own* sexual activity (infantile masturbation)", he writes that "between the symptoms and the childish impressions [i.e., masturbation] there were inserted that patient's *phantasies* (or imaginary memories), mostly produced during the years of puberty, which on the one side were built up out of and over the childhood [unconscious] memories and on the other side were transformed directly into the symptoms". [S.E. 7: 274] Now of course the contents of the conjectural phantasies are inferred by Freud himself.[1] But it is important to realise that this is not only true of the *phantasies*; he also infers the *unconscious memories* (in this instance, infantile masturbation). He makes this clear when he says that he *learned to explain* the phantasies as attempts at fending off memories of infantile masturbation. His knowledge of the infantile sexual activity does not come directly from the patient; it is again an inference. By a remarkable *tour de force* he manages to obscure the fact that the *only* secure datum he has is the original symptom itself—the rest is conjecture, based on preconceived theoretical notions.[2]

This specific instance is revealing in another important respect. By 1914, in the *History*, the story has changed so that what he had "learned to explain" in 1906 has become described as "the *discovery* that these phantasies were intended to cover up the auto-erotic activity of the first years of childhood". [S.E. 14: 18; emphasis added.] This provides an insight into the reality of so many of his

---

[1]This is spelled out, e.g., in *An Outline of Psychoanalysis* (1940), where he describes "our procedure in psychoanalysis" as follows: "We have discovered technical methods of filling in the gaps in the phenomena of our consciousness. . . . In this manner we infer a number of processes which are in themselves 'unknowable' and interpolate them in those which are conscious to us." [S.E. 23: 196–97] How the analytic technique is utilised to divine the contents of unconscious phantasies will be seen in the Dora case history later in this chapter.

[2]The point being made here is not that Freud was proposing speculative conjectures (which of course is an essential aspect of scientific endeavour) but that, as with the seduction theory episode, obfuscatory explications enabled him plausibly, but misleadingly, to claim such conjectures as "findings", "observations", or "discoveries".

claims, for what we can observe here in the making is the transformation of a conjecture into a "discovery".[3]

It is essentially by this method of inference that Freud arrives at
his "findings" in general, utilising symptoms, dreams, and appropriate associations of patients. He also makes use of what he calls
"screen memories", by which he means apparently innocent memories from childhood which supposedly mask more significant ones
from an earlier period. (In his paper "Remembering, Repeating and
Working-Through" (1914) he writes that in some cases "*all* of what
is essential from childhood has been retained in these [screen]
memories. It is simply a question of knowing how to extract it out
of them by analysis." [S.E. 12: 149]) Very frequently he uses dream
analysis for his purposes, and the importance he places on this
source of psychoanalytic material is apparent from the fact that he
devoted a considerable amount of time in the years from 1897 to
late 1899 to writing his celebrated book on the subject. An
examination of his method of dream interpretation will be deferred
until later, but some idea of his use of the art "for the discovery of
the hidden and repressed parts of mental life" [S.E. 7: 114], as well
as of his general analytic technique at that time, can be gained from
a study of his first major case history, based on a treatment which
commenced in early October 1900.

Dora

With the relinquishing of the infantile seduction theory Freud
believed he had discovered the existence of unconscious phantasies
and that he was in possession of a technique for elucidating their
contents. The first publication containing a detailed account of his
therapeutic procedure was the "Dora" case history ("Fragment of
an Analysis of a Case of Hysteria"), which he completed early in
1901.[4] [S.E. 7: 1–122] In the Prefatory Remarks he makes clear that
his purpose in writing it is to present his views on the causes and
structure of hysteria, to demonstrate that "hysterical symptoms are
the expression of [the patient's] most secret and repressed wishes"
[7–8], and to show how dream interpretation "can become the
means of filling in amnesias and elucidating symptoms" [10].

---

[3]Equally revealing is his reference to his "researches into the early years of normal people" in regard to the sexual impulses of infancy (*Three Essays on The Theory of Sexuality*, 1905). [S.E. 7: 192] Since "normal" (i.e., non-neurotic) people did
not go to him for analysis, it is evident that what he means here by research is a
process of introspective cogitation.

[4]It was not published until 1905.

Regarding the practicalities of writing up the case history he reports
that he made no notes during sessions, that he recorded the wording
of dreams immediately after the session in which they had been
recounted, and that the paper was written from memory after the
treatment was at an end.

Before looking at the actual analysis, there is one other point
concerning the Prefatory Remarks which is of interest. In his opening comments Freud states that in the paper he is proposing to
substantiate the views he had put forward in 1895 and 1896 upon
the pathogenesis of hysterical symptoms. In an obvious reference to
the fact that in "The Aetiology of Hysteria" he had implied that he
had available the clinical material which would substantiate his
claims of infantile seductions, he writes that at the time it was
"awkward" that he was obliged to publish the results of his
enquiries without there being any possibility of other workers in the
field testing and checking them. He continues: "But . . . now that I
am beginning to bring forward some of the material upon which my
conclusions were based . . . I shall not escape blame by this means.
Only, whereas before I was accused of giving *no* information about
my patients, now I shall be accused of giving information about my
patients which ought not to be given. I can only hope that in both
cases the critics will be the same, and that they will merely have
shifted the pretext for their reproaches; if so, I can resign in advance
any possibility of ever removing their objections." [7]

It was, of course, a justifiable complaint that Freud had not produced the clinical material on which his conclusions in the 1896
papers were based in spite of his implying he would do so. By
surmising it would be the same people who would now accuse him
of giving too much information about his patients, he ingeniously
manages to sidestep a perfectly legitimate criticism, while at the
same time putting himself into a position where he is able to
insinuate that his critics are "narrow-minded" and acting out of
"ill-will". In the case history itself he suggests that Dora utilised
reproaches against other people as an unconscious device to avoid
becoming aware of self-reproaches. In these opening remarks Freud
appears to be using a rather similar device to draw attention away
from a fact of which he must have been painfully aware, that in his
last major communication on the subject of his present paper he
had proclaimed a momentous discovery concerning which at the
time of writing he had yet to admit publicly that he had blundered.

The paper proper opens with a résumé of the background to the
case. Dora was eighteen at the time of her treatment, which
terminated after about three months. Freud lists her somatic
symptoms as dyspnoea (shortness of breath), a nervous cough,

aphonia (loss of voice), and possibly migraines, along with depression and "hysterical unsociability". [24] Together with her father, at whose behest she has reluctantly come to Freud, the people who feature most prominently in the account are Herr and Frau K., long-standing friends of the family. (Her mother plays only a peripheral role.) Dora is distressed because she believes that her father is having an affair with Frau K., and also because Herr K. has for some time been paying her unwelcome attention. Moreover, she senses that her father, in his own interests, has tacitly encouraged him, and is distressed at her father's making such a use of her. She reports that on two occasions Herr K. has made sexual advances towards her. When she was fourteen he had used duplicity to contrive a meeting at his place of business where he had "suddenly clasped the girl to him and pressed a kiss upon her lips", at which she had "a violent feeling of disgust" and "tore herself free from the man". [28] (Freud here remarks that "In this scene . . . the behaviour of this child of fourteen was already entirely and completely hysterical", for he would "without question consider a person hysterical in whom an occasion for sexual excitement elicited feelings that were preponderantly or exclusively unpleasurable".) The second occasion occurred when she was sixteen. She and her father were staying with Herr and Frau K. near a lake in the Alps, and Herr K. had made "a proposal" to her after a trip upon the lake. Dora had slapped his face and hurried away. [25] Nevertheless he continued to endeavour to spend his spare time in her presence and to ply her with flowers and expensive presents.

The analysis centres on the interpretations of Dora's somatic symptoms and of two dreams. Much of the account is concerned with Freud's attempt to convince his patient that she is unconsciously in love with Herr K. To this end he suggests that her repeated recriminations against her father for carrying on an affair with Frau K. point to the existence of similar recriminations against herself, and that they had the purpose of cloaking thoughts which she was anxious to keep from consciousness. Certain parallels indicated the content of these unconscious ideas. Her father had encouraged Herr K. to keep company with Dora, and had not wished to look to closely into Herr K.'s behaviour towards his daughter. In a similar way Dora had at first failed to recognise the true character of the friendship between her father and Frau K., and Freud suggests that this was in the interests of her relationship with Herr K. Her own governess had been in love with her father, and Dora had taken a great interest in Herr K.'s children. "What the governess had from time to time been to Dora, Dora had been to Herr K.'s children. . . . Her preoccupation with his children was evidently a cloak for something else that Dora was anxious to hide from herself and from other people." [37]

When Freud informs her of his conclusion that this indicated that she was unconsciously in love with Herr K., she does not assent to it. However, he has more arguments to bring to bear on her, culminating in the suggestion that the appearance and disappearance of her attacks of coughing and loss of voice were related to the presence or absence of the man she loved. He elicits that the average length of her attacks was "from three to six weeks, perhaps", and that Herr K.'s absences were for a similar period. "Her illness was therefore a demonstration of her love for K. . . . It was only necessary to suppose that . . . she had been ill when he was absent and well when he had come back. And this really seemed to have been so, at least during the first period of the attacks. Later on it no doubt became necessary to obscure the coincidence between her attacks of illness and the absence of the man she secretly loved, lest its regularity should betray her secret." [39]

It is of interest to examine this passage in the light of information given elsewhere in the paper. Freud had earlier reported that the symptoms of persistent coughing and loss of voice had started as early as her eighth year. [27] This in itself is of no significance since he argues that the unconscious utilises somatic symptoms for its own purposes. But he writes in regard to the coinciding of Dora's attacks and Herr K.'s absences that "this really seemed to have been so, at least during the first period of the attacks", and this does not bear serious examination. Are we really supposed to believe that Dora's unconscious love for Herr K. started in her eighth year, at the age of the first period of her attacks?[5] Or that she could remember from that time (ten years before) that the attacks coincided with Herr K.'s absences? Freud's words make it clear that in recent years there had been no coinciding, and the indecisive manner in which he makes the claim that at one time there had been raises the suspicion that this is in all likelihood a doubtful inference tentatiously adduced to lend support to his argument.

There is one further point to which it is worth drawing attention. Freud devotes the last paragraph relating to this interpretation to a discussion of the improvement in writing skill in the case of people who have lost the capacity to speak. He writes with regard to Dora

---

[5]That by "the first period of the attacks" Freud is referring to the time when they first started and not to a feature common to each episode is clear from the sentence which follows.

that "in the first days of her attacks of aphonia 'writing had always come specially easy to her'" (no source is given for the quotation), and concludes: "When the man she loved was away she gave up speaking; speech had lost its value since she could not speak to *him*. On the other hand, writing gained in importance, as being the only means of communication with him in his absence." [39] But though he tells us that Herr K. used to write to her at length, there is no mention of any cards or letters being sent by Dora to him in return. The whole paragraph seems calculated to create an impression that it lends support to his interpretation, but if one looks for the facts through the smokescreen of inferences it is clear that it does nothing of the kind.

Freud emphasises that the basis of a somatic symptom is as a rule constitutional or organic, and that unconscious thoughts utilise the "somatic compliance" of the symptom as a means of finding expression. [40] It follows that a given symptom may be representative of more than one unconscious idea, and a little later he is able to discover a second "determinant" of Dora's cough. He was led to it by two things, one being the fact that her cough continued while she repeatedly complained about her father, suggesting that the symptom might have some meaning connected with him; the other being that the previous explanation had not fulfilled a requirement he was accustomed to making in such cases: "According to the rule which I have found confirmed over and over again by experience . . . a symptom signifies the representation—the realisation—of a phantasy with a sexual content, that is to say, it signifies a sexual situation." [46–47] Fortunately, "an opportunity very soon occurred for interpreting Dora's nervous cough in this way". From a statement by Dora that Frau K. only loved her father because he was "a man of means", Freud infers that behind this phrase its opposite lay concealed, namely that he was "a man without means", i.e., impotent.[6] Following an admission that she knew her father was impotent, Dora acknowledges an awareness of nongenital ways of sexual gratification. She must, Freud writes, have in mind precisely those parts of the body which in her case were in a state of irritation—the throat and the oral cavity. This led to the "inevitable" conclusion "that with her spasmodic cough, which, as is usual, was referred for its exciting stimulus to a tickling in the throat, she pictured to herself a scene of sexual gratification *per os* [oral]" between her father and Frau K. [48]

---

[6]The editor notes that in German the expression is commonly used in the sense of both "not rich" and "impotent".

Not surprisingly, Dora "would not hear of going so far as this in recognising her own thoughts". However, "a very short time after she had tacitly accepted this explanation her cough vanished— which fitted in very well with my view". Having made his point, he adds: "But I do not wish to lay too much stress upon this development, since her cough had so often before disappeared spontaneously". [48] Quite what he means by saying that Dora tacitly accepted his explanation is not clear. In all probability it signifies nothing more than that she had tired of disputing his colourful interpretations.

A little later Freud extends the meaning of the symptom. He adduces material from which he infers that Dora was putting herself in her mother's place, and suggests that she was also putting herself in Frau K.'s place in the phantasy involving oral sex. She was therefore "identifying herself both with the woman her father had once loved and with the woman he loved now". [56] It followed that her affection for her father was a much stronger one than she would have cared to admit, that in fact "she was in love with him". Freud writes at this point that he has "learnt to look upon unconscious love relations like this . . . as a revival of germs of feeling in infancy" and that he had "shown at length elsewhere at what an early age sexual attraction makes itself felt between parents and children".[7] For years on end she had given no expression to "this passion for her father", but now she had revived it so as to suppress something else, namely, her love for Herr K. And with the recognition that "a part of her libido had once more turned towards her father", a further meaning of Dora's throat complaint could be derived: "it came to represent sexual intercourse with her father by means of Dora's identifying herself with Frau K." [83]

Dora gives a negative response in each instance when Freud tells her she is unconsciously in love with Herr K. and with her father. However, he is "by no means disappointed" when an explanation of his is met with an emphatic negative, for such a denial "does no more than to register the existence of a repression and its severity". [58] By interpreting associations brought forward by Dora as agree-

---

[7] A note added before publication at this point refers the reader to passages in *The Interpretation of Dreams* and *Three Essays on the Theory of Sexuality*. The latter (which in fact was not in existence when Freud wrote up the Dora case history) contains nothing other than an assertion of the Oedipal notions. The more extensive passage in the former claims a confirmation of these notions "with a certainty beyond all doubt" from the analyses of psychoneurotics, but the evidence adduced consists solely of tendentious interpretations of dream material and equally tendentious interpretations of anecdotal incidents involving children. [S.E. 4: 257]

ing with the content of his assertion, he is able to obtain "confirmation from the unconscious" of his inferences. "No other kind of 'Yes' can be extracted from the unconscious; there is no such thing at all as an unconscious 'No'." [57] Clearly, Freud has few difficulties in obtaining confirmation (one way or another) of his interpretations from the responses of his patients.

At this point he brings forward fresh arguments (for example, that a friend of hers had noted that she had gone white on meeting Herr K. in the street) in support of his contention that Dora was in love with Herr K. Nevertheless, Freud writes, she persisted in her denials for some time longer, "until, towards the end of the analysis, the conclusive proof of its correctness came to light". [59] As we shall see in due course, this "conclusive proof" turns out to be yet another interpretation, and the implication that Dora at last accepted his contention is not borne out by Freud's account of her response: "Dora had listened to me without any of her usual contradictions. She seemed to be moved; she said goodbye to me very warmly, with the heartiest wishes for the New Year and—came no more." [108–09]

Before completing this section Freud introduces us to a further complication concerning the multifarious contents of Dora's unconscious. Behind her reproaches towards her father relating to his affair with Frau K. was concealed not only her unconscious love for Herr K. but also "a feeling of jealousy which had that lady as its *object*". [60] This leads to the inference that her conscious concern involving her father was "designed . . . also to conceal her love for Frau K.". This can hardly have come as a surprise to Freud, for he had "never yet come through a single psychoanalysis of a man or a woman without having to take into account a very considerable current of homosexuality". In fact, he later concludes that Dora's "homosexual (gynaecophilic) love for Frau K. was the strongest unconscious current in her mental life". [120n] However, the premature termination of the treatment occurred before the analysis could throw light on this stratum of her unconscious.

The First Dream

The rest of the analysis revolves around the interpretations of two dreams. The first of these is recorded as follows: "A house was on fire. My father was standing beside my bed and woke me up. I dressed quickly. Mother wanted to stop and save her jewel case; but Father said: 'I refuse to let myself and my two children be burnt for the sake of your jewel case.' We hurried downstairs, and as soon as

I was outside I woke up." [64] The analysis of this dream and its
associations is too complex to deal with in detail here, and for the
most part only the conclusions reached by Freud will be presented.

On the basis of the fact that Herr K. had recently given Dora a
present of a jewel case and that the latter represented the female
genitals, and assuming that repression had caused "every one of
[the dream-elements] to be turned into its opposite", Freud is able
to interpret the dream as meaning that Dora wished to give Herr K.
a "return present". So she was "ready to give Herr K. what his wife
withholds from him", and this was "the thought which has had to
be repressed with so much energy". [70] The dream also confirmed
that she was summoning up her old love for her father in order to
protect herself against her love for Herr K.

A further interpretation was that the dream indicated that Dora
had wet her bed at an age later than is usual and that this was
because she had masturbated in early childhood. (Freud writes that
to the words of Dora's father in the dream, "I refuse to let my two
children go to their destruction" should be added from the dream
thoughts: "as a result of masturbation". [92]) At one stage in the
discussion Freud reports that they were "engaged upon a line of
enquiry which led straight towards an admission that she had
masturbated in childhood". [75] That this is rather overstating the
situation is clear from his words a short time later: "Dora denied
flatly that she could remember any such thing." But he writes that a
few days later she did something which he could only regard "as a
further step towards the confession". As she talked she kept playing
with a small reticule which she wore at her waist. Close observation
of such acts had shown him that they "give expression to unconscious thoughts and impulses" and are therefore "manifestations of
the unconscious". Dora's reticule "was nothing but a representation
of the genitals, and her playing with it, her opening it and putting
her finger in it, was an entirely unembarrassed yet unmistakable
pantomimic announcement of what she would like to do with
them—namely, to masturbate". [76–77]

Freud now invokes an incident when Dora hurriedly concealed
a letter she was reading as he came into the waiting room. he
naturally asked her who it was from, but at first she refused to tell
him. It turned out to be from her grandmother and of no relation to
the treatment. However, he infers that Dora wanted to play
"secrets" with him, and to hint she was on the point of allowing her
secret to be torn from her by the doctor. She was afraid that the
foundation of her illness might be discovered, that he might guess
that she had masturbated. Adding this incident to the reproaches
against her father for having made her ill (together with the self-

reproach underlying them), her leucorrhoea, the playing with the reticule, and the bed-wetting after her sixth year, Freud concludes that the circumstantial evidence of her having masturbated in childhood was "complete and without a flaw".[8] [78]

Since in children "hysterical symptoms . . . form a substitute for masturbatory satisfaction", he is now able to relate Dora's supposed masturbation to her dyspnoea. Her "symptomatic acts and certain other signs" give him "good reasons" to believe that as a child she had overheard her father "breathing hard while [her parents] had intercourse". He had long maintained that "the dyspnoea and palpitations that occur in hysteria and anxiety neurosis are only detached fragments of the act of copulation". In Dora's case her "sympathetic excitement" on overhearing sexual intercourse taking place between her parents may very easily have caused her inclination to masturbation to be replaced by an inclination to anxiety. Then, when her father was away and she was wishing him back, "she must have reproduced in the form of an attack of asthma the impression she had received". Her train of thought could be conjectured to have been as follows: The first attack had come when she had over-exerted herself in climbing; her father was forbidden to climb mountains or to over-exert himself because he suffered from shortage of breath; then came the recollection of how much he had exerted himself with her mother that night, and the question of whether it might not have done him harm; next came concern whether she might not have over-exerted herself in masturbating; and finally came the return of the dyspnoea in an intensified form as a symptom. [79–80]

In addition to uncovering childhood material (infantile masturbation) supposedly alluded to in the dream, Freud is also able to draw out a further connection with Herr K. after Dora belatedly relates that on waking up from the dream she had smelt smoke. At first he suggests that this indicated it had a special relation to himself, because when Dora denied that something was hidden behind this or that he would often respond, "There can be no smoke without fire!" [109] Dora objects to such a purely personal inter-

---

[8]In a note referring to "the way in which the occurrence of masturbation in Dora's case was verified" [80] Freud writes that "the proof of infantile masturbation in other cases is established in a precisely similar way". [81n] Since the "verification" in Dora's case consists of nothing more than a succession of tendentious interpretations, this sentence provides an insight into what constitutes a proof for Freud. He also claims that "the memory . . . of this piece of infantile sexual life emerges with certainty, and it does so in every instance". [81n] But this statement is contradicted by this very case history, since Dora continues to deny any memory of having masturbated in childhood.

pretation, pointing out that her father and Herr K. were smokers. Freud now argues that since the smell of smoke had only come up as an addendum to the dream, it must therefore have had to overcome a particularly strong effort on the part of the repression. Accordingly, it must relate to the thoughts which were the most obscurely presented and the most successfully repressed in the dream, that is, those concerned with the temptation to yield to Herr K. It could therefore "scarcely mean anything else than the longing for a kiss, which, with a smoker, would necessarily smell of smoke". This must hark back to the incident a few years earlier (at age fourteen) when Herr K. had given her a kiss, against whose "seductive influence" she had defended herself at the time by the feeling of disgust. Further, taking into account "indications which seemed to point to there having been a transference" onto himself, who was also a smoker, he concludes that "the idea had probably occurred to her one day during a session that she would like to have a kiss" from him. This would have been the "exciting cause" which led to the occurrence of the "warning dream" and to her intention of stopping the treatment. [109–110]

The Second Dream

The other dream whose interpretation plays a major role in the analysis is considerably longer than the first. The following is an abridged version of it: Dora was walking in a strange town. She came to a house in which she found a letter from her mother which told her that her father was dead. She then went to the station and asked repeatedly "Where is the station?". She next went into a thick wood and met a man who offered to accompany her, but she refused his request. Finally she found herself at home and was told that her mother and the others were already at the cemetery.

By means of associations to events in Dora's life, Freud is able to translate her question in the dream about the station to mean, "Where is the box [woman]?", and also "Where is the key?".[9] He interprets the latter question to be "the masculine counterpart to the question 'Where is the *box*?'" and concludes: "They are therefore questions referring to—the genitals." [96–97] A little later he associates the wood in the dream with one near the lake where the incident with Herr K. occurred and also to a wood in a picture at an

---

[9]The editor notes that the word used for "box" by Dora in the course of her associations is a depreciatory term for "woman".

exhibition she had visited the previous day. In the background of this picture there were nymphs. He continues:

"At this point a certain suspicion of mine became a certainty. The use of 'Bahnhof' [station] and 'Friedhof' [cemetery] to represent the female genitals was striking enough in itself, but it also served to direct my awakened curiosity to the similarly formed 'Vorhof' [vestibulum]—an anatomical term for a particular region of the female genitals. This might have been no more than mistaken ingenuity. But now, with the addition of 'nymphs' visible in the background of a 'thick wood', no further doubts could be entertained. Here was a symbolic geography of sex! 'Nymphae', as is known to physicians, though not to laymen (and even by the former the term is not very commonly used), is the name given to the labia minora, which lie in the background of the 'thick wood' of the pubic hair . . . If this interpretation were correct, therefore, there lay concealed behind the first situation in the dream a phantasy of defloration, the phantasy of a man seeking to force an entrance into the female genitals." [99–100]

In the course of expounding his interpretation Freud comments that "anyone who employed such technical names as 'vestibulum' and 'nymphae' must have derived his knowledge from . . . anatomical text-books or from an encyclopaedia". [99] But this statement only serves to underline the absurdity of the interpretation, since these associations occur in his own mind, and it is clear from the text that it was he, not Dora, who employed the technical terms.

Seemingly oblivious of this obvious flaw in his argument, Freud goes on to describe how he convinces himself that Dora must have at some time looked up the technical words in question in an encyclopaedia, though all Dora recollects is that she had once looked up the symptoms of appendicitis in an encyclopaedia because a cousin of hers had that illness. He now seizes on the fact that she herself had had a feverish disorder which was diagnosed as appendicitis. After demonstrating to his own satisfaction that these were hysterical symptoms, he utilises the fact that they apparently occurred nine months after the incident by the lake involving Herr K. to assert that they represented a phantasy of childbirth consequent upon that incident, and hence evidence that Dora was indeed in love with Herr K. At this point he reports, "And Dora disputed the fact no longer" [104], though it is unclear whether this is because of the persuasiveness of his arguments or simply that she was rendered speechless by the onslaught of fantastic interpretations to which she had been subjected. From the comments which follow, however, there is little doubt which of these was the case.

Freud writes that at the end of the session he expressed his
satisfaction at the result, to which "Dora replied in a depreciatory
tone: 'Why, has anything so very remarkable come out?'". At this
he tells us, "These words prepared me for the advent of fresh revela-
tions." They turn out to be nothing less than her announcement
that she is terminating the treatment, for he continues: "She opened
the [next] session with these words: 'Do you know that I am here
for the last time today?'." [105]

Conclusion of the Treatment

During this last session Dora recounts that a governess with the
K.'s had given notice while she was staying with them by the lake.
The girl had confided to Dora that Herr K. had made advances to
her on an occasion when his wife was away and that she had yielded
to them, but after a time he had lost interest in her. At this point
Freud informs us that here was a piece of material information
coming to light to help solve problems of the analysis. He is able to
tell Dora that he now knows her motive for the slap in the face with
which she had answered Herr K.'s "proposal". It was not that she
was offended at his suggestions; she was actuated by jealousy and
revenge. More inferences are then brought forward to justify his
contention that she "wanted to wait for him" and that she "took it
that he was only waiting till [she was] grown up enough to be his
wife". He concludes: "So it must have been a bitter piece of
disillusionment for you when the effect of your charges against
Herr K. was not that he renewed his proposals but that he replied
instead with denials and slanders. . . . I know now . . . that you *did*
fancy that Herr K.'s proposals were serious, and that he would not
leave off until you had married him."[10] [108]

This, then, is the "conclusive proof" promised by Freud that
Dora was unconsciously in love with Herr K. What the poor girl
thought of all this one can only conjecture. We know only that "she
came no more". It is clear that Herr K.'s unwanted attentions were
largely responsible for the depression and suicidal ideas which led
to her being induced to come for treatment in the first place, for her
father told Freud that the incident by the lake was the reason for his

[10]In a footnote early in the case history Freud had raised the questions: If Dora
loved Herr K., why did she refuse him in the scene by the lake, and why did her
refusal "take such a brutal form"? [38n] It is because he believes he now has the
answer to these questions that he triumphantly proclaims proof of his contention.

daughter's mental state and that she kept pressing him to break off relations with Herr K. and his wife. Freud quotes him as saying that Dora "cannot be moved from her hatred of the K.s. She had her last attack after a conversation in which she had again pressed me to break with them." [26] Given her distressed state, it would seem to be reprehensible that she should receive the kind of treatment to which Freud subjected her in his efforts to overcome her "resistance" to the notion that she was unconsciously in love with the man she in actuality detested.[11]

Needless to say, Freud is not short of explanations for Dora's abrupt termination of the treatment. Reading his complacent comments following his account of her departure, one has the impression of a man living in a world of his own delusions: "Her breaking off so unexpectedly, just when my hopes of a successful termination of the treatment were at their highest, and her thus bringing these hopes to nothing—this was an unmistakable act of vengeance on her part. . . . No one who, like me, conjures up the most evil of those half-tamed demons that inhabit the human breast, and seeks to wrestle with them, can expect to come through the struggle unscathed." [109] More insights relating to the second dream follow: "Screened by . . . thoughts of revenge, glimpses can be caught . . . of material derived from tender phantasies based upon the love for Herr K. which still persisted unconsciously in Dora. ('I would have waited for you till I could be your wife'—defloration—childbirth.)—Finally we can see the action of the fourth and most deeply buried group of thoughts—those relating to her love for Frau K.—in the fact that her phantasy of defloration is represented from the man's point of view . . . and in the fact that in two places there are the clearest allusions to ambiguous speeches ('Does Herr — live here?') and to that source of her sexual knowledge which had not been oral (the encyclopaedia)—Cruel and sadistic tendencies find satisfaction in this dream."[12] [110–11n]

In the light of passages such as these one is tempted to suggest that it is the physician who is subject to fantasies (though in his case they are conscious), not the patient. Quite clearly nothing, certainly no facts, could ever have shaken Freud's belief in his illusory notions, buttressed as they were by a formidable array of impreg-

---

[11]Freud produces not one iota of direct evidence that Dora was in love with Herr K., i.e., no evidence that was not based on an inference made on the *assumption* that such were her unconscious feelings.

[12]It should be noted that the two quotations in this passage are Freud's own conjectures of thoughts he supposes to be in his patient's mind and they in no way emanate from Dora.

nable psychoanalytic devices to cover every contingency and pursued with obsessional zeal. The latter is especially apparent in passages where he provides a continuous succession of interpretations, and at such times one has the impression of associations of ideas running riot. Everything is grist for his interpretive mill, and he seems to be oblivious to either absurdity or implausibility. His physician Max Schur has noted that at the time that he was influenced by the periodicity theories of his friend Wilhelm Fliess, he became so interested in the supposed significance of numbers that his preoccupation with them "had the characteristics of a severe compulsive symptom". [Schur 1972: 29] In a similar way in the Dora paper he displays a passion for making arbitrary associations which is so extreme that it too may be regarded as obsessional. [13]

Equally apparent is his preoccupation with the sexual. When he informs Dora that "jewel case" is to be interpreted as the female genitals, she responds "I knew *you* would say that". [69] Characteristically, he interprets this as confirmation of his suggestion, whereas to the reader it is clear that she is merely pointing to a self-evident fact, namely that it is difficult to conceive of any material for which he would not find a sexual connotation. One is reminded that in this connection Jung came to regard him as a "tragic figure . . . a man in the grip of his daimon". [Jung 1963: 150] He wrote that when Freud spoke of the importance of sexuality, "his tone became urgent, almost anxious. . . . A strange, deeply moved expression came over his face, the cause of which I was at a loss to understand." For Jung, "there was no mistaking the fact that Freud was emotionally involved in his sexual theory to an extraordinary degree". [147] Precisely the same impression is conveyed by certain passages in the Dora case history, and indeed the paper as a whole lends support to Jung's view. In the Postscript, Freud emphasises that a major reason for publishing it was that he was "anxious to show that sexuality . . . provides the motive power for every single symptom, and for every single manifestation of a symptom. The symptoms of the disease are nothing else than *the patient's sexual activity*. . . . I can only repeat over and over again—for I never find it otherwise—that sexuality is the key to the problem of the psy-

---

[13]The plethora of inferences made on the basis of associations, however tenuous, stems from Freud's belief in strict psychical determinism. What is extraordinary is the extent to which he augments the associations with ideas deriving from his own mind rather than from that of his patient's, and the confidence he displays in his ability "to translate into conscious ideas what was already known in [the patient's] unconscious". [49]

choneuroses and of the neuroses in general." [114–15] It is singularly ironic that the man who claimed to have solved the problem of the origins of neuroses should himself have suffered from something akin to an obsession which centred around this very solution.[14]

There is one other conclusion that can be drawn from this paper. In his *History of the Psychoanalytic Movement*, Freud uses an episode from it to demonstrate the influence of childhood experiences on events in adulthood. He refers to the scene by the lake and says that direct demands always failed to produce from his patient anything more than incomplete descriptions of it. Only after he had investigated her earliest childhood did a dream present itself which on analysis brought to her mind the "hitherto forgotten details of this scene, so that a comprehension and a solution of the current conflict became possible". [S.E. 14: 10]

Now, although in the paper itself Freud claims that the second dream "filled up a gap in her memory" [94], it is clear from the narrative that the additional information he is referring to came not from a recovered memory relating to the dream, but arose in response to questioning. [105] It was fresh information only because Dora had seen no reason to mention it before. (The reference is specifically to the last session in which Dora reports the occurrences relating to the governess employed by the K.'s which Freud utilises to "prove" that Dora was in love with Herr K.) But more important than this misrepresentation of the facts is that the words quoted above from his *History* give an indication of what Freud understands by a successful analysis. He clearly believes that he had arrived at the "solution" when he had demonstrated to his own satisfaction that his interpretation was correct. For Freud a successful analysis is one for which he is able to provide a narrative based on his theories that encompasses all the material (suitably interpreted) of the case. Although in a conventional sense the treatment did not have a favourable outcome since it was terminated prematurely, he immediately wrote it up for publication, for, as he

---

[14]In his paper "Freud, Cocaine, and Sexual Chemistry" [1983] Peter Swales argues that Freud's conviction that sexual impulses lie at the root of *all* neurotic disorders arose out of his *own* experiences with cocaine in the mid-1880s. Swales documents the evidence from Freud's writings that the latter's belief that "sexual toxins" were responsible for neuroses was directly referable to his subjective experience of cocaine as an aphrodisiac. In *Three Essays* Freud writes: "The neuroses, which can be derived only from disturbances of sexual life, show the greatest clinical similarity to the phenomena of intoxication and abstinence that arise from the habitual use of toxic, pleasure-producing substances (alkaloids)." [S.E. 7: 216]

told Fliess, "it contains solutions of hysterical symptoms". [Masson 1985: 433] In other words, in his own terms it was a success.

This first major case history raises a number of questions about Freud's analytic assumptions and preconceptions, and these will be considered in the course of this book. Perhaps the most basic in relation to this particular case has been addressed by Anthony Stadlen in a brief preliminary discussion paper, "Was Dora 'Ill'?". [Stadlen 1989] Stadlen points out that there is no indication that Freud ever questions his assumption that Dora's physical ailments were "hysterical"; he does not claim to have examined her physically before embarking on the treatment, nor sought information from her doctors. Nor does he demonstrate that Dora's distress was excessive or her behaviour unreasonable in the given circumstances. Not only had she, a girl of eighteen, been for sometime subjected to the unwelcome attentions of a man considerably older than herself, her father had supported Herr K.'s denial of untoward behaviour and connived in his designs on her in the interests of continuing his own "friendship" with Frau K. All this Freud acknowledges; he writes that Dora's reproach that her father was tacitly colluding with Herr K. so that he could remain unimpeded in pursuance of his relationship with the latter's wife was "a sound and incontestable train of argument". [S.E. 7: 35] Admitting that the psychoanalyst "is liable to feel a moment's embarrassment" when he is unable to dispute the rational nature of a patient's explanation for her disturbed state, he is forced to seek evidence of hysteria in an exaggerated response to her predicament in order to justify his preconceptions—and of course he finds it.[15] He takes the degree of bitterness she experiences in regard to her father's conduct as indicative of the presence of an unconscious motivation. He contends further that her bitterness points to self-reproaches, the source of which are feelings opposite to those she consciously expresses towards Herr K. Thus does he gain "an insight into a conflict which was well calculated to unhinge a girl's mind". [58]

Freud's procedure may be summarised as follows. He starts with the assumption that Dora is an hysteric. He then utilises his armoury of psychoanalytic techniques and preconceptions to tendentiously infer supporting evidence. This he claims as demonstrating the truth of his original contention. The circularity of such a procedure should be apparent.

---

[15]Within a week or so of the start of the treatment he reported to Fliess that the case "has smoothly opened to the existing collection of picklocks". [Masson 1985: 427]

Stadlen also questions the dubious ethical standard implicit in Freud's attitude to Dora. Herr K.'s first, carefully planned, sexual approach occurred when, in Freud's words, she was "a child of fourteen". [28] She was only sixteen at the time of the incident by the lake. On each occasion she emphatically and unambiguously rejected his advances, and took steps to avoid being alone in his company. At the outset of the treatment, Freud tells us, she insisted she wanted nothing more to do with him. In her state of distress at her father's taking Herr K.'s side and his refusal to break off relations with the K.s, she had been pressured into seeing Freud in the hope that he would "try and bring her to reason". [26] Concerned with his own preoccupations rather than with the reality of the young girl's predicament, Freud effectively acquiesces with the father's wishes and throughout the treatment bombards Dora with a stream of interpretations aimed at inducing her to doubt the integrity of her own feelings in regard to a man who had shown himself to be duplicitous and unworthy. When she breaks off the treatment his main disappointment is that *his* hopes of a successful case have come to nothing. Such is his lack of sympathetic appreciation of Dora's situation, he even surmises that if it had been revealed to Herr K. "that the slap Dora gave him by no means signified a final 'No' on her part" and if he had continued "to press his suit with a passion which left room for no doubts", the outcome of events might have been very different. [109]

In the light of the above, as Stadlen writes, Freud does not merely misdiagnose Dora's complaints, he fails to see that the primary problem is not any complaint of Dora's but her father's complaint *about* Dora. He is too preoccupied with his own preconceptions to recognise this, and therein lies his failure in the case of Dora.

CHAPTER FOUR

More Case Histories

The progress of Freud's ideas on human sexual development can be traced through his publications from 1905 onwards. It is in *Three Essays on the Theory of Sexuality* [S.E. 7: 123–245) that he first spells out in some detail his notions of the pregenital processes occurring universally in childhood. These he says he is able to derive, not only from reports of what are described as exceptional sexual impulses in childhood, but by "the uncovering in neurotics of what have hitherto been unconscious memories".[1] [176] In a footnote at this point he states, without substantiation, that he is able to make use of this source for his purposes, "since we are justified in expecting that the early years of children who are later to become neurotic are not likely in this respect to differ *essentially* from those of children who are to grow up into normal adults. . . ." (In context, "in this respect" would seem to refer to "the sexual occurrences [of childhood]" mentioned in the same passage.) Starting from the phenomenon of infantile amnesia (the virtual absence of memories from early childhood), and the likelihood that early experiences make a strong impression on the mind, he argues that the latter must have been repressed. Further, in line with the conclusions at which he had arrived in regard to adult psychoneurotics, the repression must be related to infantile sexual impulses. There follows an account of the sexual stages which, he postulates, all children have to pass through.

Within his schema he incorporates the notion that a number of sensual experiences not hitherto considered to be erotogenic in nature, such as thumb-sucking and anal sensations associated with excretion, should actually be so designated. Upon such premises he posits the occurrence of early infantile phases of oral and anal erotism, the existence of which he has "found from the study of neurotic disorders". [233] He also distinguishes three phases of infantile masturbation: the first belongs to early infancy, the second

---

[1]This statement is misleading in that it seems to imply that the supposed memories subsequently become conscious, whereas they are generally analytic constructions which elsewhere he acknowledges "quite often we do not succeed in bringing the patient to recollect". [S.E. 23: 265]

to a "brief efflorescence of sexual activity" in about the fourth year, while the third "corresponds to pubertal masturbation". The second phase, which may assume a variety of different forms, is of particular importance: "Its details leave behind the deepest (unconscious) impressions in the subject's memory, determine the development of his character, if he is to remain healthy, and the symptomatology of his neurosis, if he is to fall ill after puberty. . . . Psychoanalytic investigation enables us to make what has been forgotten conscious. . . ."[2] [189] After infancy there follows a period of prepubertal sexual latency, during which the energy of the infantile sexual impulses is diverted to social and cultural ends.[3] (In his later theory the latency period is preceded, between the ages of two and five, by a so-called phallic phase giving rise to a choice of sexual object.)[4]

Little definite information emerges in the paper in regard to his prime concern of the decade before, the aetiology of the neuroses. In his discussion of the factors interfering with sexual development he now emphasises "the innate *variety of sexual constitutions*, upon which it is probable that the principal weight falls". [235] Developmental disturbances may also result from accidental experiences in early childhood, or, more generally, as a consequence of the repression of one or other of the postulated sexual processes, diverting it into inappropriate channels via which it finds expression in symptoms. However, these factors are not to be considered as entirely separate influences, since they are mutually interrelated.

In *Three Essays*, which was completed and published in 1905, Freud takes the opportunity to acknowledge that in his 1896 "Aetiology of Hysteria" paper he had "overrated the importance of seduction in comparison with the factors of sexual constitution and

---

[2]From the earliest days of his investigations Freud had regarded masturbation as of the utmost importance. By the early 1890s he had designated it a prime cause of neurasthenia. In 1897 he reported to Fliess his "insight" that "masturbation is the one major habit, the 'primary addiction', and it is only as a substitute for it that other addictions—to alcohol, morphine, tobacco, and the like—come into existence." [Masson 1985: 287] Such was his single-mindedness in this regard that in one of his last notes at the very end of his life he writes: "The ultimate ground of all intellectual inhibitions and all inhibitions of work seems to be the inhibition of masturbation in childhood." [S.E. 23: 200]

[3]In an earlier paper he had acknowledged Fliess as the source of this notion. [S.E. 3: 281]

[4]Although not explicitly incorporated in the above schema, the notion of the innate bisexuality of all human beings is emphasised elsewhere in the paper, a postulate later to play an important role in Freud's theoretical formulations. In the 1905 edition of *Three Essays* he again identifies Fliess as his source for this notion. [S.E. 7: 220, 220n]

development", though at the same time denying that he had "exaggerated the frequency or importance of that influence". [190] However, as we have already noted, in a paper published the following year to present his views on the role of sexuality in the neuroses he asserts the contrary, that he *had* "over-estimated the frequency" of childhood seductions, as a result of the "chance" occurrence of "a disproportionately large number of cases in which sexual seduction . . . played the chief part". [S.E. 7: 274] This refashioning of his story serves to bring it more into line with the major innovation in this paper, the theory that hysterical symptoms represent unconscious phantasies having a sexual content, presented here formally for the first time. It is interesting to observe how, by a skilfully chosen form of words, he manages at one and the same time to imply he was not previously at fault ("a disproportionately large number of cases . . ."; " . . . in other respects [the seductions] were not open to doubt"), while also intimating "falsifications . . . in their memories of childhood" in an unspecified number of the very same cases, in accord with the idea he is about to put forward.[5] In essence this is that, rather than regarding hysterical symptoms as direct derivatives of repressed memories as before, he now postulates the existence of interceding unconscious phantasies (mostly produced during puberty), built out of and over repressed early memories on the one side, and transforming into symptoms on the other. With this new viewpoint "accidental influences derived from experience . . . receded into the background, [and] factors of constitution . . . gained the upper hand. . . ." [S.E. 7: 274] In justification of his changed position, Freud disingenuously asserts that "further information" which "now became available . . . led to the unexpected finding" [276] that the sexual history of the childhoods of normal people did not necessarily differ in essentials from that of neurotics, disregarding the fact that he had explicitly acknowledged this supposedly new information, and rebutted its significance in relation to his seduction theory, in "The Aetiology of Hysteria".[6] It is probably fair to say that, taken as a whole, this paper provides support for the view that

---

[5]By the next time Freud refers to the episode (in 1914 in his *History*) the supposed seductions, here declared "not open to doubt", have become almost completely discounted. [S.E. 14: 17–18]

[6]The same false assertion that he "did not then know that persons who remain normal may have had the same [seduction] experiences in their childhood" is made in *Three Essays*. [S.E. 7: 190] At the time he had specifically referred to "the observed fact that many people who remember scenes of that kind have *not* become hysterics". [S.E. 3: 209]

both Freud's clinical data and his arguments are to a considerable extent subservient to his current theoretical position.[7]

In his writings of this period, other than reiterating that the essence of neuroses "lies solely in a disturbance of the organism's sexual processes", Freud says nothing more specific concerning aetiology than the general statement in the above paper that it "comprises everything which can act in a detrimental manner upon the processes serving the sexual function". [S.E. 7: 279] In his paper on "Hysterical Phantasies", published in 1908, he asserts that the technique of psychoanalysis enables the physician to infer from the symptoms the unconscious phantasies from which the symptoms arise [S.E. 9: 162], but he does not specify the aetiological factors underlying the symptoms in a way which distinguishes the experiences of neurotics from non-neurotics. During this period and after he sought to provide clinical evidence for the infantile sexual processes he postulates, though in his subsequent writings, including the case histories, it is often by no means clear why certain supposedly universal processes, such as the castration complex, should have assumed pathological proportions in specific cases.

Little Hans

The castration complex (briefly alluded to in *The Interpretation of Dreams* and tentatively formulated in *Three Essays*) plays a significant role in Freud's account, published in 1909, of the analy-

---

[7]Precisely why Freud abandoned the infantile seduction theory is a matter of debate. Certainly, as Cioffi observes, his own published explanations are not coherent. [Cioffi 1988: 64] It may be that the answer lies in a conjunction of two main factors: 1. in the course of his lengthy ruminations he came to realise that he had been too precipitate in his espousal of his brainchild and overzealous in foisting the seductions on his patients, and 2. he recognised that in his unconscious phantasy theory he had a conception which enabled him to retain both infantile and sexual components of his speculations and his now indispensable analytic technique while discarding the problematic seduction theory, which involved him in excessive and time-consuming labours in his efforts to justify it in every case. His failure to resolve his current cases may also have played a part in eroding his faith in the theory, though, as Cioffi points out, while this might raise doubts about the *pathogenicity* of the supposed seductions, it could not of itself be sufficient reason for rejecting their *historicity*, had there been serious evidence for their occurrence. (Those who take the view that a significant factor was Freud's realisation that the seduction theory required an improbably high level of sexual abuse of young children overlook the fact that previously, in *dismissing* this very objection, he had cited documentary evidence which supposedly supported his contention that there *was* a sufficiently high incidence of such abuse. [S.E. 3: 207])

sis of a small boy who had developed a fear of horses. ("Analysis of a Phobia in a Five-Year-Old Boy", the case history of "Little Hans" [S.E. 10: 1–149]). In fact the boy was not actually treated by Freud, but by the boy's father under Freud's supervision. The father had for some time been supplying the latter with notes concerning his son's development, and it is on the basis of these notes taken during the treatment undertaken by proxy that Freud derives his analytic conclusions. Although he was frequently to cite the analysis as a source of corroborations of his theories, it has little to commend it for this purpose. In Freud's words, Hans "had to be told many things that he could not say himself", and "had to be presented with thoughts which he had so far shown no signs of possessing"; indeed, after making these observations, Freud felt compelled to state that the essence of psychoanalysis "is not to prove anything, but merely to alter something". [104] This information alone is sufficient to cast doubt on the evidential value of the case history, even without regard to its author's analytically tendentious interpretations of the notes. (In his summing-up he states revealingly that he had learned nothing new from the analysis that he had not already been able to discover from the analysis of adults, whose neuroses "could in every instance be traced back to the same infantile complexes that were revealed behind Hans's phobia". [147])

The boy had developed a fear of being bitten by a horse (and, related to this, an anxiety about going out onto the street) after witnessing a scene in which a bus-horse had fallen down. The infantile complexes supposedly revealed behind the phobia were associated with the Oedipal impulses of sexual desire for the mother and hostility towards the father. The commentary Freud supplies to the father's notes purports to demonstrate this, and to provide justification for the conclusion that the phobia was a manifestation of anxiety resulting from "the repression of Hans's aggressive propensities (the hostile ones against his father and the sadistic ones against his mother)". [140]

We shall examine a few examples of how Freud was "obliged to reconstruct the unconscious complexes and wishes, the repression and reawakening of which produced little Hans's phobia", basing his conclusions "upon the findings of analysis". [135]

Indications of the existence of Oedipal impulses come from an incident which occurred before the onset of the phobia. When Hans was about four he became fond of the landlord's fourteen-year-old daughter Mariedl, who used to play with him. On one occasion when he was being put to bed he said he wanted Mariedl to sleep with him. On having his request denied he suggested she sleep instead with his mother and father. The inferences drawn from this episode run as follows: Hans's desire for Mariedl to sleep with them meant "I want Mariedl to become one of our family". But Hans's parents occasionally allowed him to sleep with them, and "there can be no doubt that lying beside them had aroused erotic feelings in him: so that his wish to sleep with Mariedl had an erotic sense as well. Lying in bed with his father or mother was a source of erotic feelings in Hans just as it is in every other child."[8] [17]

Freud reports that soon after he was informed the boy had developed a fear of horses he arranged with the father that Hans should be told that the fear was a piece of nonsense, and that the truth was that he was fond of his mother and wanted to be taken into her bed.[9] The reason he was afraid of horses was because he had taken so much interest in their "widdlers". [28] Since "his libido was attached to a wish to see his mother's widdler", Freud also proposed that the father should inform the boy that his mother and all other female beings had no widdler at all. Not long after this, further indications of Oedipal impulses were forthcoming. Hans had been taken by his father to a zoo, where he had shown fear of the large animals, including a giraffe. About a week later he went to his parents' room after darkness fell and got into bed with them. His explanation the next morning involved a story about a big giraffe in his room and a crumpled one. The big giraffe had called out when the boy took the crumpled one away from it. When it stopped calling out the boy sat down on top of the crumpled one. (He crumpled a piece of paper to show what he meant.) That same day, Freud tells us, the father discovered the solution to the giraffe phantasy: "The big giraffe is myself, or rather my penis (the long neck), and the crumpled giraffe is my wife, or rather her genital organ." [39] The whole thing was a reproduction of a scene which had occurred almost every morning the last few days. Hans came to them and his wife could not resist taking him into bed for a few

---

[8]The paragraph relating the above inferences is enclosed in round brackets; before 1924 there were square brackets. In the paragraph, unlike the rest of this section consisting of the father's original notes, the father is referred to in the third person. These facts would seem to make it virtually certain that the passage is an interpolation of Freud's own. Nevertheless, when asked by the translators in 1923, Freud asserted that it originated with the father. [17n] However, the generalisation at the very end of the paragraph is hardly likely to have come from the father, suggesting, together with the other facts mentioned, that Freud's statement was not true.

[9]Though in the case history Freud strenuously denies suggestion played a significant role in the analysis, it is noteworthy that following Freud's proposals being put into effect, the father reported that the boy began referring to his phobia as his "nonsense". [30]

minutes. Thereupon the father warned her she should not do so, and she answered that it was all a lot of nonsense.[10] Then Hans stayed with her a little while. "Thus the solution of this matrimonial scene transposed into giraffe life is this: he was seized in the night with a longing for his mother, for her caresses, for her genital organ, and came into our bedroom for that reason." [39] Freud endorses this "penetrating interpretation", adding that it is justifiable to divine behind the phantasy "a fear that his mother did not like him, because his widdler was not comparable to his father's".[11] [40]

It is necessary for Freud's analysis of the phobia that the horse of which Hans was afraid represented his father. When the latter interrogates his son regarding the incident of the falling horse which precipitated his fear, to the question, "Was the horse dead when it fell down?" Hans first replies jokingly that it was, before saying the contrary. [50] The father notes at this point that the boy maintained a serious expression during this exchange. In his commentary Freud suggests that at the moment that Hans saw the horse fall "he perceived a wish that his father might fall down in the same way—and be dead", adding that "his serious expression as he was telling the story no doubt referred to this unconscious meaning". [52] Immediately afterwards the father is reported describing Hans playing horses and running up to him and biting him. Freud tells us that in this way Hans was accepting the above interpretation (his father had asked the boy if he had thought of him at the time) more decidedly than he could in words—"but naturally with a change of parts, for the game was played in obedience to a wishful phantasy. Thus *he* was the horse, and bit his father, and in this way was identifying himself with his father." [52] Later Freud summarises these conclusions as follows: "Behind the fear to which Hans first gave expression, the fear of a horse biting him, we had discovered a more deeply seated fear, the fear of horses falling down; and both kinds of horses, the biting horse and the falling horse, had been shown to represent his father, who was going to punish him for the evil wishes he was nourishing against him." [126]

It is on the basis of analytic evidence of this nature that Freud informs us that, in his attitude to his mother and father, Hans

---

[10]The father reports elsewhere that he tried (unsuccessfully) to stop the boy coming to their bedroom, telling him that while he continued to do so his fear of horses would not get better. [47] Clearly the boy's mother was of a different opinion.

[11]Elsewhere Freud writes that Hans "was afraid of big animals because he was obliged to think of their big widdlers", having come to the "distressing" conclusion that his "widdler" was defective in size. [34]

"confirms in the most concrete and uncompromising manner" his conjectures in regard to Oedipal impulses in male infants. He writes that Hans "wanted to have his father 'out of the way', to get rid of him", so that he might be alone with his mother and sleep with her. [111] The latter wish, we are told, originated when the boy's father was intermittently away from home, though the only evidence to be found for this in the case notes is a statement by the father that Hans was fearful when he drove away to the station for business trips, which the father interprets as a "repressed wish" that he should go away. [45] A little earlier, following an interview during which Freud had "disclosed" to the little boy that "he was afraid of his father, precisely because he was so fond of his mother" [42], the father describes how he had first divined that the boy was hostile to him. On a morning when Hans had come into his father's bed, he said (responding to questioning) that he had come because when he was not with his father he was frightened. The father soon came to recognise this as evidence of repressed hostility: "This suppressed hostile wish is turned into anxiety *about* his father, and he comes to me in the morning to see if I have gone away." [44] Freud naturally endorses this interpretation (having prompted him), and later informs us that despite the fact that the boy "deeply loved" his father, he nevertheless "cherished . . . death-wishes" against him.[12] [112]

The latter are a consequence of Hans's Oedipal desires towards his mother. Freud writes that following his occasional nights alone with her the boy "had been in a state of intensified sexual excitement, the object of which was his mother". [118] The chief evidence adduced to indicate the intensity of the excitement was an attempt at "seducing his mother", a reference to an incident when, while being bathed, Hans suggested she should put her finger on his penis, after noticing that she avoided doing so while powdering him. [19]

Freud is also able to detect other unconscious currents in Hans. At one point the boy talks about a wish to tease horses, which Freud explains as "compounded of an obscure sadistic desire for his mother and of a clear impulse for revenge against his father". [83] These would seem to be the same impulses whose early suppression he describes in his concluding discussion as possibly predisposing Hans towards his phobia: "hostile and jealous feelings towards his

---

[12]In the course of his account of the above episode the father reports Hans as saying: "Why did you tell me I'm fond of *Mummy* and that's why I'm frightened, when I'm fond of *you*?" His interpretation of this reproach is that Hans "evidently wants to get me out of the way. . . ."! (Freud describes the account of this episode as demonstrating "the progress of the father's enlightenment".) [44]

father, and sadistic impulses (premonitions, as it were, of copulation) towards his mother." [138] However, notwithstanding the presence of such intense feelings, Freud reports that the boy recovered from his phobia. But since he also tells us of phobias in children generally that "in the course of months or years they diminish, and the child seems to recover" [142], it would appear to remain uncertain to what extent the analysis was instrumental in curing Little Hans.

Before leaving the case history we must note one other episode that especially caught Freud's attention. He had already, in *The Interpretation of Dreams*, referred to the treatment of a youth during the analysis of whom he had provided an interpretation involving a surmise that the father had long before threatened the patient with castration [S.E. 5: 618–19], so the occurrence of a corresponding incident in relation to Hans naturally attracted his attention. As reported in the father's notes, when the boy was three and a half his mother found him with his hand on his penis, and threatened she would send for his doctor to cut it off. At this point Freud writes: "This was the occasion of his acquiring the 'castration complex', the presence of which we are so often obliged to infer in analysing neurotics". [8] This incident served the purpose of enabling him to fill in details not present in the brief discussion of the castration complex in *Three Essays*. Consistent with his extraordinary tendency to generalise from singular examples, he lost little time in positing an episode of a similar nature to be the common experience of all male infants, and presented the idea in 1908 in his paper "On the Sexual Theories of Children".[13] [S.E. 9: 217] However, other than to relate it incidentally to homosexuals, he does not suggest what role the trauma plays in the child's sexual development; at this stage he does not utilise it as a critical event in relation to the Oedipus complex.

In the case history of Little Hans, which he wrote up in the following year, the Oedipus complex is much discussed, as we have seen, but not in connection with the threat of castration. However, the conjunction between the two notions was effected shortly afterwards, in the account of an analysis of an obsessional neurosis which was published later the same year. For reasons which will become apparent, this account has a significance over and above its immediate subject matter, and the import of the auxiliary theme

---

[13]In that paper he makes the extraordinary assertion that when a small boy sees his sister's genitals "he *invariably* says: 'Her widdler's still quite small. But when she gets bigger it'll grow all right.'" (Freud's emphasis!) [S.E. 9: 216] Almost identical words are ascribed to Hans in the case history.

which will emerge is such that it will feature strongly in our examination of the case history and be of some concern in succeeding chapters.

The Rat Man

On 1 October 1907 Freud started treating a patient who was later to become known as the "Rat Man". The patient had been troubled over a period of many years by obsessive thoughts and compulsions, the former relating predominantly to fears concerning the safety of his father (now dead) and of his current ladyfriend. He was also subject to recurrent compulsive ideas involving rats. The ensuing case history is unique in that the original case notes covering some three and a half months of the treatment were found among Freud's papers after his death, whereas it was customary for him to destroy all his preliminary notes relating to his publications. In the course of preparing a study of the case history, Patrick Mahony [1986] was surprised to discover that there were significant differences between the Original Record [S.E. 10: 253–318], made on the evening of the day of treatment, and the published account ("Notes Upon a Case of Obsessional Neurosis" [S.E. 10: 151–249]). Most notably, he found that Freud had altered the chronological ordering and extended the duration of episodes occurring in the treatment. These latter discrepancies will be examined before we consider the case history in relation to the theoretical developments addressed above.

By correlating corresponding items in the two versions, Mahony has demonstrated that in relation to two important phases of the treatment Freud appears to have striven to create the impression that the narration was drawing on a considerably more prolonged period of time than was actually the case. [Mahony 1986: 72–78] Temporal discrepancies of this nature occur in the section pertaining to the precipitating cause of the patient's illness, and in that dealing with his "father complex" and the rat obsession. [S.E. 10: 195, 199–200, 292–93] Although the text of the case history sometimes implies that relatively extensive periods are involved, examination of the corresponding passages in the original notes indicates this not to be the case [209, 280–294]; for instance at one point Freud asserts that he learned of the patient's association of fees with rats six months into the treatment, [213] whereas this actually emerged after about two months [288]. Freud's prime concern in manipulating the time scale seems to have been to give the impression of a relatively prolonged period of treatment, in keeping with the reported duration of about a year in the case history. However, there are indications that the therapy, at least in intensive form, may not have lasted as long as Freud claims. The original process notes cover regular sessions from 1 October 1907 to 7 January 1908, followed by an unexplained break until 20 January, after which the record ceases. Textual comparisons between the two versions show that the conclusion of the clinical section of the published account correlates with material which had emerged by January 1908. Specifically, a supposedly lengthy period of "transferences", during which emerged the "solution" to the rat obsession with which Freud ends his narration (the remainder is headed "Theoretical"), actually took place between early November and 7 January, indicating that the analysis as published essentially corresponded to a period of little more than three months. Moreover, there are very few items in the published account which are not recorded in the process notes. Mahony has also drawn attention to a passage in the introduction to the 1959 English edition of Freud's paper "Character and Anal Erotism" (first published in March 1908) where Strachey writes that the latter had been in part stimulated by the analysis of the Rat Man "which had been concluded shortly before". [S.E. 9: 168] On the basis of the fictitious lengthening of episodes in the case history and the documentary evidence, Mahony suggests that it is likely that the period of intensive therapy coincided with the dates recorded in the process notes, and that the treatment continued only intermittently until April and very irregularly after that.[14] Though this surmise cannot be conclusively demonstrated, there are clearly grounds for suspecting that the effective period of therapy may have been appreciably less than that claimed by Freud.[15]

---

[14]In the introduction to the 1955 English edition of the case history, Strachey reiterates Freud's statement that the treatment lasted nearly a year. However, Mahony has demonstrated that Freud was away from Vienna in 1908 from the middle of July until the end of September, precluding the possibility of a continuous period of therapy of nearly a year from October 1907. Mahony notes that the last of Freud's irregular reports on the Rat Man case to the Vienna Psychoanalytic Society occurred on 8 April 1908, and that in that same month (during which Freud reported to Jung in relation to a proposed lecture that the case was not finished) the Rat Man commenced a period of professional employment (from 15 April to 30 September 1908).

[15]The fact that in his introduction Freud describes his published version as "fragmentary extracts" rather than a full case history does not dispose of the considerations listed above. Though it remains possible that there were regular therapy sessions for a period not covered by the extant process notes, this would leave unexplained the dearth of substantive material in the published history not in the original record, and the exaggerations of time scale.

Doubts also exist in regard to the claims in the case history of complete therapeutic success. At the close of the clinical section of the case history, after the relating of the "solution" of the rat obsession, Freud writes: "We should not be justified in expecting such severe obsessional ideas as were present in this case to be cleared up in any simpler manner or by any other means. When we reached the solution that has been described above, the patient's rat delirium disappeared." [220] As we have already noted, textual comparisons between the original record and the published account show that the phase of the treatment in question was completed by early January 1908. However, there is nothing in the process notes to indicate that the elucidation of the said solution coincided with the remission of symptoms as Freud claims. On the contrary, the notes reveal that on 2nd January the patient was still complaining of a feeling of having rats gnawing at his anus [308], and on the following day there is recorded an association exemplifying what is described as a rat "delirium" [313].[16] In his introduction to the case history Freud asserts that the treatment "led to the complete restoration of the patient's personality" [155], but this is con- tradicted by his own words in a letter to Jung in October 1909, in which he refers to "the one point which still gives him trouble", namely his "father-complex and transference" [McGuire 1974: 254], an aspect of the analysis which comprises an appreciable pro- portion of the published account.[17]

Mahony suggests that Freud exaggerated the duration and therapeutic efficacy of the treatment because he wanted the appear- ance of a complete case to impress his followers, and to promote the cause of the psychoanalytic movement. Whatever the motivation, his misrepresentations also involved a manipulation of the chrono- logical ordering of episodes in the treatment so as to enable him to utilise the case to enhance his current theoretical precepts, as we shall see in the next section.

A key episode in the analysis relates to a reconstruction of a childhood event, in regard to which Cioffi has drawn attention to a further example of dissembling on Freud's part. [Cioffi 1985: 35] In the published account the latter writes that at one stage he proposed to the patient a construction to the effect that as a small child he had been guilty of some sexual misdemeanour connected with masturbation, for which he had been soundly castigated by his

---

[16]Freud uses the term "delirium" in this context to refer to certain psychical structures related to obsessional ideas. [222]

[17]In the letter to Jung, Freud refers to his "conversations with this intelligent and grateful man", indicating he still retained some contact with him.

father. [S.E. 10: 205] This "punishment" had put an end to his masturbating but left him with an ineradicable grudge against his father as an interferer with his sexual enjoyment. Freud reports that to his "great astonishment" the patient then informed him of "an occurrence of this kind", namely a beating from his father, an event he himself did not recall but of which he had been told by his mother. However, the original record reveals that Freud did not conjecture a beating or similar punishment, but rather that as a small boy his patient had been in the habit of masturbating, and that in response his father had forbidden it, threatening, "it would be the death of you", and perhaps also threatening to cut off his penis. [263] Moreover, the incident is recorded along with two other unrelated memories in the same paragraph, and, far from registering astonishment, Freud does not identify it with the conjectured construction, or single it out for special attention. In fact, no part of this construction was confirmed by the patient (his mother subsequently stated that the boy had been punished because he had bitten someone [206]), but in writing up the case history Freud seizes on the patient's report to create the false impression that it provides support for his conjectured scenario, and hence for his fledgling theory of the castration complex. To this end, at this point he devotes a long footnote [206–08n] to an extended discussion of childhood recollections, in the course of which he almost imperceptively slips into treating the reported beating as if it were a memory of the *patient's* (when in fact it was told him by his mother). This dissimulation enables him to bring in his notion of unconscious phantasies and the supposed role of childhood memories in masking recollections of auto-erotic activities. He goes on to claim that a "deeper interpretation" of the patient's dreams in relation to this episode revealed that "his sexual desires for his mother and sister . . . were linked up with [his] chastisement at his father's hand". In such ways he insinuates an association between the reported episode and his theory of the Oedipus complex. By this means he endeavours to create an impression of having adduced clinical support for this notion, although in actuality there is nothing in the patient's report to justify this.[18]

---

[18]Curiously, some recollections and transferences reported in the case history in connection with the above incident [209] are recorded in the process notes as occurring at the time that the patient recalled a *second* beating (22 November), received after he had wet the bed when lying between his parents. [284] Possibly this second incident was not utilised because, being five or six years old at the time, the boy was no longer in the phallic phase of infancy.

We have seen in the case of Little Hans that Freud inferred
unconscious hostility towards the father as a necessary concomitant
of Oedipal desires. From the beginning of the present case history
he is clearly at pains to bring to the fore this same issue, and has
little difficulty in finding appropriate material. Following the
patient's recollection of two incidents, one from childhood and one
more recent, which had occasioned awareness of the intense distress
he would suffer should his father die and he lose "what I love most",
Freud informs him: "According to psychoanalytic theory . . . every
fear corresponded to a former wish which was now repressed; we
were therefore obliged to believe the exact contrary of what he had
asserted." [180] With the addition of "another theoretical requirement, namely, that the unconscious must be the precise contrary of
the conscious", he infers the existence of unconscious "hatred for
the father". [181] (When the patient protests that he loved his father
more than anyone else in the world, Freud answers that it is
precisely such intense love as his that was a necessary precondition
of the repressed hatred.)[19] Further tenuous inferences enable him to
divine that the source from which the supposed hostility "derived its
indestructibility" related to "sensual desires", in connection with
which the patient "must have felt his father as in some way or other
an *interference*". [182] It was on the basis of such reasoning that,
only twelve days into the treatment [263], he felt justified in
formulating the conjecture that in early childhood the patient had
indulged in masturbation and been warned by his father to stop,
possibly with a threat of castration. To conceal the degree to which
his preconceptions determined the course of the analysis, in the
published account he endeavours to create the impression that this
pivotal conjecture sprang quite naturally from material emerging in
the therapy sessions. For this purpose he chronologically transposed two incidents recorded at a later date in the process notes to a
time just prior to the presentation of the construction, claiming
them to have played a part in prompting the latter formulation.
[204, 205, 275, 302] Thus was produced what Mahony describes as
a "fictionalised reconstruction" of an episode which plays an important role in an account that purports to demonstrate clinical
support for fundamental psychoanalytic theses.

---

[19]At this point in his narrative Freud writes: "To be sure, the hatred must have
a source, and to discover that source was certainly a problem." [181] But this is
blatantly disingenuous, since he immediately proceeds to tendentiously interpret
material to purportedly demonstrate, in accordance with his analytic preconceptions, that the supposed hostility derives from the father's "interference" with
the patient's infantile erotic desires. [182, 201, 205]

From the foregoing it is clear that it would not be advisable to place much store on the evidential value of Freud's case histories. This becomes further apparent when we turn to his analysis of the patient who was to become known as the "Wolf Man", whom he started treating in the year following the publication of the account of the Rat Man's therapy. As we have noted, at this stage Freud sees his theoretical notions as requiring the occurrence of an episode in infancy to initiate the supposed pathological processes which result in neurosis, though the one he finds for the Wolf Man is rather different from that in the previous case.

The Wolf Man

The case history of the Wolf Man ("From the History of an Infantile Neurosis" [S.E. 17: 1–122]) is too complex to be fully examined here and, with the exception of one item which will be discussed in detail, we shall draw attention only to a few salient points.

The Wolf Man paper has long been regarded as a classic of psychoanalytic literature, a brilliant demonstration of its author's remarkable ability to fashion a coherent analysis out of innumerable details. In recent years it has come to have an additional claim on our attention, for its subject is the only one of Freud's patients to have come forward with his own story. Apart from writing his memoirs [Gardiner 1971], in old age he engaged in an extensive series of interviews conducted by Karin Obholtzer, and the record of these has been published. [Obholtzer 1982] We are thus now in possession of information to juxtapose against Freud's account, and this is invaluable, as the factual basis of his analysis is so interwoven with the interpretations that at times it is scarcely possible to distinguish one from the other.

Serge Pankejeff (the Wolf Man) was a Russian, born into a wealthy family. In his early twenties he suffered from severe depression, which eventually brought him to Vienna at the age of twenty-three to be treated by Freud. The analysis lasted for some four and a half years, from 1910 to 1914. For reasons which will become apparent later, the paper pertains only to a neurosis which made its appearance in early childhood, rather than to his later illness (though of course they were not unrelated). There is in fact some ambiguity on this point, since Freud tells us that the finding of the analytic solution to the childhood neurosis led directly to the successful conclusion of the treatment. [S.E. 17: 94] However, we shall not be concerned with the analysis in detail, but only with the factual basis on which Freud constructs his case history.

At the heart of Freud's analysis lies his interpretation of a dream which his patient recalled having had as a four-year-old boy: It was night, and through the open window of his bedroom the little boy saw six or seven white wolves with big tails like foxes sitting very still in a large walnut tree facing the window. He screamed in terror, and then woke up. Through a long series of associations Freud leads us to his interpretation of the dream: It represents a censored version of a memory of a coitus *a tergo* [from behind] between the boy's parents, which the boy probably viewed at the age of one and a half. (Freud describes this as the primal scene.) [29–37]

Having postulated an incident in the Little Hans case to be critical in initiating the onset of the castration complex, and contrived to represent the Rat Man's childhood beating as a similar pivotal incident, Freud was clearly determined to find an equivalent "scene" in the present case, and utilises the wolf-dream for this purpose. Although he builds his interpretation fragment by fragment, it is not difficult to discern that the elements in his constructive process are a consequence of a preconceived picture, rather than the reverse, as he affects to demonstrate.[20] This can be seen from the following (not untypical) examples of his interpretive method. The six or seven wolves represent the boy's parents, the disparity in numbers being explained as a stratagem of the unconscious to conceal the true meaning of the dream. The reported stillness of the wolves is a censored version of violent motion, as would occur in coitus. That the animals were white is an allusion to the white of the parents' bedclothes and underclothes. The wolves staring at the little boy with fixed attention is translated to mean the opposite, that is, it represents the boy staring at his parents in similar fashion. That they had notably big tails is an indication, contrariwise, of the recognition by the little boy, through his viewing of the primal scene, of the reality of castration.[21] Freud's

---

[20]In the Dora case history, Freud had surmised that as a child his patient had overheard her parents engaging in sexual intercourse. Similarly, in the Little Hans case he had sought indications that the boy had observed sexual intercourse between his parents, but he reports that the father had been unable to confirm his suspicion. [S.E. 10: 135–36] His belief that hysterical symptoms may arise from such circumstances derives from an incident recorded in *Studies on Hysteria*. [S.E. 2: 127n]

[21]Freud writes that the terror evoked by this conclusion broke out in the dream and brought it to an end. The traumatic force of the primal scene supposedly results primarily from the fact that through observing his mother naked the little boy became finally convinced of the reality of castration. This notion plays a crucial role in the analysis.

technique enables him to make associations by use of parallels, opposites, distortions, transpositions, and symbolism in a completely arbitrary fashion, and it was no exaggeration when, much later, the Wolf Man himself described the interpretation as "terribly far-fetched" [Obholtzer: 35]; in Erich Fromm's view it is "an example of obsessional thinking with complete disregard for reality" [Fromm 1982: 19], and it can scarcely be doubted that the primal scene existed only in Freud's imagination.

At one point in the case history, in the course of a general discussion of primal scenes, Freud states explicitly that in his experience "these scenes from infancy are not reproduced during the treatment as recollections, they are the products of construction" [50–51]; and the Wolf Man himself confirmed that he had not recalled the supposed event. Yet on two occasions Freud reports alleged statements made by his patient in which he describes specific details of the primal scene. [55,88] Since the Wolf Man was hardly likely to have given descriptions of an occurrence he did not remember, it would seem that Freud misleadingly embellished his account in order to give more credence to his vital interpretation of the wolf-dream.

It is likely that this is by no means the only instance of Freud's misinforming the reader. In his memoirs and the interviews with Karin Obholtzer, the Wolf Man's version contradicts that of Freud on a number of counts, as can be seen from the following list:

F: The patient was "entirely incapacitated" and "in a state of complete helplessness" at the start of the treatment. [S.E. 17: 7; 23: 217]

W: He was considerably improved by the time he came to Freud, and able to engage in a large number of social activities. [Gardiner 1971: 82, 83, 89; Obholtzer 1982: 40–41]

F: On the death of his sister the Wolf Man showed no sign of grief, and in fact rejoiced in being the sole heir to their father's property. [S.E. 17: 23]

W: He fell into a state of mental agony, and the event marked the onset of his serious depression. [Gardiner: 25; Obholtzer: 89]

F: The patient's intestinal trouble was functional in nature. [S.E. 17: 75–76, 80]

W: Some inappropriate medicine prescribed by a country doctor had permanently damaged the mucous membranes of his intestines, resulting in chronic bowel trouble. [Obholtzer: 47]

F: The intestinal symptoms cleared up in the course of the treatment. [S.E. 17: 76]

W: He emphatically denies Freud's claim. The trouble remained with him the rest of his life. [Obholtzer: 48]

F: The Wolf Man fell passionately in love with the peasant girl from whom he contracted gonorrhoea. [S.E. 17: 91, 93]

W: He was not in love with the girl, and merely gave her a present in return for her favours. [Obholtzer: 27]

F: After the fixing of a time limit there was a dramatic change in his patient's behaviour, following a long period of stagnation. [S.E. 17: 11]

W: He several times expresses scepticism about this claim. [Obholtzer: 39–40]

F: In his narration of the dream the animals were wolves. [S.E. 17: 29]

W: The animals sitting in the tree "were not wolves at all but white Spitz dogs with pointed ears and bushy tails". [*Psychoanalytic Quarterly* 1957, 26: 449] (At one point in the case history Freud himself asserts as a "fact" that the animals "were actually sheep dogs". This was at a time when he needed sheep dogs for an alternative interpretation of the dream. [S.E. 17: 57–58]).

F: The Wolf Man's sister repeatedly tormented him by showing him a picture of a wolf standing upright and striding forward, which caused him to scream that he was afraid of the wolf eating him up. [S.E. 17: 29–30]

W: There was a single occasion when his sister told him she would show him a picture of a pretty little girl, only to reveal a wolf on its hind legs about to swallow Little Red Riding Hood, and his scream was in anger at his sister's teasing rather than due to a fear of the wolf. [Gardiner: 7] It is notable that although the Wolf Man recalls wolf-hunts from his early childhood, he makes no mention of a phobia about wolves in his memoirs, and it may well be that Freud's claim to this effect is based on the one incident recounted by his patient, together with the fact that he had a nightmare supposedly involving wolves.[22]

---

[22]It is true that in a letter to Freud in 1926 the Wolf Man writes that the wolf dominated his childhood fantasies, but that is by no means the same thing as a phobia. [*Psychoanalytic Quarterly* 1957, 26: 449]

Of course, it cannot be automatically assumed that, where they conflict, the patient's version rather than Freud's represents the true story. However, there are several grounds for deeming it most likely that this is generally the case. We have seen, for example in regard to the seduction theory accounts and the Rat Man case history, that Freud has a tendency to dissemble when it suits his purpose; we shall present considerably more evidence to this effect in due course. Certainly, where there is evidence available in particular instances, it supports the Wolf Man's version. Such is the case in respect of the latter's intestinal trouble. In the case history Freud writes that the patient's bowel "recovered its normal functions after their long impairment", and later, in the same context, refers to "the final clearing up of [the] patient's symptoms". [S.E. 17: 76, 84] When questioned by Obholtzer on the same subject the Wolf Man says that he "somehow got it to come by itself, a few times. And [Freud] wrote 'We've been successful!' No such thing!" He adds emphatically that the problem "has stayed with me to the present day; my intestines don't work by themselves." [Obholtzer: 47, 48] Now, in a footnote added to the case history in 1923, Freud writes that the Wolf Man had further treatment from him in 1919 to deal with "a piece of the transference which had not hitherto been overcome". [122n] The analyst Ruth Mack Brunswick, who treated the Wolf Man for some months during 1926–27, reports that the additional period of therapy in 1919 was for the purpose of dealing with the intestinal trouble [Gardiner: 266], confirming that it had *not* been cleared up as Freud claimed. Again, in regard to the animals in the dream, Freud asserts that they were wolves, whereas in a letter written in 1926 the Wolf Man reiterates that he had recounted them to be white Spitz dogs. A delay in the publication of the case history due to the onset of the 1914–18 war gave Freud the opportunity of inserting two short sections, in one of which he proposed an alternative interpretation of the dream featuring sheep dogs. At this point he writes that "colour is lent to this view above all by the fact that the wolves in the dream were actually sheep dogs" [57–58], a clear corroboration of the Wolf Man's words. Had there not been an unforeseen delay in publication, we would not have had any intimation that the recounting of the dream may have been other than as Freud reported it.

More generally, Freud's propensity to present as fact what he infers for his analyses manifests itself with respect to his assertions concerning the patient's early boyhood relationship to his father. In his introductory survey Freud reports that it was a "very affectionate one" [17], as does the Wolf Man in his memoirs, though in later years there was some estrangement because of his father's

increasingly frequent depressive states. [Gardiner: 8] However,
Freud's analysis (as with Little Hans and the Rat Man) requires the
existence of antagonistic feelings from an early age, and in accord
with this in the main body of the history he repeatedly asserts as
fact his inference that the little boy feared his father. Freud's
propensity to posit analytic inferences as facts contributes towards
the unreliability of his accounts; we have noted above another
example of this in his discussion of the primal scene, in regard to
which he reports statements which misleadingly create the impression of their being first hand recollections of that event.

From the foregoing it is clear that there are good grounds for
doubting the trustworthiness of Freud's account of the treatment; it
appears that on occasion he is not above inventing the material he
needs for his analysis.[23] In some instances the misinformation is by
no means trivial, as for example in the case of the Wolf Man's
intestinal problem. Freud expounds at great length on his theory of
anal erotism which supposedly reveals the underlying causes of his
patient's condition. Many of these passages would have been seen
to be redundant had he disclosed the truth about it, and had he not
lent support to his interpretations by falsely claiming to have
effected a cure.[24]

Something of the flavour of the kind of interpretations to be
found in the Wolf Man paper can be obtained from a sketch of
Freud's analysis of the role played by the patient's bowel condition
in his neurosis. After a brief discussion of the Wolf Man's infantile
anal erotism, he reports that at the age of about four the boy
became apprehensive as a result of his mother giving orders that he
and his sister be protected against dysentery, which had appeared in
the neighbourhood. After hearing that with this disease blood is
found in one's stool, he became very nervous and declared (errone-
ously) that there was blood in his own stool. His dread, Freud
writes, indicates that he was trying to put into effect an identification with his mother, who suffered from abdominal troubles which
had involved haemorrhages. The meaning of this identification is
explained as follows:

---

[23]The point being made is not that Freud reconstructs inferred events (which is
an acknowledged procedure in his interpretive technique), but that at times he distorts, or even fabricates, the factual basis on which his interpretations are based.

[24]In an article responding to Obholtzer's book Muriel Gardiner defends her psychoanalytic colleagues against criticisms made by the Wolf Man, but reports
nothing bearing directly on the points raised above. [Gardiner 1983]

Dysentery was evidently his name for the illness which he had heard his mother lamenting about . . .; he did not regard his mother's disease as being abdominal but as being intestinal. Under the influence of the primal scene he came to the conclusion that his mother had been made ill by what his father had done to her; and his dread of having blood in his stool, of being as ill as his mother, was his repudiation of being identified with her in this sexual scene—the same repudiation with which he awoke from the dream. But the dread was also a proof that in his later elaboration of the primal scene he had put himself in his mother's place and envied her this relation with her father. The organ by which his identification with women, his passive homosexual attitude to men, was able to express itself was the anal zone. The disorders in the function of this zone had acquired the significance of feminine impulses of tenderness, and they retained it during his later illness as well. [S.E. 17: 78]

Freud now discusses two of the symbolic meanings faeces have for children, "gifts" and "babies". This leads him to announce that the deeper significance of the patient's early "screen memory" of a fit of rage when he was not given enough presents one Christmas is now revealed: "What he was feeling the want of was sexual satisfaction, which he had taken as being anal." He also adds "to the sexual currents that are already known to us" that the boy "was ready to give his father a baby, and was jealous of his mother, who had already done so and would perhaps do so again". [82]

Further, since both "money" and "baby" have the sense of a "gift", "money can take over the meaning of baby and thus become the means of expressing feminine (homosexual) satisfaction". This, Freud tells us, explains an incident when, seeing his father give his sister two large bank notes, the boy had rushed at his sister and demanded a share of the money with great vehemence: "What had excited him was not merely the actual money, but rather the 'baby'—and sexual satisfaction from his father." [83]

We shall leave the remainder of this passage, in which Freud utilises the notion that "faeces", "baby", and "penis" form an unconscious unity, and move on to the section where he explains the origins of the patient's intestinal trouble. He writes that "the analysis of the anxiety-dream shows us" that the boy's "homosexual attitude understood in the genital sense" was repressed at that time. The motive force of the repression "seems to have been the narcissistic masculinity which attached to the boy's genitals". [109–110] The consequences of this repression were not only anxiety symptoms, but also somatic symptoms brought about by conversion: "A portion of the homosexual impulse was retained by the organ concerned in it; from that time forward, and equally during his adult life, his bowel behaved like a hysterically affected organ. The unconscious repressed homosexuality withdrew into his bowel." [113]

Elsewhere in the case history Freud utilises the notion of unconscious homosexuality in his explanation of the fact that the Wolf Man's habitual feeling of being cut off from the world by a veil only left him after he had evacuated his bowels using an enema.[25] He sees this as a symbol of rebirth:[26]

> The stool was the child, as which he was born a second time, to a happier life. . . . The necessary condition of his re-birth was that he should have an enema administered to him by a man. . . . This can only have meant that he had identified himself with his mother, that the man was acting as his father, and that the enema was repeating the act of copulation, as the fruit of which the excrement-baby (which was once again himself) would be born. The phantasy of re-birth was therefore bound up closely with the necessary condition of sexual satisfaction from a man. So that the translation now runs to this effect: only on condition that he took the woman's place and substituted himself for his mother, and thus let himself be sexually satisfied by his father and bore him a child—only on that condition would his illness leave him. Here, therefore, the phantasy of re-birth was simply a mutilated and censored version of the homosexual wishful phantasy. [100]

Freud goes on to relate this to the primal scene. He writes that "in this condition which he laid down for his recovery the patient was simply repeating the state of affairs at the time of the 'primal scene'. At that moment he had wanted to substitute himself for his mother, and . . . it was he himself who, in the scene in question, produced the excrement-baby.[27] He still remained fixated . . . to the scene which had such a decisive effect on his sexual life. . . ." [100–01]

Finally, Freud is able "to make clear the whole meaning which underlay" the circumstances that prompted the above analysis: "He wished he could be back in the womb, not simply that he might then be re-born, but in order that he might be copulated with there by his father, might obtain sexual satisfaction from him, and might bear

---

[25]Since the unfortunate incident when he had been prescribed a medication which he was later told was normally only given to horses, the Wolf Man had had to resort to the regular use of an enema. This was administered by a manservant until the latter returned to Russia. [Obholtzer: 47]

[26]The link with birth arises because the Wolf Man reported being told he had been born with a caul.

[27]Freud had ealier conjectured that the child had interrupted his parents' intercourse by passing a stool as a sign of his sexual excitment. [80–81]

him a child." Further, the phantasy of re-birth is "in all probability regularly a softened substitute . . . for the phantasy of incestuous intercourse with the mother. . . . There is a wish to be back in a situation in which one was in the mother's genitals; and in this connection the man is identifying himself with his own penis and is using it to represent himself." [101–02]

It is clear that Freud's obsession with sexual matters had not diminished in the years which had elapsed since he had written his first case history. Nor indeed had the implausibility of most of his interpretations, though not all of them attain quite the level of absurdity of the one just outlined. In recent years even Freudians have publicly questioned the plausibility of some of them, most notably that of the wolf-dream. Nevertheless, this seems to have scarcely tempered the eulogies heaped on the case history. Describing it as "one for all time", one such friendly critic (Patrick Mahony) finds spelled out in it "an impressive multiple etiology for the Wolf Man's neurosis" among which he lists a traumatising primal scene; oral, urethral, anal, and phallic factors; and castrating experiences. [Mahony 1984: 157] Why he remains impressed by the first item when he had just cast doubts on its reconstruction, its historical reality, and its clinical interpretation, he does not explain. Nor is it clear why the undermining of what is the very foundation of the analysis should not call into question most of the other items on the list, since they supposedly acquired much of their impetus from it.

Considering interpretations such as that of the wolf-dream or of the Wolf Man's bowel trouble, one is faced with the question: In what way could they conceivably contribute to solving the patient's problems? And the same has to be asked of the analysis as a whole. The contention sometimes advanced nowadays that the therapeutic effect of an analysis derives, at least in part, from its coherence, the explanatory power of the interpretations, and the belief of the patient, fails to find validation in this case, for it exhibits these requirements to an exceptional degree. (The extraordinarily coherent structure and masterly ordering of detail is one of the notable features of the analysis, and the patient eventually came under the influence of his physician to such a degree that he later described it as like being hypnotised.) Yet it is clear from the record of his subsequent experiences that the Wolf Man continued to experience severe psychological problems, as we shall see in a later chapter.

There remains the view that in spite of its deficiencies the paper contains profound insights into the workings of the mind. This too must be regarded as highly questionable in the light of the implausible interpretations and therapeutic inefficacy of the analysis. But beyond all such considerations there is one further reason for calling into question the value of the Wolf Man case history. Its importance requires that it be given a chapter to itself.

Grusha

It is clear from the testimony of its subject that the factual basis of the Wolf Man case history cannot be regarded as reliable. This is of considerable relevance in connection with the episode which we shall now examine. It concerns an incident involving a servant girl which plays a crucial part in furnishing the "solution" to the analysis. She makes her appearance after the treatment has been in progress some four years, and the episode in question is second in importance only to the wolf-dream.

Freud approaches her arrival on the scene indirectly. He tells us first of a childhood memory of the Wolf Man's in which he was terrified by a yellow-striped butterfly, and notes that in Russian a butterfly is called *babushka* ("granny").[1] He then writes that on another occasion his patient had remarked that the opening and shutting of a butterfly's wings reminded him of a woman opening her legs. Only after these apparently unconnected observations does he describe how one day there emerged an indistinct recollection from a very early age of a nursery maid who was very fond of him. Her name was first given as the same as the patient's mother, but this was later amended. The thought of some yellow-striped pears grown on his parents' estate reminded him of her real name, Grusha, the same as that of the fruit. A little later came a recollection of a scene in which Grusha was kneeling on the floor, beside a pail and a broom. [S.E. 17: 89–91]

Freud next narrates a number of recollections of the patient's that appear to be related to the scene with Grusha, which occurred when the boy was about two-and-a-half years old. By means of his interpretive method he proceeds to infer more details of the incident, so that he is able to associate it directly with the primal scene. He tells us that she "became his mother to him; he was seized with sexual excitement" owing to the reactivation of the memory of his mother's posture in the primal scene by his view of her "with her buttocks projecting and her back horizontal". [92–93] As a consequence of this, Freud infers, he had micturated on the floor, to which the girl had responded with a threat of castration. In this way

---

[1]The Russian word for butterfly is actually *babochka*.

the compulsion which proceeded from the primal scene was transferred to the scene with Grusha, thereby introducing the element of
his fixation to women of low social status which was a feature of his
adult sexual disposition. Once the connections to the Wolf Man's
subsequent experiences had been made the treatment went forward
smoothly to its successful conclusion.

At first sight there appears to be nothing exceptional in the
passages describing the Grusha scene and its ramifications in the
context of the case history; but on closer inspection there are one or
two clues which suggest that all may not be as it seems. Most
notable is the number of times that the author insists that he played
no part in the emergence of the scene; there are no less than three
such instances, and in addition a more general assertion denying the
role of the therapist's imagination in the results of analyses. Now, if
someone repeatedly proclaims his innocence in circumstances in
which no misdemeanour is apparent, it naturally arouses suspicions, and Freud's behaviour certainly does so here. As it happens,
there are several other grounds which lead one to suspect that he
played precisely that role with respect to the Grusha scene which he
is so anxious to deny. But before turning to these it is important to
read exactly what he himself says about the episode:

> When once the Grusha scene had been assimilated—the first
> experience that he could really remember, and one which he had
> remembered without any conjectures or intervention on my
> part—the problem of the treatment had every appearance of
> having been solved. [94]
>
> The Grusha scene emerged in the patient's memory spontane-
> ously and through no effort of mine. [95]
>
> The Grusha scene was, as I have said, a spontaneous product
> of the patient's memory, and no construction or stimulation by
> the physician played any part in evoking it. [112n]

In addition to these, the following occurs in relation to material
associated with the Grusha scene: "I only mention this as an
illustration to show how inadequate the physician's constructive
efforts usually are for clearing up questions that arise, and how
unjust it is to attribute the result of analysis to the physician's
imagination and suggestion." [88–89]

Are these protestations of innocence sufficient grounds for us to
be suspicious of Freud's behaviour? Well, it so happens that
something rather similar occurs in his *History of the Psychoanalytic Movement*—only in that case his stratagem is transparent
enough for all to see. To appreciate the passage in question it is
necessary to know something of the background to the writing of

the *History*, which was completed in the spring of 1914 (a few months before he started work on the Wolf Man paper). Ronald Clark has documented the evidence that Freud's primary purpose in writing it was to attack Jung and Adler. [Clark 1980: 334–36]. In a letter to Lou Andreas-Salomé he expressed his expectation that the publication of his *History* would "put an end to all compromises and bring about the desired rupture" with Jung. He later wrote to her that he intentionally gave "the adversaries, diluters and misinterpreters" a "good clobbering" and explained his justification for being allowed "to abuse them for the pollution which the cause suffers at their hands". [Pfeiffer 1972: 16, 17] To James Putnam he explained: "I must protect myself against people who have called themselves my pupils for many years and who owe everything to my stimulus. Now I must accuse them and reject them." [Hale 1971: 176] Yet in the section of his *History* in which he recounts his version of the secessions of his psychoanalytic rivals he claims that he is doing so "without any strong personal motive", and adds that it is a "very severe drawback [*sic*]" that he "cannot entirely avoid throwing some analytic light on these two opposition movements". [S.E. 14: 49] What is significant from our point of view is that having denied any personal interest, he promptly launches into a bitter attack on Adler, accusing him of being guilty of "petty outbursts of malice", an "uncontrolled craving for priority", and being "dominated" by ambition. [51] Then, in a reference to "the inconsistencies displayed in the various public and private pronouncements made by the Jungian movement", he insinuatingly wonders "how much of this is due to lack of clearness and how much is lack of sincerity". [60] (He had earlier described Jung as a man "incapable of tolerating the authority of another", whose energies were "relentlessly devoted to the furtherance of his own interests". [43]) He also assures his readers that he will "restrict to a minimum . . . indiscretion and aggressiveness towards [his] opponents" [49]—only to go on to commit the indiscretion of quoting specific criticisms made by a patient of the Jungian analysis he had undergone.[2] [63–64] Astonishingly, Freud seems to be unaware that by explicitly making denials which manifestly contrast with his actual behaviour, his words have the opposite effect to that in-

---

[2]That Freud himself regards this as an indiscretion is clear from the fact that he finds it necessary to excuse himself, somewhat lamely, as follows: "I know the objections there are to making use of a patient's reports, and I will therefore expressly state that my informant is a trustworthy person, very well capable of making a judgement." [64n]

tended: they draw attention to his stratagem, which in this case is to undermine the standing of his rivals. It is precisely this same idiosyncratic personality trait which appears to be in evidence with regard to the Grusha scene; here again his repeated denials that he had played any part in the emergence of Grusha only serves to draw attention to the issue, and to arouse the suspicion that he has something to hide.[3]

Now that we have cause to question the truth of Freud's claim that he played no role in the emergence of the Grusha scene, the manner in which he describes the first memory of the girl appears rather strange: "One day there emerged, timidly and indistinctly, a kind of recollection that at a very early age . . . he must have had a nursery maid. . . ." [S.E. 17: 90] His use of the word "must" in particular is suggestive, as it is again a few lines later in regard to this "first love that had faded into oblivion": "But we agreed that something must have occurred at that time that became of importance later on." The latter sentence in particular gives the impression that it was *necessary* for there to have been such an incident to satisfy Freud's analysis. As we shall see later, it was crucial that an incident such as that involving Grusha had occurred, for without it the case history could not be satisfactorily completed. In such a situation it was Freud's normal practice to infer an appropriate scene which would satisfy his analysis, and to present it as a construction to his patient. On a previous occasion he had described his procedure as comparable to the solving of a jigsaw puzzle: "We become absolutely certain in the end which piece belongs in the empty gap" owing to its "relationship . . . to the content of the whole of the rest of the case history". [S.E. 3: 205] Compare this to his statement regarding the Grusha scene: "But we agreed that something must have happened at that time that became of importance later on." In the context the "must" may well say more about an idea in Freud's mind than about any recollection of his patient's. We might possibly paraphrase his attitude by saying that if the Grusha scene had not occurred it would be necessary to invent it; and as we examine more evidence it will become apparent that it is highly probable that this is indeed what happened.

---

[3]As early as 1916, W. Trotter (in his *Instincts of the Herd in Peace and War*) noted that one of Freud's "traits" was that he had the "tendency to state his least acceptable propositions with the heaviest emphasis as if to force belief upon an unwilling and shrinking mind were an especial gratification". [Trotter 1916: 76] This trait is not without significance in relation to the excessive emphasis Freud has put on his claim that the Grusha scene was a genuine memory of his patient's.

The Wolf Man's Version

We shall now turn to the patient's own words. In 1971 his memoirs were published as part of a volume edited by Muriel Gardiner with the title *The Wolf Man and Sigmund Freud*. Although he was eighty-three years old at the time, both his memory and his critical faculties were clearly undiminished. Recollections from his early life are recounted, including virtually all the major occurrences reported by Freud in his case history—with one notable exception. There is no mention of Grusha, or of any servant girl from his earliest years. Considering the crucial role Grusha comes to play in the analysis, one must presume that a considerable time must have been spent discussing her in the final stages of the treatment. Yet the Wolf Man fails to recall her in his memoirs.

Explicit reference to Grusha does occur in another book, *The Wolf Man Sixty Years Later*. This is a record of the interviews conducted by Karin Obholtzer, commencing in 1974 when the Wolf Man was eighty-seven. In spite of his age there are passages in which he discourses on the subjects of philosophy, politics, and psychoanalysis that illustrate the remarkably high intelligence and lucidity he still retained at that time. In view of its importance, the section in which Grusha is mentioned will be quoted in full: [Obholtzer 1982: 39–40)

Obholtzer: But then Freud set a final date and said that treatment must be over by then.
Wolf Man: But he wrote that things moved along after that.
O: Yes, but what happened before? Why did it come to that in the first place?
W: Well, because it lasted such a long time. Four years, that's a long time.
O: But the analysis is supposed to have stagnated.
W: Allegedly.
O: And you didn't notice anything?
W: I wasn't really aware of it.
O: Nothing struck you as odd?
W: No, nothing did. I was simply glad it was ending. Those four years were beginning to feel a little long.
O: He hints that you took refuge in resistance.
W: But he wrote that things moved along afterwards. He set the date and then it went all right, allegedly.
O: But setting a date is the ultimate weapon, when there is no other way of dealing with a patient. Treatment must have stagnated for a long time before that.

W: To judge by his comments, of course. I cannot give you any
   detailed information about that. I was not aware of that.
O: You mean you always talked about something.
W: I always talked about something. But he didn't find what he
   was after, whatever it was. But you see, all those constructs
   must be questioned. Do you believe in all those constructs of
   psychoanalysts?
O: No. But in this case what do you mean by construct?
W: Well, that scene with the white wolves: those are the parents
   and the coitus, and that's how it is all supposed to have
   started. Do you believe that?
O: No, I don't really. But my question is this: What made Freud
   say that treatment was stagnating?
W: One would have to bring Freud back to life and ask him,
   wouldn't one? I don't know what went on in his brain.
O: Didn't that story about Grusha, the servant girl who was on
   your estate in your early childhood, come to light after that?
W: That's very hazy. I no longer know precisely. I cannot
   remember. I cannot even remember this Grusha. She was a
   maid, I believe. But I cannot remember details.

The Wolf Man's response to this last question is not entirely
unambiguous; nevertheless he does state explicitly that he has no
memory of Grusha. This implies that his subsequent reference to
her as a maid relates to Freud's narrative, not to any recollection of
his own.[4] Yet her significance for the analysis is immense, as Freud
points out on several occasions. He reports that as the first years of
the treatment produced scarcely any change, he set a time limit, and
referring to the breakthrough resulting from the subsequent emergence of the Grusha scene, he writes that "in a disproportionately
short time the analysis produced all the material which made it
possible to clear up [the patient's] inhibitions and remove his
symptoms. All the information, too, which enabled me to understand his infantile neurosis is derived from this last period of the
work, during which resistance temporarily disappeared and the
patient gave an impression of lucidity which is usually attainable
only in hypnosis." [S.E. 17: 11]

---

[4] It should be noted that even if the Wolf Man had had a shadowy recollection
of a servant girl from his earliest infancy, this would not in itself weaken the case
being argued, which is that the Grusha *scene* was an invention, in contradistinction
to Freud's assertions.

One would have thought that such a dramatic transformation could scarcely have been forgotten by the Wolf Man, but we have seen the scepticism with which he responds to Obholtzer's questions regarding the alleged stagnation and subsequent breakthrough. We have already noted that in the framework of the analysis, as Freud repeatedly emphasises, Grusha plays an important role and must have been discussed at considerable length in the last months of the treatment. Any recollection the Wolf Man might have had of Grusha would have been reinforced during this period, yet he says "I cannot even remember this Grusha". In addition, his statement that Freud "didn't find what he was after, whatever it was" must be regarded as highly suggestive. It would seem to indicate that Freud was actively seeking some specific occurrence to bring cohesion to his analysis, one, moreover, that he did not find. The fact that the Grusha scene is, uniquely, such an occurrence, and that Freud dramatically proclaims it as his belated "solution" to the analysis, is therefore, circumstantially, grounds for questioning its authenticity.[5]

If the Grusha scene was indeed a construction one might have expected some reaction from the Wolf Man when he first read the case history. In the Obholtzer interviews he was in fact asked if he had believed that everything Freud had written was true. His reply was: "I didn't think about it. That was because of the transference." [Obholtzer 1982: 35] Elsewhere he explains that by this term he means he was totally under the influence of Freud, a state he remained in for some considerable time after the treatment; in his own words: "I took the faith with me." [140] In such a frame of mind he would obviously have been unable to assess the case history critically.

The Primal Scene Debate

The next line of enquiry relates to the fifth chapter of the case history, which is entirely devoted to a discussion of the nature of primal scenes. Originally Freud concluded, with some emphasis, and in opposition to the view of Jung and Adler, that such reconstructed scenes were unconscious memories of genuine occurrences.

---

[5]In view of the Wolf Man's considerable age, his failure to remember Grusha cannot, of course, be regarded as conclusive. It must be taken in conjunction with the rest of the material examined in this chapter. (His failure to recall the spectacular breakthrough in the last months of the treatment is a different matter.)

[55–56] However, although the paper was completed in November 1914, owing to the onset of the First World War its publication was delayed until 1918. This enabled him to insert two supplementary sections, and in the first of these, placed at the end of chapter 5, he reverses his position. On the basis of an alternative interpretation of the wolf-dream (that it represents a memory of sheepdogs copulating), he now comes to the conclusion that there is "no need any longer to doubt" that the primal scene "is only a phantasy". [59] Admitting that his *volte-face* had "laid [him] open to grave aspersions" on the part of his readers, he asks us to reserve judgement until he has revealed a new factor which will throw fresh light on the issue. This eventually (chapter 8) turns out to be the Grusha scene, and it is at the end of his discussion of the latter that the second supplementary section appears. Here, somewhat surprisingly, he reverts to his original view, and concludes that most probably the primal scene was a reality in the present case. [95–96]

The sole justification Freud gives for reaffirming his original view in the second supplement is the evidence provided by the Grusha scene; but reference to this scene is conspicuous for its absence in the whole of the first draft of the chapter on primal scenes. It seems inexplicable that such vital evidence should have been omitted at that stage, evidence of such significance that he "cannot deny that the scene with Grusha, the part it played in the analysis, and the effects that followed from it in the patient's life can be most naturally and completely explained if we consider that the primal scene, which may in other cases be a phantasy, was a reality in the present one". [96] It is odd that he did not make use of this argument to support his position against that of Jung and Adler, and his failure to utilise the Grusha scene for this purpose in chapter 5 is a complete mystery. It seems unlikely that the idea of using it in that context would not have occurred to him at that time, since Grusha is important precisely as a link with the primal scene, and hence, from Freud's perspective, strong confirmatory evidence for the validity of that construction.

One is reminded of the curious incident of the dog which failed to bark in the night. In this instance the curious occurrence is the allusion to the Grusha scene which fails to appear in chapter 5.[6]

---

[6]It might be argued that Freud wished to hold back the Grusha scene until it could be dramatically revealed in chapter 8 as the "solution" to the analysis. However that did not prevent him from alluding to it on three other occasions, namely in chapters 3 and 4, and in a footnote in chapter 7. [22, 41, 86n] One would have thought that at the very least a similar allusion would have been made in chapter 5 to indicate that further support for his argument would be forthcoming later.

One possible explanation is that if the Grusha scene is an invention, Freud may have been reluctant to employ it in chapter 5, for it is one thing to concoct an event for the specific purpose of solving the analysis, but quite another to then use it for a different purpose altogether, that of providing support for a general theoretical position in regard to primal scenes; in a context, moreover, where he would in effect be using one construction to justify the validity of another. If this sounds unlikely one must keep in mind that Freud's was a very complex personality, and it is conceivable that some such mental process was at work, so that at the time he felt it was inadmissible to utilise the Grusha scene for this purpose.[7]

There is thus a feasible explanation for the fact that the Grusha scene is not alluded to in the first draft of chapter 5, and it is dependent on the assumption that it was a construction, not a recollection, as Freud claimed. While one can only surmise as to the reason for the omission, its conspicuous absence in itself suggests that its presence in the analysis may not have been entirely legitimate.

Further Circumstantial Evidence

There remain to be considered two major strands of circumstantial evidence, and taken together, in the light of what has already been brought forward, they turn out to be surprisingly strong. The first relates to the significance of the Grusha scene in the context of the analysis. The problem Freud faced was to find a link between the primal scene and a characteristic feature of the Wolf Man's adult sexual behaviour, namely his tendency to be compulsively attracted to women of lower social rank. At the same time he needed to incorporate an element which maintained the connection between the mode of intercourse in the primal scene and his patient's predilection for coitus from behind.[8] The Grusha scene is presented as the "solution" to this problem: "It provides an important link between the primal scene and the later compulsive love which came to be of such decisive significance in his subsequent career, and it

[7]The fact that he eventually came to use the Grusha incident in the primal scenes debate in the second supplementary section in chapter 8 does not invalidate the argument, since it was added some four years later when he needed it in order to try to extricate himself from the extraordinary muddle he had managed to get himself into on the issue.

[8]Paul Roazen has drawn attention to the fact that Ruth Mack Brunswick claims that the Wolf Man practiced anal intercourse as well as *coitus a tergo*, and suggests that if true this may have influenced Freud's reconstruction of the supposed infantile neurosis. [Roazen 1989: 187]

further shows us a condition upon which his falling in love de-
pended and which elucidates that compulsion." [92] And again:
"When once the Grusha scene had been assimilated . . . the problem
of the treatment had every appearance of having been solved. . . . all
that remained to be done was to collect and co-ordinate." [94]
However, it is difficult to reconcile this supposed solving of the
analysis, leading to the emergence of "all the material which made it
possible to clear up his inhibitions and remove his symptoms" [11],
with the Wolf Man's assertion that Freud was unable to find what
he wanted. Clearly he did (eventually) find precisely what he
wanted, but the Wolf Man's words must add to the suspicion that it
came from his own imagination and not from his patient.

The second part of the circumstantial evidence relates to the
significance of the paper itself. Ronald Clark, in his biographical
study, and James Strachey, Freud's editor and translator, both
emphasise the importance for Freud of the case history in his
conflicts with Jung and Adler. According to Strachey, "The
primary significance of the case history in Freud's eyes at the time
of its publication was clearly the support it provided for his
criticisms of Adler and more specifically of Jung." [S.E. 17: 5] This
is also evident from the number of critical allusions, both explicit
and implicit, to his psychoanalytic rivals in the paper. In Clark's
words, he hoped it "would provide a weapon with which to beat his
enemies". [Clark 1980: 290]

A few years earlier, in 1911, Alfred Adler had left the psychoanalytic movement as a result of several long and bitter disputes,
and the extent of Freud's animosity towards him can be seen in his
letters to various colleagues. To Jung he wrote that he had "forced
the whole Adler gang (six of them) to resign from the Society"
[Hale 1971: 447], and even three years later he was writing to Lou
Andreas-Salomé of Adler's "specific venomousness" and referring
to him as a "loathsome individual". [Pfeiffer 1972: 19] The depth of
Freud's feeling may be gauged from the fact that more than twenty
years afterwards, on learning that Adler had died while attending a
meeting of the British Association for the Advancement of Science,
he could still write that "for a Jew boy out of a Viennese suburb,
death in Aberdeen is an unheard of career in itself, and a proof of
how far he had got on. The world really rewarded him richly for his
service in having contradicted psychoanalysis." [Jones 1957: 223]
Carl Jung's secession in 1914 was hardly less acrimonious, and
when it came Freud wrote to Abraham, "I cannot suppress a
cheer", and a little later exulted, "So we are at last rid of them, the
brutal, sanctimonious Jung and his disciples". [Abraham and
Freud 1965: 184, 186]

These quotations give some indication of the hostility Freud felt towards his psychoanalytic rivals. That such feelings went beyond the bounds of professional rivalry is indicated by the fact that he displayed a similar excessive rancour even towards those with whom he had previously enjoyed an especially close friendship. Such was the case with Josef Breuer, his mentor and collaborator earlier in his career. For no reason that Freud's colleague and biographer Ernest Jones could discern, after their friendship had come to an end he displayed considerable animosity towards Breuer, in spite of the generosity and sympathy the latter had previously extended towards him. Sulloway remarks on the "vitriolic and unattractive side of Freud" revealed by his bitter remarks about his former friend [Sulloway 1979:99], and Roazen recounts a reminiscence of Breuer's daughter-in-law relating to an incident long after the break, when Breuer saw Freud approaching him in the street: "Instinctively, he opened his arms, Freud passed, professing not see him." [Roazen 1975: 80]

Freud's friendship with Wilhelm Fliess was even more intimate, but it too ended in considerable ill-feeling. When, many years later, Abraham reported to him that Fliess had expressed concern over his deteriorating state of health, Freud's response was: "This expression of sympathy after twenty years leaves me rather cold." [Jones 1957: 122]

His own estimation of his behaviour, as expressed in a letter to James Putnam (8 July 1915), is in sharp contrast to that detailed above: "I believe that when it comes to a sense of justice and consideration for others, to the dislike of making others suffer or taking advantage of them, I can measure myself with the best people I have known. I have never done anything mean or malicious. . . . When I ask myself why I have always aspired to behave honourably, to spare others and to be kind wherever possible and why I didn't cease doing so when I realised that in this way one comes to harm and becomes an anvil because other people are brutal and unreliable, then indeed I have no answer. . . . So one could cite just my case as a proof of your assertion that such an urge towards the ideal forms a considerable part of our inheritance. If only more of the precious inheritance could be found in other human beings!" [Jones 1955: 314–15]

Now this hardly accords with what has been related above, and it seems he was unaware of the considerable disparity between his self-estimation and the reality of his behaviour towards many of his former friends and associates. All of this suggests that his excessive bitterness towards erstwhile colleagues may have tended towards the pathological.[9] This would explain the extent of the vilification he directed towards Jung and Adler, and adds a new dimension to his motive for writing the Wolf Man paper.

In addition, there is one sentence in his *History*, written before the Wolf Man's treatment was completed, which shows just how fully Freud had committed himself to publishing the case history. In the course of criticising Adler's "twisted interpretations and distortions of the disagreeable facts of analysis" [S.E. 14: 54], he writes: "Careful dissection of a neurosis in early childhood puts an end to all misapprehensions about the aetiology of the neuroses and to all doubts about the part played by the sexual instincts in them." [55–56] As the editor notes at this point, this is precisely the main thesis of the Wolf Man analysis, the actual title of which is, significantly, "From the History of an Infantile Neurosis". In the case history itself Freud draws attention to this dispute, claiming that the emergence of the Grusha material at the conclusion of the analysis saved him from being obliged to correct his preconceived opinion in a direction favourable to Adler's position that motives of power, rather than sexuality, may be instrumental in the development of neuroses.[10] [S.E. 17: 22]

Freud's assertion in his polemical *History* that the close study of a childhood neurosis (clearly that of the Wolf Man) confirms his view of the sexual aetiology of the neuroses was written some six months before the termination of the treatment.[11] In the case history he writes that all the information which enabled him to understand the infantile neurosis was derived "in a disproportionately short time" during the "last period" of the analysis. [S.E. 17: 11] One has to consider whether such an extraordinarily productive conclusion to the analysis really occurred (apparently unremarked by the patient himself), or whether, having earlier virtually committed himself to disproving Adler's view, he belatedly

---

[9]In this light, Freud's *cri de coeur* to Abraham in 1914, "All my life I have been looking for friends who would not exploit and then betray me", sounds distinctly paranoid. [Abraham and Freud 1965: 186] Many of his early disciples eventually seceded from the movement, usually in acrimonious circumstances, and Sulloway writes of the "vilifications" directed by Freud against the defectors. [Sulloway 1979: 482]

[10]The Wolf Man's tendency to be attracted to women of lower social status could be interpreted on Adlerian lines as an intention to debase. The belated emergence of the Grusha episode enabled Freud to subsume this aspect of the Wolf Man's behaviour into his Oedipal impulses by identifying the servant girl with the patient's mother.

[11]The *History* was written in January and February and published in February 1914. [S.E. 14: 3] The Wolf Man's treatment ended in July 1914. [S.E. 17: 3]

derived from his own imagination the infantile scene which he needed to satisfactorily complete the analysis in his own terms.[12]

Further Doubts Concerning Freud's "Solution"

There is still to be considered the fact that in the paper Freud explicitly refers to discussions about Grusha and to statements apparently made by the patient about her. Could it be that this material was also invented? That this is without doubt quite possible can be demonstrated by quoting the claims Freud made about another scene which was definitely *not* recalled by his patient: "When the patient entered more deeply into the situation of the primal scene he brought to light the following pieces of self-observation. He assumed to begin with, he said, that the event of which he was a witness was an act of violence, but the expression of enjoyment which he saw on his mother's face did not fit in with this; he was obliged to recognise that the experience was one of satisfaction. What was essentially new for him . . . was the conviction of the reality of castration. . . . For now he saw with his own eyes the wound of which his Nanya had spoken. . . ." [45–46] And again: "Then suddenly . . . the analysis plunged back into the prehistoric period, and led him to assert that during the copulation in the primal scene he had observed the penis disappear, that he had felt compassion for his father on that account, and had rejoiced at the reappearance of what he thought had been lost." [88]

Now, elsewhere in the case history it is stated explicitly that the primal scene was a reconstruction and was not recollected by the patient [50–51], so the above must all have originated from Freud, despite the assertions to the contrary. There is no less detail here than in the case of the Grusha scene, and it is therefore quite feasible that the latter, and the bulk of the material associated with it, was invented by Freud.

---

[12]Freud's description of the striking period initiated by the emergence of the Grusha material, during which "resistance temporarily disappeared and the patient gave an impression of lucidity which is usually attainable only in hypnosis" [S.E. 17: 11], strains credibility. Not only is such an occurrence unique in his descriptions of specific cases, the almost miraculous manner in which the patient's "resistance . . . gave way" would seem to fly in the face of the very function of the resistance. It is left to readers to decide whether they are prepared, as Freud exhorts them, to "rest assured that [he is] only reporting what [he] came upon as an independent experience, uninfluenced by [his] expectations". [12]

It is possible that some of that material may have genuinely emerged during the treatment, though in a different context, and been incorporated into the narrative at that point. In fact, there is some evidence that this is indeed what happened in the case of the peasant girl from whom the Wolf Man contracted gonorrhoea. According to the case history, he had "fallen in love in a compulsive manner" [91] with the girl, and in the course of associating the episode with the Grusha scene Freud recounts more details. The Wolf Man was walking through the village which formed part of his family's estate when he saw the girl kneeling by a pond washing clothes, and her posture, evoking the memory of the Grusha scene, induced him to fall in love "instantly and with irresistible violence". [93] Now, the peasant girl herself certainly existed, but when Obholtzer quotes Freud's description of their supposed first meeting at the pond, the Wolf Man interrupts to tell her "that isn't correct, that has nothing to do with washing". [Obholtzer 1982: 134] Likewise, the Wolf Man's account of his feelings towards the girl contradicts that of Freud. Asked if he gave her some money, or if he was in love, he replies, "No, no, you always gave something, that was a matter of good manners". [27] So it looks suspiciously as if Freud concocted the scene by the pond, suitably embellished by the instantaneous attack of falling in love, so that he could link the genuine information the Wolf Man had given him about the peasant girl with the fabricated Grusha scene.

Freud's account in the case of another link with the Grusha scene, that relating to the patient's future wife, is also challenged. According to Freud, "Even his final choice of [love] object, which played such an important part in his life, is shown by its details (though they cannot be adduced here) to have been dependent upon the same condition. . . ." [93] (namely, a preference for coitus from behind). However, when Obholtzer quotes this sentence to the Wolf Man, he tells her, "That's incorrect". [Obholtzer 1982: 134]

But even without the Wolf Man's denial of two of the items associated with the Grusha incident, there would be reason to be suspicious of the whole section, with its complex of interrelating material, for everything interlocks too perfectly to be entirely plausible. This can be seen clearly from a summary of the passages in question. The story began with the memory of the young boy chasing a striped butterfly and recoiling in fear. Then came the timid and indistinct recollection that he must have had a nursery maid who was very fond of him, and whose name he first thought to be the same as his mother's. Though this turns out to be erroneous it showed that in his memory she had become "fused with his mother". [90] Her real name came to mind when he recollected a type of pear grown on his parents' estate which had yellow stripes on its skin. The word for 'pear' was '*grusha*', and this had also been the name of the maid. So "behind the screen memory of the hunted butterfly the memory of the nursery maid lay concealed". [90] There soon followed the memory of Grusha kneeling on the floor; beside her was a pail and a short broom made from a bundle of twigs.

Freud next supplies what he calls the "missing elements" relating to this scene. He reports that in the first months of the treatment his patient had told him of how, in his eighteenth year, he had fallen in love with a peasant girl, from whom he contracted gonorrhoea. He had at first been reluctant to give Freud the name of the girl, but it was eventually revealed to be Matrona, "which has a motherly ring about it". [91][13] The Wolf Man's shame about the name would be explicable "if it should turn out that the affair with Matrona had something in common with the Grusha scene". Sure enough, this is indeed the case, for a little later we are told that his first sight of Matrona was of her kneeling by a pond, washing some clothes. He fell instantly in love with the girl "with irresistible violence, although he had not yet been able to get even a glimpse of her face". [93] Her posture and occupation evoked the memory of Grusha, and the shame relating to the content of the scene with Grusha became attached to the name of Matrona.[14]

Before the episode with Matrona there had been another young peasant girl, a servant in the house, who had long attracted the Wolf Man. He had been able to keep from approaching her until he came upon her one day "kneeling on the floor and engaged in scrubbing it, with a pail and a broom beside her". The reminder of Grusha was too much for him, and "he was overwhelmed by his love". [93]

Then follows the reference to the Wolf Man's "final choice of object", his future wife, chosen as "an offshoot of the compulsion which, starting from the primal scene and going on to the scene with Grusha, had dominated his love choice". [93]

---

[13]It is interesting to note that the reluctance of the Wolf Man to give the name of the servant girl Matrona has a precedence in the case of the Rat Man. [S.E. 10: 272–73] It is tempting to surmise that it was from that case that Freud got the idea.

[14]The shame was presumably because, having become "seized with sexual excitement" at the sight of Grusha's buttocks (evoking the memory of those of his mother in the primal scene), the two-and-a-half-year-old boy "micturated" on the floor. This act, the infantile equivalent of "an attempt at seduction", provoked Grusha to respond with "a threat of castration, just as though she had understood what he meant". [93]

Given the doubts as to the authenticity of the Grusha scene, one can only remark on how beautifully it inter-relates with the primal scene before it and the comparable events after it (the two episodes involving peasant girls, and the Wolf Man's future wife's low social status [nurse] and her supposed habitual posture during coitus). Equally, one can only admire the remarkable way that Freud is able to interpret and associate so many details of the analysis. But both achievements, impressive as they are, only serve to strain credibility beyond breaking point.

Also relevant here is another of Freud's idiosyncrasies, his tendency to reach a state of total conviction about his own ideas even when they are based on the flimsiest of foundations, and to be so transported by the intellectual excitement of working out his analyses that he sometimes loses all contact with reality. Such is the case with the numerous details he supplies of the primal scene; it is as if he becomes so caught up in the creations of his own mind that they take on a reality regardless of the flimsiness of the evidence to support them, and of the amount of invention necessary to sustain them. Something of the sort appears to have occurred in regard to the Grusha scene and its ramifications, for the whole section reads more like a work of the imagination than a description of real-life events. One's impression is that, having fabricated the Grusha scene, Freud set about incorporating it into the analysis with his usual enthusiasm and ingenuity. But he got carried away by his task and did the job *too* well by making the narrative virtually seamless, and, characteristically, he failed to see that by doing so he was going beyond the bounds of credibility.

One final strand of argument may be added in support of the thesis that Freud made up much of this narrative. There are several incidents whose whole *raison d'être* is the "primal scene", but since there is not the slightest evidence that this event occurred, these related incidents cease to have any meaning. The Grusha scene, and the two incidents with the peasant girls, one already shown to be doubtful, depend for their significance *purely on the fact that they involve girls in a kneeling posture which evoked the memory of the mother's position in the primal scene.* But if the latter only existed in Freud's imagination, which can scarcely be doubted, the subsequent incidents make no sense. This suggests that their presence in the narrative is solely to justify the central thesis of the analysis (the interpretation of the wolf-dream) and that they were concocted by Freud specifically for this purpose; for without the underpinning of the primal scene the logic of the narrative collapses.[15]

Taking the evidence presented above as a whole, it seems likely that the Grusha scene, the "solution" to the analysis, was a product of Freud's imagination, and that his repeated claims to the contrary which first aroused suspicion are false. It may be that either towards the end of the treatment, or possibly when he was preparing to write up the case history, he realised that he needed an incident to link the primal scene with his patient's strong propensity to be sexually attracted to women of lower social rank. He could scarcely have presented the new scene as a construction, as this would have meant that the two key episodes in the Wolf Man's infancy were both constructed, leaving his analysis lacking in credibility.[16] He may even have convinced himself that some such incident must have occurred, and in his overwrought state of mind it might have seemed a minor transgression to act on this conviction rather than be left with an analysis he could not complete. One can imagine that his aim of demonstrating that the "heretics" Jung and Adler had been in error had assumed overriding importance, and that in his mind the primary goal of preserving the psychoanalytic movement in his own image would have legitimised his behaviour. Under the pressure of the dramatic events with which he was obsessively involved at that time, he succumbed to the temptation which presented itself and fabricated the "solution" to what was destined to become, ironically, his most famous case history.

---

[15]It might be argued that, on the contrary, the primal scene was constructed, at least in part, to make sense of the later events. This view is difficult to sustain when one considers that of the four supposed derivatives cited by Freud, two are explicitly denied by the Wolf Man, and a third is the one being called into question here. We have to take Freud's word for the remaining episode, another scene with a servant girl whose kneeling posture caused the Wolf Man to be "overwhelmed by his love". [93]

[16]On the other hand, to make the alleged recollection from such an early period credible, he had to present it as hazy and incomplete, while including the essential elements of a servant girl and the kneeling posture.

CHAPTER SIX

Fabrications

The material we have examined thus far points to something that has been becoming apparent for some years, though it has yet to be widely acknowledged. Freud's legendary reputation for probity does not stand up in the face of the close scrutiny to which his life and work are now being subjected. In large measure, what Cioffi has called "the myth of Freud's superlative integrity" [Cioffi 1979: 504] derives from the image he himself projected in his writings, augmented by the picture presented in the famous biography written by Ernest Jones, his faithful colleague and friend. Yet behind what Thomas Szasz describes as his "base rhetoric" [Szasz 1979: 123], it has always been possible to discern a far more complex, even devious, figure than has traditionally been depicted. In a field where replication of specific clinical claims is difficult, if not impossible, indications that a researcher's reports may not be entirely trustworthy are of more than passing concern. Doubts on this score become a relevant factor in the appraisal of the researcher's work. For this reason the next two chapters will be concerned with material which bears on this question, before we resume our examination of the development of Freud's ideas.

The "Screen Memories" Paper

Undaunted by the collapse of the infantile seduction theory, at the end of the 1890s Freud remained committed to his analytic technique of reconstruction, a procedure by means of which he believed he could reliably infer the contents of unconscious ideas not accessible to recall by his patients. He was particularly concerned to reconstruct memories from early childhood, and a key concept in this regard was his notion of "screen memories". These were recollections from childhood which he believed served to hide more significant experiences from an earlier period, the memory of which had been repressed. In presenting his thesis in the 1899 "Screen Memories" paper, he explains that psychoanalytic investigation of seemingly innocuous childhood memories had taught him that "an unsuspected wealth of meaning lies concealed behind their apparent innocence". [S.E. 3: 309][1] He would not content himself with mere assertion, but would now give a detailed report of one particular instance which seemed to him the most instructive out of a considerable number of similar ones. At this point he informs his readers: "Its value is certainly increased by the fact that it relates to someone who is not at all or only very slightly neurotic." [309] What we are not told is that on the other hand its value is substantially *reduced* by the fact that the subject under discussion is none other than Freud himself, for the editor notes that "there can be no doubt that what follows is autobiographical material only thinly disguised", a conclusion demonstrated originally by Siegfried Bernfeld and confirmed by Ernest Jones. [Jones 1953: 27] However, according to Freud, the subject's profession "lies in a very different field", though "he has taken an interest in psychological questions ever since I was able to relieve him of a slight phobia by means of psychoanalysis"—which must go down as the most dubious of all the suspect claims of therapeutic success made by Freud!

The bulk of the paper is cast in the form of an extended dialogue ("reproduced as accurately as possible" [320]) between Freud and the invented acquaintance. The aim of the paper is to present an explication of his thesis while at the same time creating an impression that a degree of corroboration is forthcoming from an independent source. In the course of the discussion the interlocutor concurs with Freud's views and himself contributes information and interpretations which serve to exemplify them.

One reason for the subterfuge is that he required a non-neurotic subject so as to be able to show, as he says in the paper, that the processes he posits are operative in the mental lives of normal people as well as in those of his patients, while at the same time he was aware that the value of the exposition would be enhanced by recounting it as relating to someone other than himself. Certainly the credibility of his thesis gains from the pertinent contributions made by his disinterested and perspicacious interlocutor. No doubt he also felt that the erotic nature of the inferred phantasy was too intimate for him to reveal that he himself was the subject of the account. In his biography Jones reports that Freud withheld the paper when it might otherwise have been reprinted in collections where it would naturally belong. [Jones 1953: 27–28] When it was

---

[1]In essence the theory posits that childhood memories are actually phantasies composed of elements of genuine events, but also deriving from memory traces of earlier sexual experiences in a guise sufficiently innocent that they evade the repression to which such memories are subject.

eventually republished in the complete edition of his works in 1925, he tried to conceal his subterfuge by making alterations in the text of *The Interpretation of Dreams* where he had referred to the same incidents in his early life to which he had also alluded in the 1899 paper.[37–38]

The *Aliquis* Incident

In 1901 Freud published the first edition of *The Psychopathology of Everyday Life*, in which he expounds the psychoanalytic theory of the mental processes involved in the occurrence of slips of the tongue and equivalent errors. Much of the material consists of anecdotes illustrating applications of his method of analysis, and he notes that he has had to fall back mainly on self-observation for his examples. To illustrate the procedure applied to the forgetting of foreign words, however, he recounts an episode involving a young man whose acquaintanceship he had renewed while on a holiday trip the previous summer. [S.E. 6: 8–12] In the course of their conversation the acquaintance had made an error (omitting the word *aliquis*) in quoting a line from Virgil, and Freud describes how, at the behest of his friend, he had taken advantage of the opportunity which presented itself to demonstrate the use of his technique to uncover the disturbing thought at the root of the mistake. In a paper in which Freud's account of this incident plays a central role, Peter Swales has subjected the quoted dialogue to a close scrutiny and demonstrated that in his views, experiences, and knowledge the young man bears a striking resemblance to Freud himself.[2] This strongly suggests the possibility that the analysee may have been, as in the 1899 paper discussed above, a product of Freud's imagination, and that the episode as described did not actually take place.

There is in fact no way of distinguishing between the presentation in this case, in the "Screen Memories" fabrication, and in an instance when Freud openly utilises an invented person for the purpose of exposition, as he does in the *The Question of Lay Analysis*; in all of them the form of the dialogue is remarkably similar. Swales argues that, in the light of the fact that two years earlier Freud had without doubt fabricated an incident and presented it as an actual occurrence complete with dialogue, the extent of the correlations he has documented between Freud and

---

[2]See "Freud, Minna Bernays, and the Conquest of Rome" (1982).

his subject in this instance tilts the balance of probabilities in favour
of his thesis, and that it now requires a greater act of faith to accept
Freud's account than to believe the encounter to have been a
fabrication.[3]

The thesis becomes more problematic, however, when the conclusion of Freud's exposition, that the slip in memory related to a
worry about having made a woman pregnant, is taken into account.
Nevertheless, Swales utilises other material from Freud's writings,
including information deriving from the latter's self-analyses of a
dream and a slip of the pen which occurred during the relevant
period, to marshall support for the case that there *was* such a
woman, namely his sister-in-law Minna Bernays, who lived in the
Freud household and accompanied him alone for a period during
his summer holiday in 1900. He therefore argues that the *aliquis*
analysis was *genuine*, but that it relates to Freud, not to an
acquaintance.[4]

To accept Swales's argument as a whole would obviously mean a
major re-evaluation of Freud's personal life. However, the first, and
stronger, part of Swales's case could, less contentiously, be taken to
indicate the likelihood that the episode was a product of Freud's
imagination, a suggestion first mooted by the writer Frederick
Raphael in a review of Sebastiano Timpanaro's book *The Freudian
Slip* in 1976. Having too often, as Freud notes, to draw on self-
observation because of his wish to steer clear of material provided
by his neurotic patients, and with the precedent of the 1899 paper in
mind, he may have concocted the dialogue to provide an appropriate illustration of his thesis in relation to the forgetting of foreign
words.[5] Certainly, as Swales observes, the impression one gains of
the analysis is that it is too pat, too good to be true. On the basis of

---

[3]To add to the parallels with the "Screen Memories" episode, in the later narration Freud explicitly draws attention to the value of the analysis, in that it supposedly relates to a person other than himself who is not suffering from a nervous
illness [S.E. 6: 12], just as he had (mendaciously) in the 1899 paper.

[4]No direct evidence exists of an affair between Freud and his sister-in-law,
though Jung is reported to have claimed that Minna confided to him in 1907 that
their relationship was very intimate. [Billinsky 1969: 42–43] Peter Gay has recently
revealed that when he was permitted to peruse the correspondence between Freud
and Minna (deposited in the Library of Congress in 1986–87), he discovered that
the letters written between 1893 and 1910 were missing. [Gay 1990: 178–79]

[5]Appiganesi and Forrester [1992: 50] find plausible Swales's case that the
"acquaintance" was Freud himself, and suggest that, in the light of the latter's
known concern that there should be no further increase in the size of his family, the
account may relate to an anxiety he experienced in regard to a potential pregnancy
of his wife, Martha.

the slightest of errors and in the face of his interlocutor's scepticism, Freud relentlessly draws from him the associations which unerringly lead to the successful unveiling of his secret, and to the triumphant vindication of the analytic procedure. Swales's meticulous research has, at the very least, thrown serious doubt on the authenticity of the episode as described.[6]

Hysterical Attacks

Whatever the full truth about the *aliquis* incident, there is little doubt about the next little example to be considered. In his paper on "Hysterical Attacks", written in 1908, Freud refers to the possibility of a reversal of the chronological order within the phantasy which is supposedly being portrayed by a convulsive attack, and continues:

> Supposing, for instance, that a hysterical woman has a phantasy of seduction in which she is sitting reading in a park with her skirt slightly lifted so that her foot is visible; a gentleman approaches and speaks to her; they then go somewhere and make love to one another. This phantasy is acted out in the attack by her beginning with the convulsive stage, which corresponds to the coitus, by her then getting up, going into another room, sitting down and reading and presently answering an imaginary remark addressed to her. [S.E. 9: 231]

Now this is quite clearly a hypothetical example invented to illustrate Freud's surmise that what he calls hysterical convulsive attacks can be regarded as a representation of a phantasised sexual situation with a reversal of temporal and physical elements. It is in fact an embellished version of ideas presented in more schematic form to the Viennese Psychoanalytic Society on 8th April 1908. From the paper itself it is clear that the conjectured phantasy supposedly underlying the convulsion is a highly speculative ana-

[6]Alan Elms [1982] has challenged Swales's conclusions in an article in which he acknowledges that there is a remarkable resemblance between the subject of Freud's story and Freud himself. He suggests flaws in Swales's arguments (including the fact that Freud specifically stated that he was drawing on the experience of someone other than himself and that scientific honesty was an extremely important aspect of his self-concept), but fails to deal either adequately, or in some cases at all, with many of Swales's points. His own suggestion that the young man could hve been Freud's younger brother Alexander is supported by evidence with far less to commend it than Swales's and in general he fails to do justice to the comprehensiveness of the latter's argument.

lytic interpretation of its manifestations deriving entirely from Freud's imagination. However, in 1909 he added the following footnote to *The Interpretation of Dreams*:

> Hysterical attacks sometimes make use of the same kind of chronological reversal in order to disguise their meaning from observers. For instance, a hysterical girl needed to represent something in the nature of a brief romance in one of her attacks— a romance of which she had had a phantasy in her unconscious after an encounter with someone on the suburban railway. She imagined how the man had been attracted by the beauty of her foot and had spoken to her while she was reading; whereupon she had gone off with him and had had a passionate love-scene. Her attack *began* with a representation of this love-scene by convulsive twitching of her body, accompanied by movements of her lips to represent kissing and tightening of her arms to represent embracing. She then hurried into the next room, sat down on a chair, raised her skirt so as to show her foot, pretended to be reading a book and spoke to me (that is, answered me). [S.E. 4: 328n]

From his introductory words, but most clearly from the later reference to himself, Freud is indubitably presenting this incident as a genuine occurrence. But since it almost exactly parallels the entirely imaginary episode conjectured in the passage quoted above it is difficult to conclude other than that it is an invented situation which Freud is passing off as authentic. By implicitly presenting the phantasy as if it derives from the girl rather than from himself, he appears to be engaging in a disingenuous attempt to gain credence for his notion that distortion by inversion occurs in manifestations from the unconscious. While trivial in itself, this example illustrates the difficulty there can be on occasion in distinguishing imaginative invention from authentic description in Freud's reports.

A Case of Paranoia

There are indications that Freud may have practised deception of considerably greater magnitude in his paper "A Case of Paranoia Running Counter to the Psychoanalytic Theory of the Disease", published in 1915. [S.E. 14: 261–272] Five years earlier he had written an analysis [S.E. 12: 1–82] of an autobiographical account by Daniel Paul Schreber of a serious mental breakdown, among the symptoms of which were acute paranoid delusions. As he explains in the 1915 paper, he had there put forward the view that paranoia arises as a result of a struggle against an intensification of homosexual trends. In now presenting an analysis of a second case of paranoia, that of a young woman, he describes how at first sight it fails to satisfy his theory that "the delusion of persecution invariably depends on homosexuality". [S.E. 14: 266] However, when more of her story comes out he is able to demonstrate that the case is not a refutation of his theory after all.

The story as recounted by Freud is that some years previously a lawyer had consulted him regarding a young woman who had come to him for protection against the molestations of a young man with whom she had been having a love affair. She alleged that the man had arranged to have someone photograph them together in a compromising situation in his rooms, so that he had it in his power to force her to resign the post she occupied. However, the lawyer "was experienced enough to recognise the pathological stamp of this accusation" and sought Freud's opinion on the matter. [263]

Shortly afterwards Freud was introduced to the young-looking and attractive thirty-year-old woman, who told him her story. She had been on the staff of a large business concern for many years, living quietly with her mother, her father being long dead. Recently an employee in her office had paid her attentions, and she had been drawn into a love affair. Eventually she consented to visit him in his rooms; they kissed and embraced as they lay together, and "he began to admire the charms which were now partly revealed". [264] Suddenly she was frightened by a noise, a kind of knock or click, which her friend could only suggest might have come from the clock in his room. On leaving the house she had met two men on the stairs one of whom was carrying an object which, under its wrapping, looked like a small box. She immediately began to suspect that it was a camera and that her friend had arranged to have someone photograph them together from behind a curtain. From that moment she pursued her lover with reproaches and pestered him for explanations and reassurances. Eventually she called on the lawyer, told her story, and handed over the letters the man had written her about the incident. Freud later had the opportunity to see the letters, which consisted mainly of regrets that the relationship should have been spoiled by an unfortunate, morbid idea.

At this point Freud comments that since the persecutor (the young man) was not of the same sex as the victim of paranoia, the case seemed to refute his theory of that disease. However, rather than give up his theory so easily, he asked the girl to call on him a second time, and when she did so she revealed that she had omitted to mention that she had visited the young man's rooms on one previous occasion. Nothing noteworthy had happened, but the next day at work he had appeared in the office to discuss something with

the elderly lady who was her superior. She suddenly felt a conviction that he was telling her of their "adventure" of the previous
day, and that the two of them had themselves been having a love
affair for some time. She took her lover to task about his betrayal,
but he denied the "senseless accusation" and was able to free her
from the delusion. She regained sufficient confidence in him to
repeat her visit to his rooms a short time later, an event which led to
the second delusion already described.

We shall leave Freud's solution to the problem for the moment
and consider the story thus far. A close scrutiny of the text discloses
that the narrative contains a number of contradictions and improbabilities. Let us first note the contradictions:

1. Freud states that the young woman was thirty years old, "had
never sought any love-affairs with men" [264], and in fact had "kept
away from men up to the age of thirty" [268]. Yet elsewhere in the
narrative he reports that the elderly lady superior "knew about the
girl's love *affairs*, disapproved of *them*." [267; emphases added.]
What affairs? She was supposed to have had none before her
involvement with the man in her office.

(That the old lady's disapproval was in regard to affairs with
men is clear both from the context and the fact that the occurrence
of overt homosexual relations would have contravened Freud's
theory of paranoia. As he writes, the girl "had lived quietly with her
old mother" [264], and it was to her that she supposedly had "her
homosexual attachment" [268].)

2. The lawyer consulted Freud because "he recognised the
pathological stamp" of the girl's accusation. [263] But later we are
told that the lawyer's view was that there was no paranoia and that
her story was "an actual experience which had been correctly
interpreted" by the girl. [266]

Now the improbabilities:

1. The elderly lady had a "great liking" for the girl. [266] Would
she *really* be likely to have shown disapproval of the love affairs of
a young woman for whom she had much affection, rather than
taking a benevolent interest? It seems improbable—but, as we shall
see, Freud needed this disapproval for his solution. (Of course it is
made even more improbable by the fact that the girl is supposed to
have had no affairs!)

2. The first indication of the girl's paranoia was her suspicion
that her lover and the white-haired lady were having a long-
standing affair. However, she was easily talked out of the delusion
by her lover, so it hardly qualifies as paranoia. One can understand
that as the first sign of a paranoid illness, she might falsely suspect
the two of conspiring against her, but it seems scarcely credible that

she would believe that her lover was having an affair with an old lady, especially as the impulse underlying the belief was so weak that she was quickly reassured. So why would Freud put forward such an unlikely notion? Again, because he needed it as part of his solution. (It was necessary that the superior should be an old lady, because she had to represent the girl's mother in the solution.)

3. Freud states that the events in question had taken place some years before. His normal practice was to write up a case history for publication soon after the treatment was terminated. In this instance there was a particularly good reason for publishing it, since, as the editor notes, it serves as confirmation of his views, put forward in the 1911 Schreber paper, concerning the homosexual impulse at the root of paranoid delusions, while addressing an obvious weakness therein. Writing up this brief case history was a matter of only two or three days, so it seems odd that he should delay several years before doing so.

4. In his brief discussion of the theoretical ramifications of the case following the account of the first interview with the girl, Freud writes that the psychoanalytic view was that homosexuality is an essential element in paranoia, and that further interpretation led to "the necessary conclusion that the persecutor must be of the same sex as the person persecuted". [265] He notes that in psychiatric literature "there is certainly no lack of cases in which the patient imagines himself persecuted by a person of the opposite sex", but adds: "It is one thing, however, to read of such cases, and quite a different thing to come into personal contact with one of them." His own observations and analyses and those of his friends had up to that time "confirmed the relation between paranoia and homosexuality without any difficulty", but the present case "emphatically contradicted it"; in this instance (at that stage) there was "no trace of a struggle against a homosexual attachment".

It is clear that Freud is telling us that such an instance, in which the persecutor is of the opposite sex to the patient, was the first of its kind he had personally encountered. Now one must presume that paranoid illness is not particularly rare (as he says, there is no lack of cases in the psychiatric literature). At that time he had been practising psychoanalysis for some twenty years. Yet he asks us to believe that prior to this case, by some statistical quirk, he had only come across cases in which the persecutor was of the same sex as the patient; moreover, his words appear to imply that this is true of his psychoanalytic colleagues as well. But this seems rather unlikely; possibly he felt obliged to make the claim because otherwise it would appear that he had previously maintained his theory in the face of clinical facts which apparently refuted it. He may also have

wished to create the maximum dramatic effect from his story,
which, we shall argue, could well have been a product of his imagination rather than an authentic case.

We shall now turn to Freud's solution to the problem posed by
this case. It depends on an identification, from the fatherless girl's
point of view, of the old lady with her mother. This occurs as a
result of the disapproving attitude of the old lady who comes to
represent "the hostile and malevolent watcher" (ego ideal) and thus
takes on the role of the mother. (The ego ideal derives from the
authority of the mother alone in the absence of the father.) The
delusion of an affair between the old lady and girl's lover (who in
spite of his youth came to represent her father at this point)
demonstrated the strength of her (homosexual) mother-complex.[7]
This is brought out by the incident of the delusional noise (when the
lovers were lying together) which is "an indispensable part of the
phantasy of listening" associated with a young child eavesdropping
on parental sexual intercourse (the primal scene): "The patient's
lover was still her father, but she herself had taken her mother's
place." The apparent contradiction of the expectation that paranoia
derives from the repression of a homosexual impulse is disposed of
by the occurrence of the first paranoic episode which draws in the
elderly lady. She becomes "the *original* persecutor", the one who
disapproved of the girl's love affairs, and hence representative of
the homosexual attachment from which the girl wishes to escape.
The conflict between the homosexual mother-complex and the
attraction towards the young man was the source of the symptoms
of paranoia. In Freud's words, "the patient protected herself against
her love for a man by means of a paranoic delusion". The key to the
understanding of the case history is that it was on the basis of this
delusion that "the advance from a female to a male object was
accomplished". [267–271]

We shall shortly discuss whether the inconsistencies enumerated
earlier alone constitute sufficient grounds for querying the authenticity of the case history. Before doing so it is necessary to consider
other material relevant to this question, starting with the motivation Freud might have had for fabricating it at that particular time.
Not long before, he had published two other papers containing
theories whose direct relationship to the solution of the paranoia
case is unmistakable. The papers in question are "The Disposition

---

[7]Apparently because it indicates an *identification* (deriving from an excessive
attachment) with her mother who, in the guise of the old lady, was having an affair
with the young man, who in turn had come to represent her father.

to Obsessional Neurosis" (1913), which deals specifically with the problem of the choice of neurosis, and, more especially, "On Narcissism" (1914). In the former, Freud ascribes the disposition to paranoia to a fixation relating to the very early narcissistic stage of libidinal development. [S.E. 12: 318] (In the 1915 paper he argues that the girl's regressive change from homosexual dependence on the mother to identification with her points to "the narcissistic origin of her homosexual object-choice and thus to the paranoic disposition in her". [S.E. 14: 269]) However, Freud's motivation for writing the case history of the paranoic young woman is most clearly revealed in the paper on narcissism. It is in this paper that he first introduces the concept of the ego ideal, which he says can be recognised in the form of the "delusions . . . of being *watched*, which are such striking symptoms in the paranoid diseases". [S.E. 14: 95] (In the 1915 paper the girl experiences precisely this delusion.) He also writes that the ego ideal arises from the critical influence of parents [96] (represented in 1915 by the disapproving elderly superior identified with the mother). Again, in the 1914 paper he states that the ego ideal binds a considerable amount of homosexual libido which may be transformed into paranoia. [S.E. 14: 101] (In 1915 this same idea is expressed in terms of a powerful homosexual attachment to the mother, the struggle to free herself from which [by relating to a man] results in a paranoic delusion.)

It is evident that the object of the 1915 paper is to provide clinical vindication of the ideas expressed in the Schreber and narcissism papers. The essential processes involved in the young woman's illness can be summarised as follows, given the premiss that her attachment to her mother is homosexual in nature: Her overpowerful ego ideal (which binds her homosexual libido) is recognisable in the delusion of being watched, which is symptomatic of paranoia (the disposition for which has its source in the very early narcissistic state of her libidinal development), and the delusion arises as a result of the struggle to free herself from the homosexual attachment to her mother, i.e., the struggle to release the libido bound to her homosexual fixation, which would enable her to relate to a man.

That everything Freud needed fits together so perfectly that it can be coherently expressed in this way underscores just how closely the case history is congruent with the theories presented in the papers to which it relates, most notably that on narcissism of the previous year. Perhaps the reason he put the time of the events recounted a few years into the past was because he realised that it would have been too implausible for such a case to have turned up right on cue. Had the events actually occurred as Freud claims, one might have expected some reference to the case in the narcissism paper, given the features it has in common with the relevant section of that paper. It was his custom to use his own cases (both published and unpublished) to lend support to his theoretical postulates, and the fact that he does not do so in this instance in spite of the parallels enumerated above can only add to the doubts concerning the authenticity of the paranoia case history.[8]

Also noteworthy is the occurrence in the narrative of an incident which enables Freud to bring in as an inherent part of the analysis his notion of the "primal scene", which had played such an essential role in the Wolf Man paper written up only the previous autumn. It was on this subject that he had engaged in a dispute with Jung, and here we have another thread to our story, one of considerable significance.

In papers published in 1912 and 1913 Jung had taken issue with certain of Freud's ideas put forward in the Schreber case history. [S.E. 14: 79–80] In particular, in 1912 he had challenged Freud's libido theory and suggested that in the case history Freud had implicitly modified his concept of libido in the direction of his own view that it represented psychical energy in general, and not just sexual energy. Now, Freud was never tolerant of criticisms of his basic premises, and to make matters worse it was the arch-heretic Jung, with whom he was currently engaged in a bitter wrangle, who had the audacity to claim that he had moved over to Jung's view on a point of fundamental theory. The narcissism paper was clearly intended, in part, as a rebuttal to Jung's assertions (Clark describes it as another "weapon" against him [Clark 1980: 336]). Both Strachey [S.E. 14: 70] and Jones [1955: 341] aver that one of Freud's motives for writing the paper was to counter Jung's challenge arising from the Schreber analysis, and indeed he devotes several pages to this issue. Fortunately, the very next year he was able to provide another case history furnishing support for ideas presented in the narcissism paper, and containing an analysis of a case of paranoia interpreted in terms of his own concept of libido.

---

[8]This point is underlined by the fact that Freud does in fact make use of this case history in the discussion of paranoia [S.E. 16: 246] in the *Introductory Lectures on Psychoanalysis*, published in 1917. Should anyone feel that this suggests that the case was authentic after all, on the grounds that Freud is unlikely to have compounded his deception in this way, it should be noted that he had no compunction about utilising, in *The Psychopathology of Everyday Life*, his "Screen Memories" paper, in which he had fabricated an individual and lengthy dialogue. [S.E. 6: 43–44] In that paper, it will be recalled, he went out of his way to impress on his readers that the material derived from someone other than himself, even going so far as to claim to have relieved the fake subject of the paper of a phobia.

That the emotional impetus for writing up the case history derived in large measure from the dispute with his psychoanalytic rival is one of a number of parallels with the Wolf Man paper of the previous year. Reminiscent of the latter is the means used by Freud to bring out the representative function of the elderly lady superior. The only quoted description of her as given by the girl is that "she has white hair like my mother". [S.E. 14: 266] In the earlier case history the patient remembered at first (mistakenly) that Grusha's name was the same as his mother's, and another peasant girl was called Matrona, "which has a motherly ring about it". [S.E. 17: 91] (In these instances Freud was trying to add plausibility to the analysis in which the girls were associated in the patient's mind with his mother.) Again, in both case histories an important psycho-analytic theory seemed to be at risk until fresh disclosures by the patient resulted in Freud's view being vindicated. Finally, as in the case of the Grusha section of the Wolf Man paper, parts of the paranoia paper read like a fictional narrative. This is especially true of the opening paragraphs, which remind one more than anything of the Sherlock Holmes detective stories: "Some years ago a well-known lawyer consulted me about a case . . ."[9] The second paragraph is reminiscent of Conan Doyle (alias Dr. Watson) creating an atmosphere of authenticity by confiding that he had altered certain details of the case to protect the client's anonymity: "Before I continue the account, I must confess that I have altered the *milieu* of the case to preserve the incognito of the people concerned. . . ." When the attractive young woman comes to his consulting room she recounts her remarkable story, which initially perplexes Freud because it fails to conform with his theory. However, on further investigation the brilliant analyst/detective is able to unravel the plot and demonstrate he was right after all, so bringing the case to a triumphant conclusion.

It is of interest to speculate as to the reasons why the case history should take the form it does, on the assumption that Freud did in fact concoct it himself. Motivated by an urge to respond further to Jung's criticisms, and also anxious to demonstrate that the ideas put forward in the narcissism paper were more than just theoretical speculations, Freud would have realised that another analysis of a case of paranoia was the most appropriate vehicle for his purposes. It had been his theoretical analysis of Schreber's paranoid delusions with which Jung had joined issue; the paper in which he had initially responded to Jung had been the one on narcissism, in

---

[9]Freud knew and admired the Conan Doyle stories.

which he had developed his ideas on paranoia; and he needed to demonstrate that his theory of the homosexual basis of paranoia remained valid in the face of the obvious objection that there are many cases which seem to contradict it, namely those in which the delusional persecutor is of the opposite sex to the victim. Previously the subject had been a man; this time it was natural that it should be a woman. Having decided on this, it was easy for him to introduce the element of homosexuality essential to his story, for he had only to make her fatherless, with the natural consequence of excessive attachment to the mother which for Freud is indicative of a homosexual relationship. To bring in the more tenuous hetero-sexual element which was to be the nub of the story there obviously had to be a young man to whom the woman could relate. With precise knowledge of the specific ideas he needed to utilise in his analysis, his fertile imagination would have supplied the narrative without too much difficulty. With the precedent of an analogous situation in the Wolf Man case history still fresh in his mind, his penchant for story telling almost inevitably led him to make the dramatic twist which is inherent to the analysis the basis for what is essentially a tale of detection. His recollection of how one of his female patients had experienced a delusional noise may have provided him with the idea which served as the basis of the second delusion.[10] He was even able, as a bonus, to utilise this same incident to bring in the primal scene phantasy which had been intrinsic to the recent Wolf Man analysis.

Given that this is a feasible scenario, and that there is con-siderable circumstantial evidence consistent with the thesis that the case was concocted by Freud, it is, of course, of primary impor-tance to consider more closely whether the contradictions in the narrative constitute sufficient grounds for questioning the authen-ticity of the case history. Of the internal contradictions in the text only one is of major proportions; it is, however, of such significance that in itself it is enough to raise serious doubts about the genuineness of the narrative. Given the subject matter of the paper, it is obviously crucial to Freud's case that, as he twice emphasises, the girl had had no love affairs with men. Equally crucial to his argument is that the old lady superior should be critical of the girl, since she was supposed to have come to represent the girl's mother (thus becoming a surrogate ego ideal), so that the "persecutor"

---

[10]In a letter to Jung in 1911 he had reported that a female patient of his had dreamt someone was knocking on her door, but on waking had found that no one had knocked. [McGuire 1974: 391] He relates this incident in the case history.

and the homosexual object effectively become one and the same person, as Freud's theory required. But the only disapproval she displayed is reported by Freud to be in relation to the girl's "love affairs" in a context which clearly indicates he is referring to affairs with men. Both these items are essential to Freud's argument, but they are mutually contradictory. Had the contradictions been only minor, lapses of memory could feasibly have accounted for them, but in this instance the inconsistency undermines the very heart of his case. If he had been describing a genuine occurrence, it is almost inconceivable that such incompatible statements would have occurred in the narrative. It has been observed that one reason for sticking to the truth is that one is then not faced with the problem of remembering precisely what has been invented, and hence with the danger of introducing inconsistencies in one's story. Freud's difficulty would have been that, not having the solid foundation of a genuine occurrence to fall back upon, he was liable to lapses of this nature.[11] If the case had been authentic, it is difficult to understand how he could have made an error of such proportions. However, were he making up the narrative as he went along, it is conceivable that he would fail to notice he had introduced inconsistencies in the text, in the same way that novelists have been known to introduce contradictions in their narrative which the attentive reader spots immediately.

That the errors were not observed by Freud before he sent the paper off for publication may be related to the fact that he wrote an astonishing number of papers in 1915, no less than sixteen altogether. [Jones 1955: 208–09] (For reasons not known seven were never published.) In addition, in the early part of the year he was occupied in editing two psychoanalytic journals, and in October he began a series of lectures given to an audience drawn from different faculties in the University of Vienna. These were written out after each lecture and became the early chapters of the first part of the *Introductory Lectures on Psychoanalysis*, published in the following year. Given this immense work load, it is less surprising that he made errors in writing up the paranoia paper, for it was probably done hurriedly, with little time devoted to checking it over.

Now, of course it is not possible to actually *prove* that the case history was fabricated. Taken in isolation one might consider the

---

[11]It is interesting to note that in a 1907 addition to *The Psychopathology of Everyday Life*, Freud writes that his occupation with psychoanalysis had resulted in his scarcely being able to tell lies any more: "As often as I try to distort something I succumb to an error or some other parapraxis that betrays my insincerity. . . ." [S.E. 6: 221]

evidence to be suggestive, the thesis to be plausible. But we also know that Freud practised deception in the "Screen Memories" paper, and to some degree in the Rat Man case history, and there are doubts about the authenticity of the *aliquis* episode. He also presented as factual an appreciable amount of material in the Wolf Man paper which is clearly not authentic, and it is probable that the Grusha scene was fabricated. Again, his retrospective accounts of the seduction theory episode are a farrago of false and disingenuous statements. Moreover, as we shall see in the next chapter, there is abundant evidence of dissimulation elsewhere in his writings; his accounts of the early history of psychoanalysis, for instance, contain gross distortions of the facts both in relation to events and to individuals. The stridently polemical tone of his *History of the Psychoanalytic Movement* (1914), in which the worst of the excesses occur, give some indication of the intensity of his feelings in relation to the dispute with Jung, which was just coming to a head at that time. As we have noted, the divergence of their views had arisen initially with respect to a difference of opinion concerning conclusions to be drawn from Freud's analysis of paranoia in the Schreber case, and as Jones observes, the impetus for the writing of the narcissism paper in which Freud responded to Jung was precisely this acrimonious dispute. [Jones 1955: 341] The paper "A Case of Paranoia" of 1915 not only supplied corroborative material to elements in the narcissism paper directly related to the disputed issue, it also, in Strachey's words, "serve[d] as a confirmation of the view put forward by Freud in his Schreber analysis" [S.E. 14: 262], thereby effectively constituting a double riposte to Jung. Taking all this into consideration along with the evidence presented above, there are undoubtedly substantial grounds for suspecting that Freud may have fabricated "A Case of Paranoia".

The Seduction Theory Revisited

In view of the evidence indicating that Freud was not averse at times to inventing material to lend support to his theories, it is of interest to return to the events leading up to the public announcement of the infantile seduction theory in 1896 to see if this knowledge may throw fresh light on some curious aspects of that episode.

It is apparent from the correspondence with Wilhelm Fliess that Freud arrived at the theory implicating premature sexual experience in the aetiology of neuroses in the first half of October 1895.

[Masson 1985: 141, 144][12] The first two of the seduction theory papers were completed by the beginning of February of the following year. The first case which he thought provided evidence to support his conjecture was triumphantly reported on 2 November 1895 (had there been any other of such a nature before that date there can be little doubt that he would have reported it to Fliess). This means that, as reported in the first seduction theory papers, in the course of some three months all his current cases (thirteen hysteria, six obsessional neurosis) supposedly provided him with evidence of infantile sexual experiences occurring for the most part before their fifth year.[13] [S.E. 3: 152, 155, 163, 164, 168]

By the time he presented his lecture on the seduction theory in mid-April 1986, the number of cases of hysteria for which he claimed to have corroborated his theory had increased by five. [S.E. 3: 199, 207] In his papers he reports that before reaching the critical event he had to laboriously trace a number of other sexual scenes experienced at a later age, and that the intricacies of his procedure were such that "an account of the resolution of every single symptom would . . . amount to the task of relating an entire case history". [S.E. 3: 196–97] Yet he apparently achieved all this with his five new patients in two-and-a-half months or less.[14]

In relation to the six reported cases of obsessional neurosis the intricacies were even greater. Whereas the patients suffering from hysteria were said to have experienced an infantile scene of passive

---

[12]The theory postulated that hysteria is the consequence of premature sexual shock and obsessional neurosis of premature sexual pleasure. Apart from a reference to sexual traumas below the age of understanding in a list of conjectured aetiological factors in an undated draft paper [Masson 1985:38], there is no indication in the correspondence to Fliess of any specific theory along these lines until the letter of 8 October 1895, in which Freud reports he is "on the scent" of the preconditions for hysteria and obsessional neurosis. Nor had he reported any instances of infantile seductions prior to that time.

[13]It is possible that the three reported cases of hysteria combined with obsessional neurosis may have been included in both groups. [S.E. 3: 152]

[14]Thornton has raised questions about the five extra patients. Two weeks after giving the lecture on his seduction theory in April, Freud told Fliess that he was troubled by the fact that "this year for the first time my consulting room is empty, that for weeks on end I see no new faces, cannot begin any new treatments, and that none of the old ones are completed". [Masson 1985: 185] In psychoanalytic terms anyone commencing treatment in the previous two or three months would surely be regarded as a new patient (his treatments were by that time extending to periods of a year or more). The words quoted here might be interpreted as implying that there had been no such new patients, though it is not possible to be sure on this point. The possibility that the later number may have been boosted by the inclusion of obsessionals who were also hysterics is precluded by the fact that such patients had already been included in the original thirteen. [S.E. 3: 152]

seduction, for the obsessionals he claimed to have traced not only such a passive scene but also a later premature experience involving sexual pleasure. [S.E. 3: 168–69] However, such clinical findings were never mentioned again once he had given up his theory of a differential aetiology along these lines following his abandonment of the seduction theory.

Further complications were reported in the seven cases in which female patients had been sexually abused in infancy by slightly older brothers. It the "Heredity" paper, Freud writes that in these cases the young boys had themselves been the victims of identical practices by female adults. [S.E. 3: 152] He reiterates this in "Further Remarks", stating that in a few cases "it was possible to trace with certainty" that the boy had been sexually abused in infancy by someone of the female sex. [S.E. 3: 164–65] One is left to ponder how he could make such confident claims about the early childhood of people who were not even his patients.[15]

Although in the seduction theory papers Freud twice alluded to the material of his analyses in terms which implied he would in due course provide "a detailed presentation" of it, he never actually did so. [S.E. 3: 162, 203] That he remained very conscious of this omission is indicated by the fact that he refers to it in a paper published in 1898 [S.E. 3: 262] and again in the prefatory remarks to the Dora case history, written up in 1901 [S.E. 7: 7].[16] The considerations detailed above, together with his reticence about producing the clinical material at issue, warrant searching questions about the precise nature of that material. At the time he reported the occurrence of brutal assaults and a remarkable variety of culprits, neither of which claims were ever mentioned again in his later accounts. In regard to the identity of the assailants he was already changing his story in 1897, little more than a year later, when he wrote the abstract of "The Aetiology of Hysteria" in which he stated that they were generally close relatives, in contrast to the nursemaids, governesses, domestic servants, and teachers who featured so prominently in the "Further Remarks" paper. In 1897 his

---

[15]Of the two cases which Freud specifies in this context only one involves a sibling relationship, and in this instance the brother was not in analysis. [S.E. 3: 206]

[16]In the 1898 paper, in acknowledging that a full presentation of this clinical material was "still wanting", he explains that this is mainly because "in endeavouring to throw light on what is recognised as the actual state of affairs, we come upon ever fresh problems for the solution of which the necessary preliminary work has not been done". [S.E. 3: 263] Apart from sounding somewhat obfuscatory and evasive, these words hardly accord with his claim in the "Heredity" paper that he had carried out "a complete psychoanalysis" of his thirteen cases of hysteria. [152]

theories were in a state of transition, with parents beginning to take a crucial role. This no doubt (regrettably) accounts for the changing story, but since the emendation occurred in such a short time, one is left wondering whether the original clinical claims were considerably more nebulous *even in his own terms* than he professed in his papers.

When Freud reported to Fliess on 6th February 1896 that he had just sent off his "Further Remarks" paper, he told him he had not forwarded a copy to him because it was identical with part of a draft paper he had enclosed with a letter on 1st January.[17] In the February letter he refers to the subject matter of the papers as "these latest new ideas". [Masson 1985: 170] But if he had just been achieving the epoch-making clinical results proclaimed in the seduction theory papers, it seems odd that even at this late stage he should be reporting to Fliess on his *theoretical* conceptions rather than on his remarkable clinical findings. One would have expected under such circumstances that he would have been emphasising to his friend the successful clinical corroborations of his momentous solution to the problem of the neuroses rather than dwelling on his theoretical formulations. It is almost as though his certainty of the correctness of his solution is such that the clinical corroborations are secondary in his mind. We can, of course, never know the precise nature of the material of his analyses which he took as corroborative of his theory, but it could scarcely have been other than flimsy, given the improbably comprehensive extent of his claims and the ease with which he discarded most of them. One gains the impression that his imaginative reconstructions arising from his theoretical preconceptions were increasingly taking precedence over his actual clinical experience. In this regard the fact that, as the Fliess correspondence indicates, he was occasionally resorting to the use of cocaine for the relief of migraines, nasal problems, and depression during the 1890s may be of some relevance. [Masson 1985: 49, 106, 126, 132][18] Thornton has argued that the somatic symptoms Freud complained of during this period, which Jones and Schur attribute to neurosis, are consistent with the known effects of the drug. [Thornton 1983: 193–95] Crews, follow-

---

[17]In fact, the published paper is by no means identical with part of the draft paper in question. In the former Freud goes into considerable detail concerning the nature of his clinical findings, whereas the draft paper is almost entirely theoretical, with only a passing reference to clinical results.

[18]In *The Interpretation of Dreams*, with reference to a dream he had in July 1895, Freud writes that he was making "frequent use" of cocaine at that time to reduce nasal swellings he was finding troublesome. [S.E. 4: 111]

ing Thornton, regards it as plausible that Freud's research and writings at this time were influenced by the disorienting effects of cocaine, and questions whether he was always capable of distinguishing between observation and fantasy. [Crews 1986: 63]

Possibly also of relevance to the discussion are comments (quoted by Thornton) in a paper on cocaine addiction published in *The Lancet* in 1893. A United States physician, Dr. J. B. Mattison, reported that among the doctors he was treating even those not severely affected by the drug were subject to adverse personality changes, and he cites the case of one individual whose "moral sensibilities and social responsibilities were obtunded [blunted]". [Thornton 1983: 186] In this context it is interesting to note that Clark Glymour detects, in Freud's writings, a sudden change in the late 1890s from his earlier intellectually honest and coherently argued papers to the "rhetorical trickery and evasiveness" and "near-chicanery" to be found in *The Interpretation of Dreams*, written in the years 1897–99. [Glymour 1983: 69] The above discussion suggests that the change may be located a little earlier, with the seduction theory papers of 1896.

Clearly any views about Freud's state of mind at that period can only be surmise, but we do know it was such that he felt able to disregard scientific ethics to the extent that he invented an individual and fabricated dialogue in the "Screen Memories" paper of 1899 in order to better promote his ideas. From the items examined in this chapter and the previous one we have seen that there are strong indications that there were other occasions when he resorted to imaginative invention for this purpose. That these were not the only circumstances in which he fell below the highest standards of reporting and behaviour will be evident from the material we shall be examining in the next chapter.

CHAPTER SEVEN

Miscellaneous Items

By the early 1900s Freud's theoretical ideas were conceived with the aim of explaining normal human development as well as the origins of nervous illness, but his reputation both as researcher and physician could not but be influenced by the success he was perceived to achieve in treating the latter in his practice. Although there is no evidence that he kept records in this respect, from the very beginning of psychoanalysis he was inclined to make extensive claims for the efficacy of his therapeutic procedure. However, before looking at these we shall examine the cases of two patients who have figured prominently in psychoanalytic history for whom we have information which rather conflicts with that reported in Freud's published works.

The famous Anna O., as we have seen, was not Freud's patient but one of Josef Breuer's, his older colleague, who treated her from 1880 to 1882. Nevertheless, Freud later referred to Breuer's procedure in this case as having "brought psychoanalysis into being" [S.E. 11: 9], and there are numerous other references to it in his writings which underline its importance in the genesis of his own system of treatment. He persuaded an apparently somewhat reluctant Breuer to write up the Anna O. case history belatedly for publication, thirteen years after he finished treating her, in their joint *Studies on Hysteria*. In his account Breuer describes how the patient was induced to recall significant past events in order to free her of numerous symptoms, and writes that he succeeded in this aim, though he does acknowledge that "it was a considerable time before she regained her mental balance entirely". [S.E. 2: 41]

In his *Introductory Lectures on Psychoanalysis*, Freud uses her case to support his contention that symptoms have a sense, and in doing so he refers to it as a "successful cure". [S.E. 16: 257] Elsewhere in his writings he states that the treatment was "a great therapeutic success" [S.E. 18: 235], and that Breuer was able to "restore [his patient] to health" [S.E. 19: 193]. However, thanks to the researches of Ellenberger [1972] we now know the truth to have been rather different. Following the cessation of the treatment, Anna O. was transferred by Breuer to a sanatorium, the location of which has been traced by Ellenberger. He discovered from its records that many of the symptoms of the patient (whose real name was Bertha Pappenheim) were still present, and that the documents prove that "the famed 'prototype of a cathartic cure' was neither a cure nor a catharsis". There can be no doubt that Freud knew the full story: in a letter to Stefan Zweig in 1932 he wrote that for months after her transfer to the sanatorium she struggled to regain her health [E.L. Freud 1961: 409], and in a letter to his fiancée in 1883 he reported that a year after discontinuing the treatment Breuer confided to him that she was quite unhinged and that he wished she would die and so be released from her suffering [Jones 1953: 247]. Nevertheless, there is no hint of this in his published reports, in which he invariably presents the case as having had a successful outcome, in contrast to what is now known to have been the actual state of affairs.

Misleading claims of therapeutic efficacy are also to be found in the Wolf Man case history. We have already noted that Freud stated that the Wolf Man's intestinal trouble cleared up in the course of his treatment, and that this was emphatically denied by the patient. With regard to the latter's general condition also he originally conveyed the impression of complete success, writing that in the last stage of the treatment the patient's "fixation to the illness gave way" making it possible "to clear up his inhibitions and remove his symptoms". [S.E. 17: 11] He amended this in a footnote added to the case history in 1923, in which he reports that when the Wolf Man left him in 1914 he considered him cured, but that the patient returned in 1919 for treatment for "a piece of the transference which had not hitherto been overcome". This was "successfully dealt with", and subsequently the patient "felt normal and . . . behaved unexceptionably". [S.E. 17: 121–22n] In a reference to the case in 1937 he states that fifteen years had passed "without disproving the truth of that verdict", but that "certain reservations have become necessary". His "good state of health" had been interrupted by several attacks of illness of which he was treated by another analyst and which related to "residual portions of the transference", or to "pieces of the patient's childhood history" that had come away "like sutures after an operation".[1] These events he refers to as part of the "history of this patient's recovery". [S.E. 23: 218]

The Wolf Man's view, recorded by Obholtzer, is rather different. Concerning a "very serious relapse" he experienced a few years after seeing Freud for the second time he commented: "It was a genuine

---

[1]The other analyst, who treated the Wolf Man from October 1926 to February 1927, was Ruth Mack Brunswick.

illness. And if I had become completely well through Freud's treatment, it should have been impossible for me to slip into such a state." [Obholtzer 1982: 57] Of his tendency to be attracted to women of low intelligence and social status he said, "I should at the very least have been cured of that. It ruins one's entire life." [119] In the light of the experiences he describes in the interviews it is hardly surprising to find that he states that he does not believe in psychoanalysis, and it seems clear that his cannot be regarded as a successful treatment, even in the modified terms Freud eventually described.

In his 1937 reference to the case, Freud reiterates the claim made in the original paper that when he first came for treatment the Wolf Man had been "entirely incapacitated and completely dependent upon other people". [S.E. 17: 7] This does not square with the Wolf Man's words in his memoirs, where he recounts that in his first months in Vienna he engaged in a variety of social activities, visiting restaurants, theatres, and other places of entertainment, sometimes playing cards in coffee houses until the early hours. In fact, he reports that by the time he arrived in Vienna his condition had improved considerably, a statement he also makes in a letter to Muriel Gardiner in 1970: "I should mention also that when I came to Professor Freud at the beginning of 1910, my emotional state was already much improved under the influence of Dr. D., the journey from Odessa to Vienna, etc. Actually Professor Freud never saw me in a state of really deep depression, such as I was suffering from when I went to Dr. Mack, for instance." [Gardiner 1971: 83–84, 89n]

That Freud may have had a general tendency to exaggerate the degree of illness suffered by his patients is indicated by his words in an article he wrote in 1907, where he claims he had been able to test his therapeutic method "only on severe, indeed on the severest cases". His material had at first "consisted entirely of patients who . . . had spent long years in sanatoria", and psychoanalytic therapy had been "created through and for the treatment of patients permanently unfit for existence". [S.E. 7: 263] But some of the cases referred to in the letters to Fliess and in *Studies on Hysteria* hardly seem to measure up to this description, and Ronald Clark goes so far as to say that the cases reported in *Studies* seem to be those of patients whose troubles were due to lack of motivated work, and were slight rather than so severe as to render the victims unfit for existence. [Clark 1980: 136]

With regard to the effectiveness of psychoanalytic therapy, Freud's general statements are characteristically both extravagant and inconsistent. As early as February 1898, in "Sexuality in the

Aetiology of the Neuroses", he claimed that he "owed a great number of successes to [psychoanalysis]" [S.E. 3: 282], although privately he had confessed to Fliess on 21 September 1897 his "continual disappointment in [his] efforts to bring a single analysis to a real conclusion" [Masson 1985: 264]. By 1916, in *Introductory Lectures*, he was averring that under favourable conditions psychoanalysis achieves "successes which are second to none of the finest in the field of internal medicine". [S.E. 16: 256] Similar assertions are to be found in a 1923 encyclopaedia article [S.E. 18: 250] and in *A Short Account of Psychoanalysis* (1924), where he refers to the "undeniable therapeutic success [of psychoanalysis], which far exceeded any that had previously been achieved" [S.E. 19: 202].[2] However, in *New Introductory Lectures* (1933), while still insisting that compared with other therapeutic procedures psychoanalysis "is beyond any doubt the most powerful", his assessment is rather more modest. Stating that he has "never been a therapeutic enthusiast", he now writes: "Psychoanalysis is really a method of treatment like others. It has its triumphs and its defeats, its difficulties, its limitations, its indications"; and he goes on to say that the results of the first ten years of the Psychoanalytic Institute of Berlin "give grounds neither for boasting nor for being ashamed". [S.E. 22: 153, 151, 152]

Though Freud always stressed the limitations of analytic therapy in regard to the range of psychiatric disorders and type of patient for which it was appropriate, he originally expressed highly optimistic views of the potential of his therapeutic procedure. For instance, in *Introductory Lectures* he writes that as a result of successful analytic treatment "the patient's mental life is permanently changed, is raised to a high level of development and remains protected against fresh possibilities of falling ill". [S.E. 16: 451] However in his late paper "Analysis Terminable and Interminable" (1937) he repudiates this position and in a somewhat pessimistic dissertation on the realistic goals of analytic therapy concedes that such an outcome is a rare occurrence. [S.E. 23: 220]

From an overview of Freud's pronouncements considered chronologically one gains the impression that as the technique of analysis grew more sophisticated its achievements became more modest. At first sight this might seem to be simply the result of his legitimately modifying his position in the light of experience. That he cannot, however, be so easily exonerated is apparent on more

---

[2]Freud does not cite any evidence to support these categorical assertions. Nor is this surprising, since none existed.

than one ground. From the beginning in his writings the impression is given of a degree of therapeutic efficacy beyond that which he could have been sure he could achieve, and of successful results he could not have substantiated. We have cited above evidence that his claims of success were not always reliable. To this must be added the fact that as early as 1900, as he confessed in a letter to Fliess, he was already recognising the "apparent interminable nature of the treatment" [Masson 1985: 409], yet publicly he kept his own counsel in respect of his reservations until he aired them in the 1937 paper (by which time anyway the tendency of analyses to become indefinitely long must have been only too widely apparent).[3] Overall the conclusion to be drawn is that his concern was more with the promotion of psychoanalysis than with the dissemination of accurate information.[4]

The Cocaine Episode

It was pointed out in the last chapter that doubts about Freud's probity mostly arise in relation to events from the mid-1890s onwards, and that his intermittent use of cocaine prior to and during this period may just possibly be of some significance. While this must remain in the realms of surmise, it is nevertheless worthwhile returning to the early cocaine episode not only for its intrinsic interest but also because it provides another example illustrative of the fact that his words cannot always be regarded as reliable.

The historical background is that after reading a report by a German Army doctor describing the remarkable power of cocaine to revive exhausted soldiers and to enhance their endurance, Freud procured a sample of the drug in the spring of 1884 for experimental purposes. Testing small doses on himself, he soon discov-

---

[3]In a letter to Jung in 1906 he justified his having kept to himself "certain things that might be said concerning the limits of therapy and its mechanism" on the grounds that "it is not possible to explain anything to a hostile public". [McGuire 1974: 12]

[4]The paper "Analysis Terminable and Interminable" was published in a psychoanalytic journal in 1937. In his general exposition *An Outline of Psychoanalysis*, written the following year, he presents a generally more optimistic view, while not glossing over the difficulties involved in the therapeutic procedure (the most serious of which he attributes to resistances related to the patient's "need to be ill or to suffer"). There is no specific indication of the doubts he had expressed the previous year about the prophylactic power of psychoanalysis; on the contrary, as Strachey notes, there is a passage which implies a reiteration of his earlier position on this issue. [S.E. 23: 179, 215]

ered it relieved depression and digestive disorders, substantially improved his capacity for concentrated work, and had aphrodisiac properties. He began administering cocaine to patients and colleagues, and even sent the occasional small sample to his fiancée, Martha. On the basis of his experiences he wrote an article ("On Coca") in July 1884 extolling the remarkable curative properties of the drug, and advocated its use as a safe means of withdrawal from morphine addiction.

The latter recommendation relates to the tragic case of his talented friend and colleague Ernst von Fleischl-Marxow, who had become addicted to morphine as a consequence of using it to relieve intractable nerve pain in the aftermath of an amputation of his right thumb arising from an infection contracted during research. Jones reports that after reading an article on this use of the drug, Freud offered it to Fleischl in May 1884 in the hope that he might be able to dispense with the morphine. He notes that Fleischl immediately administered it to himself in the form of subcutaneous injections. [Jones 1953: 99]

In March of the following year Freud presented a lecture on cocaine to the Psychiatric Association, in the course of which he alluded to the Fleischl case as an example of its use as a means of rapid withdrawal from morphine addiction. His conclusion, based on his experiences, was that he had "no hesitation in recommending the administration of cocaine for such withdrawal cures in subcutaneous injections of 0.03–0.05g. per dose, without any fear of increasing the dose". [Byck 1974: 117] This paper was one of several he published in 1885 championing the cause of the drug, but his views were becoming subject to increasingly vocal opposition. By 1886 the terrible effects of cocaine addiction were becoming widely publicised, and in a paper written the following year he was obliged to acknowledge the dangers, at least with regard to its use as an antidote to morphine addiction. Nevertheless, he still recommended its application in moderation for other purposes, though he considered it advisable to abandon as far as possible subcutaneous injections.[5] [175]

It is in respect to the latter that there lies an addendum to this episode. In 1885 he had stressed that "subcutaneous injections—

---

[5]The promising results that had been achieved initially with Fleischl soon proved to be deceptive. By April 1885 he was again in a desperate state and taking enormous doses of cocaine (though the paper containing Freud's optimistic report on the successful use of the drug for morphine withdrawal remained unamended when it was published in August of the same year). Fleischl lingered on in terrible pain before his death some six years later. [Jones 1953: 100–01]

such as I have used with success in cases of longstanding sciatica—
are quite harmless", and in relation to the treatment of morphine
addiction advocated such injections, as we have seen, with "no
hesitation". [109] But we find a different story recounted in *The
Interpretation of Dreams*. In a section dealing with one of his own
dreams which he believed related to his "unfortunate friend who
had poisoned himself with cocaine" he writes: "I had advised him to
use the drug internally [i.e., orally] only, while morphia was being
withdrawn; but he had at once given himself cocaine *injections*." A
little later, in another reference to his "dead friend who had so
hastily resorted to cocaine injections", he is even more explicit: "As
I have said, I had never contemplated the drug being given by
injection." [S.E. 4: 115, 117]

The fact that over a period he had actually used injections on
patients, and then, following the many reports of the terrible reactions to cocaine, had singled out the utilisation of this particular
method of administering the drug as the reason for the adverse
effects, makes it rather unlikely that he would have forgotten this
specific detail of that sobering episode. Jones reports that Freud
suppressed the paper in which he had strongly advocated the use of
injections; no copy of it is to be found in his collection of reprints
and he did not include it in the list of his papers he had to provide
when applying for the title of Professor in 1897 (shortly before he
wrote the relevant passage in the dream book). [Jones 1953: 106]
Although unconscious repression has been proposed (by Jones and
others) to explain the erroneous statement, Freud's deliberate
attempt to suppress the incriminating paper suggests a more mundane explanation.

The Frink Affair

An episode from somewhat later in his career which throws a fresh
light on Freud's clinical judgement as well as his ethical standards
concerns the American psychiatrist Dr. Horace Frink, a founding
member of the New York Psychoanalytic Society. Although Jones
mentions it briefly (and inaccurately) in his biography, the full story
has only recently come to light through the efforts of Frink's
daughter Helen Frink Kraft, stimulated by her rediscovery of letters
pertaining to the episode. [Edmunds 1988] In February 1921 her
father arrived in Vienna to undergo a training analysis with Freud.
Some years earlier he had become involved in a love affair with one
of his patients, the bank heiress Angelika Bijur, wife of a New York

millionaire. In the course of the analysis Freud encouraged Frink to separate from his then wife, Doris, to seek fulfilment with Angelika. In response to pleading letters from Frink urging that he needed her to bring his analysis to a successful issue, in July Angelika joined him in Vienna, where she found him in a state of depression. She records that Freud advised her to divorce her then husband, Abraham Bijur, to remedy her incomplete existence, and told her that if she threw Frink over he would never try to come back to normality and would probably develop into a homosexual, though in a highly disguised way.[6] The couple immediately sought divorces from their respective spouses, and a subsequent letter expressing misgivings was met with an assurance from Freud that he knew he was right in his advice. Nevertheless, after his return to New York Frink was overwhelmed by guilt and depression. The following year, after both wives had filed for divorce, his condition worsened and he went to Vienna for treatment with Freud from April to July 1922, and again for three weeks in November and December, during which latter period he was manic and experienced hallucinations. However, he suddenly recovered, and Freud assured him that the analysis was complete and he should go ahead with the marriage; according to Angelika, Freud contended that Frink was now using the analysis to maintain his neurosis. The marriage took place at the end of December 1922.

In January 1923 Frink, as the protégé of Freud, was unanimously elected president of the New York Psychoanalytic Society while on his honeymoon. However, his emotional difficulties persisted, and he was still struggling with them when in April he heard the news that his former wife was dying. She had left New York more than a year previously at his request and had suffered considerable distress on the break-up of the marriage. She died of pneumonia in May 1923, leaving their two children to be cared for by Frink. The latter's mental state now deteriorated badly, and eventually, in May 1924, he committed himself to the Phipps Psychiatric Clinic under the care of his former teacher, Adolf Meyer. Angelika, disillusioned and despairing of the marriage, proceeded with plans for a divorce. Later that year Frink twice attempted suicide, and was again hospitalised before being reunited with his children in 1925. The final period of his life was spent quietly in tranquil surroundings, the family finances being secured in the

---

[6]In November 1921 Freud wrote to Frink that he had asked Angelika not to repeat that he had advised her to marry Frink on the threat of a nervous breakdown. It gave a false impression of the kind of advice compatible with analysis.

divorce decree. He married again in 1935, and died of a heart attack the following year at the age of 53.

An apt commentary on the part Freud plays in this sorry affair comes in an open letter to him by Angelika's former husband, Abraham Bijur, which the latter planned to publish in New York newspapers. In it he highlights the fact that Freud had sanctioned Frink's divorcing his then wife and marrying his patient, yet had never see Frink's wife and learned to judge her feelings, interests, and real wishes. He asks in respect of himself how Freud could give a judgement that ruins a man's home and happiness without at least knowing the victim so as to see if a better solution cannot be found.[7] Equally worthy of note is a poignant letter Doris Frink sent to Horace in 1921 in which she affirms she is concerned only for his happiness, but she cannot feel it lies where Freud thinks it does.[8]

An extraordinary letter sent by Freud to Frink in November 1921 indicates that the latter resisted his analyst's diagnosis of latent homosexuality. It also lends credence to the suspicion that while promoting the marriage to Angelika, Freud may have had it in mind as a source of funds for the psychoanalytic movement in the United States. He writes: "Your complaint that you cannot grasp your homosexuality implies that you are not yet aware of your phantasy of making me a rich man. If matters turn out all right let us change this imaginary gift into a real contribution to the Psychoanalytic Funds." [Edmunds 1988: 45] Now a "phantasy" of a patient was almost invariably divined by interpretation by Freud himself, and the matters intimated must surely be the plans for marriage to Angelika. It is difficult to interpret the words as other than a flagrant attempt to manipulate his susceptible patient into providing financial support for the movement, and as such a serious breach of the norms of professional conduct.

Historical Distortions

Given the numerous instances of dubious behaviour recorded in the above pages it is hardly surprising that a close examination of Freud's historical accounts of the development of psychoanalysis should reveal them to be untrustworthy. We have already noted

---

[7]Abraham Bijur died of cancer in May 1922 before he could publish the letter.
[8]In a letter to Frink in September 1921 Freud brushed off the latter's concern for his wife, assuring him on the basis of her "cool and reasonable" letters that she would be able to weather the storm.

that his *History of the Psychoanalytic Movement* was written as a polemic under the pressure of the dramatic events relating to the secession of Freud's heir-apparent, Carl Jung, so perhaps it is predictable that it contains possibly the greatest amount of factual distortion of all his works. One lengthy passage in particular stands out in this respect, and this will now be summarised and examined in some detail, although to full appreciate the persuasive power of Freud's writing it is essential to read it in its original form. [S.E. 14: 21–24]

Following a section in which he had described the early stages in the development of psychoanalysis, Freud writes that he did not at first perceive the peculiar nature of what he had discovered. He unhesitatingly sacrificed his growing popularity as a doctor by making a systematic enquiry into the sexual factors involved in the causation of his patients' neuroses, thereby bringing out new facts which confirmed his conviction of the importance of the sexual factor. To communicate these discoveries to his colleagues he "innocently" addressed a meeting of the Vienna Society of Psychiatry and Neurology with Krafft-Ebing in the chair, hoping they would be treated as ordinary contributions to science. But the silence with which his communications were met, the void which formed around him, the hints that were conveyed to him, gradually made him realise that assertions on the part played by sexuality in the aetiology of the neuroses cannot be counted upon meeting the same kind of treatment as other communications. He understood that from then on he was one of those who have "disturbed the sleep of the world", and that he could not count on objectivity and tolerance. However, since his conviction of the accuracy of his observations and conclusions grew even stronger, and neither his confidence in his own judgement nor his moral courage were "precisely small", he was prepared to accept the fate that sometimes accompanied such discoveries.

His picture of the future was that he would succeed in maintaining himself by means of the therapeutic success of his new procedure, but science would ignore him completely during his lifetime. Some decades later it was inevitable that someone else would come across the same discoveries and would achieve the recognition for them, while he himself would receive honour as a forerunner whose failure had been inevitable. Meanwhile he settled down to what seemed in retrospect "like a glorious heroic age", a state of "splendid isolation", which at least had the advantages that he did not have to read any publications, nor listen to ill-informed opponents. He learnt to restrain speculative tendencies and to follow the advice of his master Charcot to look at the same things again and again until they themselves began to speak. His publications, which he was able to place with a little trouble, could always lag far behind his knowledge and be postponed as long as he pleased, for there was no doubtful priority to be defended. *The Interpretation of Dreams*, for instance, was finished in all essentials at the beginning of 1896, though not written out until the summer of 1899. The analysis of "Dora" was over at the end of 1899 (the editor notes that this should read 1900) and written out in the following two weeks, but not published until 1905. In the meantime his writings were not reviewed in the medical journals, or if exceptionally they *were* reviewed, they were dismissed "with expressions of scornful or pitying superiority". References to him in publications were short and unflattering—words such as "eccentric", "extreme", or "very peculiar" were used to describe him. On one occasion an assistant at the clinic in Vienna where Freud gave his university lectures told him, after completing the course, that with his chief's knowledge he had earlier written a book opposing his views. He now very much regretted that he had not first learnt more about them by attending the course, for in that case he would have written much of it differently. He had in fact enquired at the clinic whether he had not better first read *The Interpretation of Dreams*, but had been advised against doing so—it was not worth the trouble. In spite of his change of view this person, a regular reviewer for a medical journal, did not think it necessary to draw attention to his revised opinion of psychoanalysis.

In the face of such experiences Freud was saved from becoming embittered by the fact that psychoanalysis enabled him to account for the behaviour of his opponents and to appreciate that their attitude stemmed from a "distressing contradiction of the security of their own sense of conviction". He was able to see that their opposition was in fact a necessary consequence of analytic premisses. Just as his patients were unable to acknowledge the facts he had discovered due to internal resistances, so also in the case of healthy people these resistances were bound to appear as soon as they were confronted with what was repressed. It was therefore hardly surprising that they should be able to justify their rejection of his ideas on intellectual grounds, though it was actually "affective in origin". The difference was that with his patients he was in a position "to bring pressure to bear on them so as to induce them to get insight into their resistances and overcome them", whereas one was without this advantage in dealing with people who were ostensibly healthy. One came across the same thing with one's patients—the arguments they advanced were just the same, and "not precisely brilliant". How these healthy people could be compelled to examine the matter "in a cool and scientifically objective spirit" was an unsolved problem which was best left for time to clear up. It has often happened in the history of science that a proposition which has called forth nothing but contradiction has come later to be accepted even though no new proofs have been brought forward. It was hardly surprising, however, that during the years when he alone represented psychoanalysis he should not develop any respect for the world's opinion or any "bias towards intellectual appeasement".

A close scrutiny of the above account reveals much that is either false or at the very least grossly misleading. Consider the claim that Freud sacrificed his popularity by making systematic enquiries into sexual matters. A letter written to Fliess on 6th October 1893 gives a rather different picture, for there he writes: "The sexual business attracts people who . . . go away won over after having exclaimed, 'No one has ever asked me about that before!'." Two years later, in November 1895, he is able to report an increase to "nine to eleven hours of hard work, six to eight analytic cases a day", and in the following month writes that because of the success of his practice he is in a position to dictate his fees. Though there was a decline in the spring of 1896, possibly because of the aggressive approach with which he sought confirmations of his sexual theories, less than a year later (February 1897) he reports that he is working about twelve hours per day. A dropping off occurred the following year, but there seems to be no evidence of any prolonged period of decline, and it is clear that, at the very least, he greatly exaggerated the effect on his practice of his espousal of sexual theories. [Masson 1985: 57, 152, 154, 185, 230, 328]

In his account of the meeting chaired by Krafft-Ebing, which he "innocently" addressed, he omits to mention the crucial fact that the paper he read was "The Aetiology of Hysteria", in which he gave his most detailed exposition of the infantile seduction theory. [Clark 1980: 157] Since he himself renounced that very theory (though not publicly) within eighteen months, his indignation at its reception, with the implication of grossly unfair treatment by his colleagues, is hardly to be taken seriously, and the whole account can only be described as disingenuous. The suggestion that it was his emphasis on the importance of the sexual factor which was responsible for his adverse reception is scarcely credible, for the chairman, Krafft-Ebing, was himself an eminent sexologist who was renowned for his book *Sexual Pathology*, published in 1886. In the words of William Johnston, a writer who has studied this period of Austrian intellectual history: "Whatever else may have isolated Freud in Vienna, it was not his scrutiny of sex. In a city where Sacher-Masoch, Krafft-Ebing, and Weininger were read with nonchalance, Freud's pansexualism hardly shocked anyone." [Johnston 1972: 249] So the passage which follows the account of the meeting, in which he casts himself as both martyr and hero, is a masterly display of rhetoric, bearing little relation to the truth. Ellenberger [1970: 450] writes that "the assertion that Freud was ostracised in Vienna is unfounded", and there is no evidence of the "trouble" in gaining publication to which Freud alludes. There is even an indication that his "splendid isolation" was largely, if not wholly, of his own making. In a letter to Fliess dated 16th April 1896 (that is, *before* he received the adverse response to his "Aetiology of Hysteria" lecture) he wrote: "In accordance with your suggestion I have started to isolate myself in every respect and find it easy to bear." Again, on 28th April he told Fliess: "Of all the advice you gave me, I followed the one concerning my isolation the most completely." [Masson 1985: 181, 183]

Equally dubious is his claim concerning the therapeutic success of his new procedure. As we have already noted, it is contradicted in his letter to Fliess of 21st September 1897, in which he refers to the continual disappointment of his efforts to bring a single analysis to a real conclusion; and in February the following year he reported that his cases of hysteria were proceeding very poorly. [Masson 1985: 264, 299]

So far as the response to his publications is concerned, Ellenberger writes: "Contrary to the usual assertion, his publications did not meet with the icy silence or disparaging criticism that are said to have existed. Actually the reception was mostly favourable. . . ." [1970: 455] Concurring in general terms with this view, Cioffi points out that the situation at the time was considerably more complex than customarily presented by Freud and his followers. From an examination of a representative sample of writings from the early part of this century he concludes that while there certainly were extreme responses of the kind traditionally depicted, these constituted a minority view compared with the many reasoned and balanced critiques which were more typical. [Cioffi 1973: 1–24] A survey of the evidence now available also leads Sulloway to conclude that "strong opposition was not the initial reaction to Freud's theories; nor was any opposition premised upon the purported triumvirate of sexual prudery, hostility to innovation, and anti-semitism that dominates the traditional historical scenario on this subject." In short, the notion "that Freud's theories were given an inadequate, hostile, and irrational reception by his contemporaries" is a "myth".[9] [Sulloway 1979: 453, 494]

The story about his having postponed publication of two of his books is also more than a little misleading. He elaborates on this in his paper on the "Anatomical Distinction Between the Sexes" (1925), where he claims that he held back publication of *The Interpretation of Dreams* and the "Dora" case history "for four or five years" to allow time for his findings to be "either confirmed or corrected". [S.E. 19: 248] With regard to the dream book the evidence of the Fliess correspondence tells a different story. His first allusion to the idea of writing a book on dreams occurs in a letter of 16th May 1897. Then on 5th November he writes that he intends to start on it soon, and on 9th February of the following year states that he is deep into it. Progress reports follow at intervals until he is able to announce on 11th September 1899 that he has finished. The work was published in early November, some two months later. Although undoubtedly Freud was noting dreams over a considerable period of time, it remains the fact, as Strachey tells us [S.E. 4: *xix–xx*], he worked on the book from late in 1897 until September 1899, and his claim to have suppressed it for several years is manifestly false. Nor is his story in regard to the publication of the Dora case history a candid version of events. He completed it in January 1901, and, as Strachey says [S.E. 7: 10, 10n], he clearly intended to publish it straight away. In a letter to Fliess dated 25th January he states that it had already been accepted by Ziehen, the editor of the *Monatsschrift für Psychiatrie und Neurologie*, and on 9th June he announces that it has been sent off and will probably appear by the autumn. However, for reasons which are not entirely clear, it was not actually published until 1905. Ernest Jones writes that Freud told Ferenczi in 1909 that the editor of a second journal had refused to publish it (probably on the ground of medical discretion), and surmises that Freud had wanted a "second string" in case Ziehen changed his mind on reading the paper. He in fact suggests that Ziehen may indeed have had some doubts on the question of discretion,

---

[9]While by no means entirely dissenting from the views of Ellenberger and Sulloway, Norman Kiell [1988] has expressed some reservations about their conclusions, and criticises some of the claims of Bry and Rifkin [1962], whose research first drew attention to this issue. However, an examination of the original material, now available in the volume edited by Kiell, does not bear out the latter's contention that the aforementioned have overstated their case. In general the numerous reviews are respectful in tone and frequently generous in their appreciation of Freud's writings. Not without reason many contain critical passages, but these are, in the main, entirely pertinent.

and this may have been why Freud withheld the manuscript for another four years. [Jones 1955: 286–87] Freud himself told Fliess on 11th March 1902 that he withdrew the paper because a little earlier he had lost his "last audience" in him. This clearly relates to a letter of 19th September of the previous year, where he writes that he has lost his "only audience" because Fliess had suggested that Freud's interpretations were merely the projections of his own thoughts. In this same letter he asks, "For whom do I still write?". [Masson 1985: 456, 450] Whatever the full story it is clear that his later versions leave something to be desired.[10]

To embellish his fanciful version of events, Freud recounts the episode in which an assistant at the Clinic in Vienna where he gave his University lectures admitted to him that he had written a book criticising his ideas without knowing much about them, and without having read *The Interpretations of Dreams*. It is interesting to note that some years later, in his *Autobiographical Study*, Freud informs us that "The man in question, who has since become a professor, has gone so far as to repudiate my report of the conversation and to throw doubts in general upon the accuracy of my recollection. I can only say I stand by every word of the account I then gave." [S.E. 20: 48] One is tempted to comment that if that account is of the same degree of veracity as the rest of the passage from which it comes, there seems little doubt about which version in this dispute is likely to be the more trustworthy.

For the remainder of the passage we are in the realms of rhetoric, with the image of the heroic Freud standing alone, not only gallantly combatting the emotionally-based arguments of his opponents, but also able to explain why they were unable to appraise his ideas with the same "cool and scientifically objective spirit" which, by implication, he himself brought to his disputes.[11]

---

[10]In the case history itself Freud writes that he postponed publication for reasons of medical discretion. [S.E. 7: 8] This is not consistent with the explanation he gave Fliess, nor with that in the 1925 paper. The less specific statement in his *History* is misleading because it is in the context of the supposed "trouble" he had in placing his publications, whereas the decision to withhold it would seem to have been his own.

[11]The question arises as to the extent to which Freud was aware of the degree to which he was falsifying the historical record and misrepresenting his critics. Barely a year after publishing his inaccurate and tendentious *History*, in which he had maligned his psychoanalytic rivals in an unprincipled manner, he wrote the letter to James Putnam in which he extolled himself as a paragon of virtue, a man who has "always aspired to behave honourably, to spare others and to be kind wherever possible", and who had concluded that he was "better than others" in regard to "ethical aspirations". In the same letter he complains that by behaving in this

Both the *History* and the *Autobiographical Study* contain a considerable number of factual distortions of the kind to be found in the above passage. For instance, in the second of these he writes that the theory in *Studies on Hysteria* scarcely touched on the problem of aetiology, and that he only subsequently learned from his rapidly increasing experience that factors of a sexual nature were invariably present, adding: "I was not prepared for this conclusion and my expectations played no part in it. . . ." [S.E. 20: 23–24] Yet we have noted that as early as 1888 he had written an article in which he had stated his view that sexual factors played a role in all neuroses [S.E. 1: 51], and by February 1894 was, in his own words, "single-mindedly" searching for an exclusively sexual aetiology in all cases of neurasthenia, hysteria, and obsessional neuroses. [Masson 1985: 66][12] Of Breuer's position concerning the significance of sexuality he states that "he was the first to show the reaction of distaste and repudiation", and that he "shrank from recognising the sexual aetiology of the neuroses". [S.E. 4: 12; 20: 26] While it is true that Breuer could not accept an *exclusively* sexual aetiology, the notion that he shied away from implicating sexual experiences as a cause of neuroses is demonstrably false. In *Studies*, among several references to the subject, he writes that "it is perhaps worthwhile insisting again and again that the sexual factor is by far the most important and the most productive of pathological results". [S.E. 2: 246–47] He also affirms that *"the great majority of severe neuroses in women have their origin in the marriage bed"* (Breuer's emphasis), adding a footnote criticising clinical medicine for ignoring "one of the most important of all the patho-

---

virtuous way "one comes to harm and becomes an anvil because other people are brutal and unreliable". [Jones 1955: 314–15] In the light of his actual behaviour towards erstwhile friends and colleagues, and the fact that his repeated recriminations against his opponents were frequently gross exaggerations (he regarded virtually all critics of his ideas as "enemies"), there would seem to have been an element of paranoia in his personality. (An earlier indication of this trait occurs in a letter to Fliess written not long after he had reported his success in isolating himself, in which he asserts "Word was given out to abandon me", which sounds more than a little unlikely. [Masson 1985: 185]) Against the background of what is now known of the historical record, the passage from the *History* examined above shows signs of this same trait, and it is possible that his tendency to misrepresent the facts in such instances may owe more to pathology than to deliberate mendacity.

[12]In *Freud Evaluated* Macmillan has demonstrated the crucial role that Freud's expectations played in his findings of sexual aetiologies. [Macmillan 1991: 122–143, 200–231] Those expectations, as Swales has cogently argued in his paper "Freud, Cocaine and Sexual Chemistry" [1983], almost certainly derived from his experiences with cocaine.

genic factors". [S.E. 2: 246] Jones reports that Breuer's cooperation in publishing *Studies* was ensured only with the strict understanding that the theme of sexuality was to be kept in the background [Jones 1953: 275], but in view of the words quoted above this seems unlikely. Breuer had become, in Sulloway's words, "the first major victim of psychoanalytically reconstructed history". [Sulloway 1979: 100]

There is a well-known story of Freud's to the effect that Breuer precipitously ended his treatment of Anna O. when he realised she had developed a strong emotional attachment to him [S.E. 20: 26; E.L. Freud 1961: 408–09], but Ellenberger has documented that there are discrepancies between Freud's (and Jones's) accounts and the ascertainable facts. [Ellenberger 1972: 271, 273] In addition there are clear indications that Freud's later version that Anna O. suddenly developed a phantom pregnancy which so horrified Breuer that "he took flight and abandoned [her] to a colleague" [E.L. Freud 1961: 409] is a reconstruction based on retrospective inferences. The most we can be sure about on the available evidence is that Breuer took to heart his wife's concern at the amount of time and energy her husband was devoting to his patient.[13]

Another of Freud's victims was the eminent sexologist Albert Moll, who had written extensively on the subject of the sexual impulse in children in his book *Libido Sexualis*, published in 1897. Freud marked passages on this topic in his own copy [Sulloway 1979: 303], yet not only did he state in his *Three Essays on the Theory of Sexuality* (1905) that not a single author had previously recognised the regular existence of the sexual instinct in children, he also added a footnote in 1910 in which he deliberately negated Moll's work. [S.E. 7: 173, 173–74n] In 1908 he even accused Moll of plagiarism, thereby, in Sulloway's words, designating him "the plagiarist of a discovery that he supposedly refused to recognise, and for which his own priority over Freud was well established by almost a decade". [Sulloway 1979: 472][14]

The great French psychologist and psychotherapist Pierre Janet received similar dismissive treatment. Although Freud had at one time acknowledged the worth of his pioneering theories on the subject of hysterical symptoms [S.E. 8: 172], he later downgraded

---

[13]In a detailed examination of the episode in his *Life and Work of Josef Breuer*, [1989] Albrecht Hirshmüller concludes that the Freud-Jones account of the termination of the treatment of Anna O. should be regarded as a myth. [126–131]

[14]Freud's antagonism towards Moll stemmed from the fact that his perceptive criticisms of psychoanalysis were not easily dismissed, since he was a sexologist of considerable eminence who had made a special study of childhood sexuality.

his ideas, and in the *Autobiographical Study* he states that Janet had "destroyed the value of his own work by declaring that when he had spoken of 'unconscious' mental acts he had meant nothing by the phrase—it had been no more than a *façon de parler*" [S.E. 20: 31]. Now, the notion of unconscious fixed ideas had been first utilised by Janet several years before Freud published on the subject, as part of a system which Janet called "psychological analysis", and the implication that he had renounced his belief in the importance of unconscious processes is another of Freud's misrepresentations.[15] In fact, it seems likely that his later tendency to play down the value of Janet's work stems from certain parallels it had with his own early endeavours. Ellenberger reports that in 1913 Janet contended that many of the so-called novel ideas of psychoanalysis were but renamed existing concepts, [Ellenberger 1970: 817] and he was later to be more specific in asserting priority in regard to a number of these. [Clark 1980: 134] However, this claim was of doubtful validity, regardless of the fact that some of Janet's theories were published several years before *Studies on Hysteria*. In view of his collaboration with Breuer in the late 1880s, Freud's assertion that psychoanalysis developed independently of Janet's work is essentially true, even though Breuer's theoretical ideas were undoubtedly influenced by the Frenchman.

Regardless of the similarities between some of their basic concepts, the ways in which Janet and Freud utilised them were very different, and there is no comparison between the form that psychoanalysis eventually took and the considerably more limited scheme evolved by Janet. In particular, Freud came to lay especial emphasis on the importance of infantile sexuality, and it is his theories on that subject to which we shall now turn as we resume our examination of the development of his ideas.

---

[15]In an earlier version of why Janet had forfeited credit for his ideas Freud writes that he had "expressed himself with exaggerated reserve, *as if* he wanted to admit that the unconscious had been nothing more to him than a form of words, a makeshift, *une façon de parler*". [S.E. 16: 257; emphasis added.]

CHAPTER EIGHT

The Oedipus Theory
and Female Sexuality

When one reads Freud's expositions in general, and his descriptions of the sexual processes of early childhood in particular, it is by no means apparent, from his confident assertions, that the bulk of his "findings" are essentially conjectural, and that the clinical evidence for them frequently rests on such tenuous foundations as to be virtually nonexistent. We have noted earlier that his evidence for the major sexual processes in childhood which he postulates is heavily dependent on his questionable unconscious phantasy theory together with the analytic technique of reconstruction, and that this is so is again made clear in a passage in the *Introductory Lectures on Psychoanalysis* (1916–17) where, in the course of discussing the paths to symptom formation, he warns the reader that there is something new and surprising to learn: "By means of analysis, as you know, we arrive at a knowledge of the infantile experiences to which the libido is fixated and out of which the symptoms are made. Well, the surprise lies in the fact that these scenes from infancy are not always true. Indeed, they are not true in the majority of cases, and in a few of them they are the direct opposite of the historical truth." [S.E. 16: 367] What is happening in such cases, he explains, is that the patient has been "engaged in bringing to light the phantasies with which he has disguised the history of his childhood". [368]

From the perspective of our knowledge of the events pertaining to the infantile seduction theory and its renunciation, which clearly serve as the prototype for the above explication, the remarkable nature of the passage is apparent.[1] He states explicitly that the supposed experiences are arrived at "by means of analysis"; in other words they are constructions—conjectures—posited by himself. He then tells us that these products of his own imagination are, in the majority of cases, not true. So having decided that his *own* constructions are untrue he concludes that they are not genuine occurrences, but are phantasies *of his patients!*

---

[1] In *History* he writes in regard to the seduction theory episode: "Analysis had led back to these infantile sexual traumas by the right path, and yet they were not true." [S.E. 14: 17]

Although at first sight one might be tempted to draw the conclusion from this convoluted argument that Freud is engaged in a gigantic confidence trick, there can be no question that he was utterly convinced that the constructed phantasies (which by his own description have to be divined by the analyst) represented processes occurring in the minds of his patients.[2] Nevertheless, in his published writings the subject is treated with an ambiguity which suggests a deliberate attempt at clouding the issue. The true version of his procedure is generally to be found in his technical papers, as in the one on "Hysterical Phantasies", where he writes: "The technique of analysis enables us in the first place to infer from the symptoms what these unconscious phantasies are and then to make them conscious to the patient." [S.E. 9: 162] However, on other occasions he seems to be maintaining the fiction that such phantasies are actually reported to him by his patients, as for example in the passage in *Introductory Lectures*, where having just explained that the supposed infantile experiences are "brought to light by analysis" (i.e., are analytical constructions) he describes them as "invented stories" and in the same context refers to "all the things that are *told to us* today as phantasy". [S.E. 16: 367, 368, 371; emphasis added.] The ambiguity blurs the distinction between the respective contributions of the analyst and patient and creates an impression that the latter materially contributes to the constructions, whereas it is clear from Freud's writings that in practice they are essentially his own speculative conjectures.[3]

---

[2]From letters written by Freud in 1901 we learn that Fliess expressed his scepticism in regard to the analytic technique, concluding, in Freud's words, that "the 'thought-reader' perceives nothing in others but merely projects his own thoughts into them". [Masson 1985: 440, 450] However, there is no indication that Freud ever entertained any doubts about the technique, which after all had enabled him to reinterpret rather than retract the emphatically proclaimed clinical results adduced in 1896 in support of the seduction theory. Only in his discussion of primal phantasies in the Wolf Man paper does he address the challenge that the analyst's constructions "are phantasies not of the patient but of the analyst himself". His argument (in essence the oft-repeated one appealing to the coherence of the analytic material) displays no evidence of self-doubt, even though he effectively concedes that without prior commitment to the psychoanalytic methodology it would "be impossible to arrive at a decision" on the issue. [S.E. 17: 52–53]

[3]Precisely this same ambiguity, so blatant that it suggest deliberate obfuscation, occurs in his accounts (both contemporary and retrospective) of the seduction theory episode. In his *Autobiographical Study* we are told that the patients "reproduced" the sexual scenes, and also that he believed "these *stories*". [S.E. 20: 33, 34] In the *History* he writes that "*analysis* had led back to these infantile sexual traumas", yet also states that he accepted as true "the *statements* made by patients" regarding the supposed traumas. Again, in the same passage he says that

Further indications that the evidence for Freud's "findings" is more than a little tenuous (and also that his words are not altogether trustworthy) come from his writings on the subject of the sexual processes he claims occur in young children, of which the Oedipus complex is the most fundamental. In a passage from the 1920 edition of *Three Essays* he tells us that "If mankind had been able to learn from a direct observation of children, these three essays could have remained unwritten". [S.E. 7: 133] However, this directly contradicts his earlier contention in *Introductory Lectures* that what he had inferred about the sexual life of children from the analyses of adults *had* been "confirmed point by point by direct observations of children" [S.E. 16: 310], and also that in *An Autobiographical Study* where he writes that from 1908 onwards it became possible to confirm these discoveries "fully and in every detail by direct observations upon children" [S.E. 20: 39]. In fact we find ourselves involved here in a circular argument, for the "direct observations" are invoked as corroboration of "what we inferred" concerning the early years of childhood from the "analysis of symptoms in adults" [S.E. 16: 310], and explicitly as "good evidence of the trustworthiness of [psychoanalysis]" [S.E. 7: 193–94n]; but we are also told elsewhere that "the certain conviction of the existence and importance of infantile sexuality can, however, only be obtained by the method of analysis, by pursuing the symptoms and peculiarities of neurotics back to their ultimate sources" [S.E. 14: 18], and again, that these beginnings of sexual life "can only be confirmed by investigators who have enough patience and technical skill to trace back an analysis to the first years of a patient's childhood" [S.E. 7: 133].

So on the one hand we are asked to accept alleged direct observations of sexual processes in young children as vindication of his method of analysis, while on the other hand we are told we need to accept his method of analysis in order to be convinced of the existence of these same sexual processes! Such contradictory statements concerning one of the fundamental tenets of psychoanalysis can only cast further doubt on the value of the supposed

---

"hysterical *subjects* trace back their symptoms to traumas that are fictitious", when quite obviously it is the physician who does that. [S.E. 14: 17; emphases added.]

The ambiguity is necessary because on the one hand in his post-seduction theory analyses the phantasies remain unconscious and have to be reconstructed using his interpretive technique, but on the other hand he is concerned to provide an explanation for his "error" which does not raise awkward questions about the reliability of that technique, so he has to perform a precarious balancing act in which he gives an impression that the seduction theory patients *told* him about the supposed sexual scenes, while at the same time *also* saying that they were arrived at by analysis.

findings. Moreover, he also seeks to nullify in advance the arguments of anyone who disputes the validity of his claims. In the passage referred to above, from the introduction to the fourth edition of *Three Essays*, he asserts: "None, however, but physicians who practice psychoanalysis can have . . . any possibility of forming a judgement [on his writings concerning infantile sexuality] that is uninfluenced by his own dislikes and prejudices." [S.E. 7: 133][4]

It is abundantly clear from the preceding pages that what Freud calls his findings in regard to young children rest largely on the shifting sands of the highly speculative phantasy theory and his equally doubtful interpretive technique. As far as the unconscious phantasy theory is concerned, the only direct empirical evidence to support it is that provided by the dubious clinical claims made in regard to the seduction theory episode (which is why he uses it as a model in *Introductory Lectures*). The analytic technique of interpretation is suspect from the start, since it was essentially this technique, in its early form, which played a substantial role in producing the spurious confirmations of the erroneous seduction theory. In Freud's hands it amounted to little more than a means of satisfying what are, in effect, self-fulfilling prophecies. The conjectures that supposedly reveal the contents of the unconscious phantasies, and which constitute most of his findings, naturally derive from his theories. The analytic technique is so versatile that it can come up with virtually any clinical material he needs to support these theories; in other words, his "findings of psychoanalysis" (sometimes also misleadingly described as "observations") are, for the most part, essentially his own wish-fulfilments.

The tenuous and speculative nature of these supposed findings is obscured by the brilliantly persuasive style of Freud's expositions, in which they are almost always presented as solidly grounded facts. That they are indeed largely tenuous speculations is nowhere more clearly revealed than in his writings on the sexual processes he postulates to occur in infancy, and it is to these that we shall now turn.

---

[4]Freud himself did not seem to be completely clear about the nature of the evidence for his theories of infantile sexuality. On occasions when he wished to demonstrate the supposed emotional resistance to his ideas, he claimed the facts were "self-evident", asserting, for example, that the "early infantile sexual life" culminating in "straightforward sexual desire" can "be confirmed so easily that only the greatest efforts could make it possible to overlook it". [S.E. 14: 18; 19: 220; 20: 39] However, at other times, such as when he was affirming the unique power of the psychoanalytic method, he asserted in regard to "the beginnings of human sexual life" that "none, however, but physicians who practice psychoanalysis can have any access whatsoever to this sphere of knowledge". [S.E. 7: 133; 17: 107]

The Oedipus Theory

In a footnote added to his *Three Essays* in 1920, Freud writes: "It has justly been said[5] that the Oedipus complex is the nuclear complex of the neuroses, and constitutes the essential part of their content. It represents the peak of infantile sexuality, which, through its after-effects, exercises a decisive influence on the sexuality of adults. Every new arrival on this planet is faced by the task of mastering the Oedipus complex; anyone who fails to do so falls a victim to neurosis. With the progress of psychoanalytic studies the importance of the Oedipus complex has become more and more clearly evident; its recognition has become the shibboleth that distinguishes the adherents of psychoanalysis from its opponents." [S.E. 7: 226n]

In essence the Oedipus theory, as propounded by Freud in 1925, postulates that in the first years of infancy "boys concentrate their sexual wishes upon their mother and develop hostile impulses against their father as being a rival, while girls adopt an analogous attitude"; thus "a child's first object-choice is an *incestuous* one". The sexual life of man comes in two waves, the first of which reaches a peak in the fourth or fifth year of childhood. This early growth of sexuality is overcome by repression, leading to a period of latency which lasts until puberty, when the early conflicts are reanimated. At the infantile stage "the contrast between the sexes is not stated in terms of 'male' or 'female' but of 'possessing a penis' or 'castrated'. The *castration complex* which arises in this connection is of the profoundest importance in the formation alike of character and of neuroses." [S.E. 20: 36–38]

Lest anyone should fail to appreciate their full import, Freud emphasises that his ideas must be taken literally: "None of the findings of psychoanalytic research has provoked such embittered denials, such fierce opposition—or such amusing contortions—on the part of critics as this indication of the childhood impulses towards incest which persist in the unconscious. An attempt has even been made recently [he writes this in 1914] to make out, in the face of all experience, that the incest should only be taken as 'symbolic'." [S.E. 4: 263n]

Freud insisted that "psychoanalytic experience" had put these ideas "beyond the reach of doubt and has taught us to recognise in them the key to every neurosis" [S.E. 21: 184], so it is of some interest to attempt to ascertain how he arrived at them and what evidence he adduces in their support.

---

[5]By himself, in *Totem and Taboo* (1913) [S.E. 23: 156].

Such information as is available in regard to the genesis of the Oedipus theory derives from the Fliess correspondence, but even there one finds no clear indication of its origin. Freud's letters and draft papers during 1896 and 1897 show him wrestling with his ideas on the seduction theory and the aetiology of neuroses. By the spring of 1897 he is starting to formulate his conception of unconscious phantasies, and in a draft paper sent to Fliess with a letter dated 31st May 1897 he posits the notion of hostile impulses (death wishes) directed against parents. From a letter of 14 August we learn of his intention to undertake a systematic self-analysis, the first fruits of which he announces on 3rd October. He relates that the self-analysis "has continued in dreams and has presented me with the most valuable elucidations and clues". Among other items he reports that "between the ages of two and two-and-a-half" his "libido towards *matrem*" was aroused on the occasion of a journey with her from Leipzig to Vienna, during which we must have spent the night together and there must have been an opportunity of seeing her *nudam*". [Masson 1985: 268] The reliability of this account is indicated by the twofold use of the words "must have"; in his commentary on the self-analysis Schur describes this as a "reconstruction" [Schur 1972: 120]. As Clark notes, it is not clear from Freud's letters which events he records are recollections, which are dreams, and which are interpretations of dreams. Following Schur, he refers to "the discrepancies between establishable facts and Freud's reconstructions of them", and concludes that the evidence for his recollections "was hardly more reliable than that which had supported the seduction theory". [Clark 1989: 166–67]

The first direct allusion to the Oedipus theory occurs in a letter dated 15 October 1897: "A single idea of general value has dawned on me. I have found, in my own case too, [the phenomenon of] being in love with my mother and jealous of my father, and I now consider it a universal event of early childhood." He goes on to suggest that the unconscious impulses relating to this phenomenon account for "the gripping power of *Oedipus Rex*", everyone in the audience having been "once a budding Oedipus in phantasy".[6] [Masson 1985: 272]

---

[6]The synopsis of Sophocles's play is as follows: The baby boy, Oedipus, is left to die because an oracle has predicted that he is destined to murder his father, the King of Thebes. The baby is rescued and grows to adulthood, only to fulfil the prophecy when he inadvertently returns to his original homeland and kills his father without being aware of his identity. He subsequently marries his mother, and when in due course he discovers the truth of his unwitting crimes, he blinds himself and forsakes his home.

It seems likely that in the course of his attempts to incorporate the unconscious phantasy theory in his rapidly evolving ideas on the origins of neuroses at that period he had concluded that parents must play a major role in the story. His recollection of his childhood attachment to his mother, which was exceptionally close, reinforced this belief and led to one of his "absolute and exclusive formulations". However, the recognition of a young child's attachment to his mother and occasional jealousy of his father hardly constitutes an original observation. It is not necessarily the case that excavation of repressed material was required for him to recall his early relationships with his parents, and there is certainly nothing to demonstrate that any *sexual* impulses are involved. This is pure surmise and arises out of his predilection for finding exclusively sexual explanations in his investigations of the neuroses.

Pertinent to this issue is the fact that during 1897 Freud was losing faith in the seduction theory, yet could not plausibly abandon it while still affirming the authenticity of the infantile seductions he had reported so emphatically the previous year. He may have come to perceive that a theory of unconscious phantasies involving parents would enable him to maintain his clinical claims (with appropriate retrospective modifications), and at the same time legitimise both his continued adherence to the analytic technique and his withdrawal from a theory he no longer felt he could sustain.[7]

Of direct clinical evidence adduced in support of the Oedipus theory there is little to be found in Freud's writings, other than the largely spurious seduction stories of his early patients interpreted as phantasies of parental seduction.[8] Much of the corroborative material comes from dream interpretations, but this has no evidential value since he invariably finds what his theories predict to be present in the unconscious. In *An Autobiographical Study* he claims of his "surprising discoveries" concerning infantile sexual impulses that "from about 1908 onwards it became possible to confirm them fully and in every detail by direct observations upon children". [S.E. 20: 39] This is specifically a reference to the analysis

---

[7]That the Oedipus theory may have derived from considerations such as the above, in combination with ideas arising in the course of his self-analysis, is suggested by the fact that it originally pertained only to the incestuous phantasies of young males, yet his clinical practice dealt predominantly with female patients.

[8]In fact Freud only employed the seduction theory episode to support his Oedipus theory in regard to women, enlisting supposed phantasies of paternal seduction for this purpose. Neither at the time, nor retrospectively, did he claim equivalent reports of maternal seduction from his early male patients.

of the five-year-old boy, "Little Hans", whose case history was published in 1909. As we have seen, as evidential value this again leaves much to be desired. The analysis was not even undertaken by Freud, but by an enthusiastic and uncritical follower (the boy's father), with some direction from the former. The notes which the father passed on to Freud show that at times he blatantly led the boy to say what he (the father) wanted and virtually put words into his mouth. In Freud's analysis the supposed confirmations of the sexual theories, as customary in the case histories, only appear as such as a result of tendentious interpretation. But purely on the grounds of Freud's acknowledgement that "Hans had to be told many things that he could not say himself", and "had to be presented with thoughts which he had so far shown no signs of possessing" [S.E. 10: 104], it is clear that the case history (the only child analysis published by Freud) does not provide the confirmatory evidence claimed for it.

Female Sexuality

The above discussion refers essentially to Freud's theories of infantile sexuality in relation to males. He turned his attention to female sexuality only late in his career, and for a period gave considerable thought to the matter. It is instructive to trace the development of his ideas through the three essays he devoted to the subject for what they reveal about his method of psychoanalytic research.

In the first of these, entitled "Some Psychical Consequences of the Anatomical Distinction Between the Sexes" (1925), he starts with a brief discussion of the early sexual life of boys, stating that in their case the situation of the Oedipus complex is the first stage which can be recognised "with certainty", and that he has shown elsewhere how its destruction is brought about by fear of castration. However, the prehistory of the Oedipus complex is far from clear, other than that there is invariably a masturbatory activity, the suppression of which sets the castration complex in action. One complicating factor is that "even in boys the Oedipus complex has a double orientation, active and passive, in accordance with their bisexual constitution; a boy also wants to take his *mother's* place as the love object of his *father*." [S.E. 19: 249–250]

In little girls, however, the Oedipus complex raises one problem more than in boys. Although in his writings before 1925 he had always asserted that the first attachment of female infants is to their father, he now tells us that in the case of girls as well as boys "the

mother is the original object". The question he now has to grapple
with is how it happens that at the Oedipal stage "girls abandon [the
mother] and instead take their father as an object". [251]

As usual he is at pains to make clear that what follows is not
simply speculation on his part, but is grounded in clinical observations. He refers to women patients "who cling with especial intensity and tenacity to the attachment to their father and to the wish
in which it culminates of having a child by him", and adds that
there is good reason to suppose that the same wishful phantasy was
also the motive force of their infantile masturbation. A thorough
analysis of these cases brings to light that "the Oedipus complex has
a long prehistory and is in some respects a secondary formation".
He now contrasts the experiences of the two sexes, reporting that
"when a little boy first catches sight of a girl's genital region, he
begins by showing irresolution and lack of interest" but after some
threat of castration has obtained a hold upon him a recollection or
repetition of the observation "arouses a terrible storm of emotion in
him". This "leads to two reactions . . . horror of the mutilated
creature or triumphant contempt for her". A little girl, however,
behaves differently at the sight of the male genitals. "She makes her
judgement and her decision in a flash. She has seen it and knows
that she is without it and wants to have it." But such single-
mindedness of purpose in young females "may put great difficulties
in the way of their regular development towards femininity, if it
cannot be got over soon enough. The hope of some day obtaining a
penis in spite of everything and so of becoming like a man may
persist to an incredibly late age and may become a motive for
strange and otherwise unaccountable actions." Alternatively, "a girl
may refuse to accept the fact of being castrated, may harden herself
in the conviction that she *does* possess a penis, and may subsequently be compelled to behave as though she were a man." The
psychical consequences of envy for the penis are various and far-
reaching: "After a woman has become aware of the wound to her
narcissism, she develops, like a scar, a sense of inferiority." [251–53]

The next section shows that Freud is feeling his way towards an
explanation for the change of sexual object which marks the onset
of the Oedipal phase. It appears that it often happens that soon
after the girl has discovered that her genitals are unsatisfactory she
begins to show jealousy of another child on the ground that her
mother is fonder of it than of her, which serves as a reason for her
giving up her attachment to her mother. Freud acknowledges that
"the situation as a whole is not very clear, but it can be seen that in
the end the girl's mother, who sent her into the world so insufficiently equipped, is almost always held responsible for her lack of

a penis". [254] After a digression on the subject of masturbation, Freud brings us to the Oedipus complex. It seems that "now the girl's libido slips into a new position along the line—there is no other way of putting it—of the equation 'penis-child'. She gives up her wish for a penis and puts in place of it a wish for a child; and *with that purpose in view* she takes her father as a love-object." [256]

Freud has now completed this preliminary excursion into what he elsewhere calls the "dark continent" of female sexuality. [S.E. 20: 212] All that remains to be done is to "cast an eye over our findings", which "in their essentials . . . are self-evident". [S.E. 19: 256–57] The difference between the sexual development of males and females "is an intelligible consequence of the anatomical distinction between their genitals and of the psychical situation involved in it; it corresponds to the difference between a castration that has been carried out and one that has merely been threatened." Among his more tentative conclusions is "the notion (though I hesitate to give it expression) that for women the level of what is ethically normal is different from what it is in men". Character traits which his analysis is now able to explain include the fact that "they show less sense of justice than men" and are "less ready to submit to the great exigencies of life", but though he says "we must not allow ourselves to be deflected from such conclusions by the denials of the feminists", he does concede that "the majority of men are also far behind the masculine ideal". [257–58]

When he takes up the subject again in "Female Sexuality" (1931), Freud repeats that his observations have been made on women who have a strong attachment to their father.[9] Writing of their early "erotic life", he reports that he was struck by the "intense and passionate" nature of the original attachment of the infant girl to her mother, and by the fact that "the duration of this attachment had also been greatly underestimated", lasting in several cases "well into the fourth year—in one case into the fifth year". He adds: "Our

---

[9]He adds about such women "nor need they be in any way neurotic", and follows this remark by saying that it is upon such women that he has made the observations he is about to report. [S.E. 21: 225] His words here reflect a quandary he never managed to resolve convincingly. On the one hand, he wanted to present his developmental conceptions as universally applicable; on the other hand, the subjects on which his investigations were ostensibly based were neurotics who had come to him for treatment. In the above instance, if it were indeed true that his observations were made largely on non-neurotic father-fixated women, then this would seem to imply that they were pupils undergoing training analyses, a remarkably narrow group on which to base such wide-ranging conclusions.

insight into this early, pre-Oedipus, phase in girls comes to us as a surprise." [S.E. 21: 225–26]

Following a brief review of the intrinsic differences between male and female infantile sexuality, in the course of which he affirms his view that bisexuality is a feature of the innate disposition of all human beings, Freud raises an issue he had not made explicit in the earlier preliminary paper. Having at that time proposed that in normal young males the fear of castration leads to the complete dissolution of the Oedipus complex and utilised this notion to explain the process of socialisation, he requires a corresponding developmental conception to account for the equivalent process in women. This problem implicitly informs much of what follows, though, as we have seen above, he considers that insofar as the ideas he advances are not fully adequate for the task, this is consonant with the actuality of the social limitations of womankind.

He begins his investigation by disclosing the three possible lines of development that the infant girl may follow after "she acknowledges the fact of her castration, and with it, too, the superiority of the male and her own inferiority". "The first leads to a general revulsion from sexuality. . . . The second line leads her to cling with defiant self-assertiveness to her threatened masculinity [*sic*]. To an incredibly late age she clings to the hope of getting a penis some time. That hope becomes her life's aim. . . . Only if her development follows the third, very circuitous, path does she reach the normal female attitude, in which she takes her father as her object and so finds her way to the feminine form of the Oedipus complex." [229–230] There follows a brief digression mostly concerned with the possible consequences of these different outcomes, at the end of which Freud writes: "This account of how girls respond to the impression of castration and the prohibition against masturbation will very probably strike the reader as confused and contradictory. This is not entirely the author's fault." The reason is, he explains, that "it is hardly possible to give a description which has general validity", for "we find the most different reactions in different individuals, and in the same individual the contrary attitudes exist side by side". [233]

Since he wrote his first paper on female sexuality, he has had time to think up a few more reasons (in his own words, "which analysis brings to light") why the infant girl turns away from her mother to her father: "that she failed to provide the little girl with the only proper genital, that she did not feed her sufficiently, that she compelled her to share her mother's love with others, that she never fulfilled all the girl's expectations of love, and finally, that she first aroused her sexual activity and then forbade it." Somewhat surprisingly, after this long list of grievances he adds: "all these motives seem nevertheless insufficient to justify the girl's final hostility." [234] (The "final hostility" he is referring to here is in the Oedipal phase at age four or five when, according to the account in *Introductory Lectures*, a little girl has "a need to get rid of her mother as superfluous" [S.E. 16: 333].) In the end he can only suggest that perhaps "the attachment to the mother is bound to perish, precisely because it was the first and was so intense; just as one can often see happen in the first marriages of young women which they have entered into when they were most passionately in love." [234]

There follows a brief discussion of ambivalence, with the conclusion "that the little girl's intense attachment to her mother is strongly ambivalent, and that it is in consequence precisely of this ambivalence that (with the assistance of the other factors we have adduced) her attachment is forced away from her mother". Since in the course of this discussion he has declared that in the first phases of erotic life ambivalence is the rule, he realises he is now faced with a difficulty, for he has to explain how it is "that boys are able to keep intact their attachment to their mother, which is certainly no less strong than that of girls." His answer is that boys are able to deal with their ambivalent feelings towards their mother by directing all their hostility onto their father, though he adds that "it is probably more prudent in general to admit that we have as yet no clear understanding of these processes". [235] In his *New Introductory Lectures on Psychoanalysis*, completed in the following year, he provides a more considered solution to the problem, and we shall see how he deals with it when we turn to that book shortly.

In the course of considering the nature of the sexual aims of the little girl during the time of exclusive attachment to her mother, Freud informs us of "the very surprising sexual activity of little girls in relation to their mother" which "is manifested chronologically in oral, sadistic, and finally even in phallic trends towards her". However, he explains that it is difficult to give a detailed account of these because "sometimes we come across them as transferences onto the later, father-object, where they do not belong and where they seriously interfere with our understanding of the situation. We find the little girl's aggressive, oral and sadistic wishes in a form forced on them by early repression, as a fear of being killed by her mother—a fear which, in turn, justifies her death wish against her mother. . . ." [237]

Freud now quotes with approval an interpretation by another analyst, Ruth Mack Brunswick. He notes that some of his women patients (apparently *all* those who had shown a strong attachment to their mother) told him that, during the pre-Oedipal phase, when their mother gave them enemas or rectal douches they used to offer the greatest resistance and react with fear and screams of rage. Though such a reaction from children between the ages of about one and three might not be thought of as requiring any complex explanation, Brunswick, it seems, "was inclined to compare the outbreak of anger after an enema to the orgasm following genital excitation". This interpretation, Freud writes, led to his gaining an understanding of the little girls' behaviour in terms of the excitation of sadistic-anal responses. [237–38]

He now reports that one of the consequences of the pre-Oedipal attachment to the mother is that "girls regularly accuse their mother of seducing them", though it seems odd that prior to this paper he had never mentioned such a common occurrence. The accusations supposedly derive from phantasies occasioned by the genital sensations experienced when being cleaned.[10] He goes on to add that the fact that the mother thus initiates the child into the phallic phase is probably the reason why, in phantasies of later years, the father so regularly appears as the sexual seducer. At first sight this seems to be an extraordinary non sequitur, but there follows a typical psychoanalytic sleight of hand by way of explanation: "When the girl turns away from her mother, she also makes over to her father her introduction into sexual life." [238]

Among further details relating to the sexual activities of the pre-Oedipal period we are told, in reference to the arrival of a baby brother or sister, that "the little girl wants to believe that she has given her mother the new baby, just as the boy wants to". Freud admits that "no doubt this sounds quite absurd"; but "this is only because it sounds so unfamiliar". [239]

It seems that Freud is not claiming that he is reporting only his own clinical experiences, for he notes that "an examination of the analytic literature on the subject shows that everything that has been said by me here is already to be found in it". [240] So apparently there is some independent confirmation of his findings in this difficult field of research. But this impression being created by Freud is undermined from an unexpected quarter, for at this point the editor directs our attention to the fact that the "recent works by other writers discussed in what follows appeared *after*

---

[10]The contention that Freud's analytic technique can be utilised to provide virtually any findings he wishes gains credence from his words in the corresponding context in his later *New Introductory Lectures*: "And *now* we find the phantasy of seduction once more in the pre-Oedipus pre-history of girls; but the seducer is regularly the mother." [S.E. 22: 120; emphasis added.] In this instance the supposed phantasies are adduced to underwrite his new theoretical departure that the first attachment of an infant girl is to her mother.

Freud's earlier paper on the anatomical distinction between the sexes (1925)". [240n][11] In reference to these other authors' papers in the editor's note introducing Freud's paper, James Strachey somewhat naively comments that "it is a curious thing that he seems to treat them as though they had arisen spontaneously, and not, as is clearly the case, as a reaction to his own somewhat revolutionary paper of 1925—to which, indeed, he here makes no reference whatsoever". [223] It would appear, contrary to Freud's intimation, that his fellow analysts were taking their cue from their leader.

It remains only to turn to Freud's final words on this subject in *New Introductory Lectures on Psychoanalysis*, which he completed in 1932. He presents the relevant chapter as "an example of a detailed piece of analytic work" and commends it specifically on the grounds that "it brings forward nothing but observed facts, almost without any speculative additions". [S.E. 22: 113]

As befits what is essentially a paper written in the form of a lecture, it is presented in a more popular style than the previous papers, and no doubt because it is to receive much wider circulation, it is more obviously designed to carry an audience with it. In essence it repeats the ideas we have already met, with some embellishment. For instance, the pre-Oedipal wish of the infant girl "to get the mother with child and the corresponding wish to bear her a child" is now "established beyond doubt by analytic observation". Freud tells the reader that "the attractiveness of these investigations lies in the surprising detailed findings which they bring us. Thus, for instance, we discover the fear of being murdered or poisoned . . . in relation to the mother". It is in this section that he reminds us of the seduction theory "episode", and goes on to report that "now we find the phantasy of seduction once more in the pre-Oedipus prehistory of girls; but the seducer is regularly the mother". Such a phantasy "touches the ground of reality", however, for the mother's activities over the child's bodily hygiene may have roused pleasurable sensations in her genitals. [120]

When we come to the crucial question of what brings the "powerful attraction of the girl to her mother to an end", we are informed that "the attachment to the mother ends in hate". [121][12]

---

[11]Actually, one of them [Abraham 1921] *was* published before the publication of the new theory, but of this paper Freud says "one would be glad if it had included the factor of the girl's original exclusive attachment to her mother". [241]

[12]He adds: "A hate of that kind may become very striking and last all through life." There then follows another of the psychoanalytic sleights of hand which enable Freud to cover any eventuality: "it may be carefully overcompensated later on." In other words, should one observe a close affection of a daughter for her mother, one should not be deceived. It may merely be a manifestation of overcompensated hate.

The motives for this turning away, of which in the previous paper we were only told "analysis brings to light", have now become "a long list of accusations and grievances against the mother". [122] He goes on to repeat these in greater detail (with one notable exception), until again coming up against the same objection as before: "All these factors . . . are, after all, also in operation in the relation of a *boy* to his mother and are yet unable to alienate him from the maternal object. Unless we can find something that is specific for girls and is not present or not in the same way present in boys, we shall not have explained the termination of the attachment of girls to their mother." He continues "I believe we have found this specific factor. . . ." [124] Although in the previous paper he had said of all the reproaches listed that they "seem nevertheless insufficient to justify the girl's final hostility" [S.E. 21: 234], he now takes one of these "insufficient" motives and proclaims it to be the specific factor he is looking for: "It was, however, a surprise to learn from analyses that girls hold their mother responsible for their lack of a penis and do not forgive her for their being put at a disadvantage." [S.E. 22: 124] (Why this should be a surprise to Freud compared with his other remarkable findings is not clear. In the previous paper it was not this reproach, but the *second* one, that her mother did not give her enough milk, which he had found "rather a surprising one". [S.E. 21: 234])

Having settled on the female version of the castration complex as the solution to his problem, he now develops all its ramifications, starting with the moment when little girls see the genitals of the other sex (when they will "often declare that they want to 'have something like it too'") and fall a victim to "envy for the penis". How far-reaching the effects of this experience may be on a woman's future life can be gathered from the fact that what a "mature woman . . . may reasonably expect from analysis—a capacity, for instance, to carry on an intellectual profession—may often be recognised as a sublimated modification of this repressed wish [to get the longed-for penis]". [125] (It is little wonder that of such cases Freud is later to write: "At no other point in one's analytic work does one suffer more from an oppressive feeling that all one's repeated efforts have been in vain, and from a suspicion that one has been 'preaching to the winds', than when one is trying to persuade a woman to abandon her wish for a penis on the ground of it being unrealisable." Appropriately enough, this comment appears in a paper entitled "Analyses Terminable and Interminable". [S.E. 23: 252])

Freud assures us that "one cannot very well doubt the importance of envy for the penis" [125], and as in his previous paper

presents the three possible lines of female development, which we
have already touched on. Eventually he comes to the process by
which the young girl takes her father as a sexual object: "The wish
with which the girl turns to her father is no doubt originally the
wish for the penis which her mother has refused her and which she
now expects from her father." However, it turns out that "the
feminine situation is only established . . . if the wish for a penis is
replaced by one for a baby. . . ." This provides the basis for future
satisfaction: "Her happiness is great if later on this wish for a baby
finds fulfilment in reality, and quite especially so if the baby is a
little boy who brings the longed-for penis with him." [128] He might
have added: doubly so in that case, for by then she already has her
husband's penis. (In an earlier paper he had written that ultimately
the infantile wish for a penis in non-neurotic women "changes into
the wish for a man, and thus puts up with the man as an appendage
to the penis". [S.E. 17: 129])

It hardly seems necessary to make any direct comment on these
imaginative flights of fancy which constitute Freud's ideas on the
development of female sexuality, but there are some general points
to be made. The first is to again draw attention to the fact that in
the book, which Freud knew was destined for wide circulation, he
makes the astonishing claim that he is bringing forward "nothing
but observed facts, almost without any speculative additions". It is
just possible that his brilliant style of presentation in *New Introductory
Lectures* might induce some people to take this assertion at its
face value, but for the more sceptical reader who has examined the
two previous papers, which contain essentially the same material, it
is a claim scarcely to be taken seriously.

The second point concerns the relationship between his clinical
experience and his theoretical writings. We have seen that from the
very beginning of his analytic career, with the infantile seduction
theory, there was a somewhat tenuous relationship between the
actual material he was dealing with and his theoretical account of it.
With the advent of the theory of unconscious phantasies this
relationship became ever more tenuous, as we saw in the Dora case
history, in which all of Dora's supposed phantasies were actually
constructions of Freud's. In his writings he strives to give the
impression that everything is based on clinical observations, but the
factual material he presents, for instance in the case histories, often
bears little relationship to the theories: it is the highly imaginative
interpretations which do that. This is nowhere more apparent than
in the papers on female sexuality, perhaps most blatantly when he
suddenly informs us of "the very common phantasy which makes
the mother or nurse into a seducer", [S.E. 21: 232] following his

belated abandonment of the view that the first attachment of infant girls is to their father. A short time later the story becomes that girls regularly *accuse* their mother of seducing them. [238] Reading through these papers one frequently gains the impression that such "findings" emanated from Freud's imagination in the course of speculative cogitation rather than as a response to his patients' productions. No doubt he later presented them to his current patients as constructions and sought to persuade them that they experienced the latter as phantasies at an unconscious level. How they reacted to them one can only speculate, but it is little wonder that the process of trying to persuade patients to accept insights such as these takes many years of struggle before resistances can be overcome.

Male Sexual Development

We cannot take leave of Freud's ideas on infantile sexuality without noting the final phase of his views on the sexual processes occurring in young boys, arrived at after "whole decades of unremitting observation" [S.E. 19: 141]. In early infancy there is a pre-Oedipal stage of affectionate identification with the father. In this period the infant invariably engages in masturbatory activity, one of the consequences of which may be habitual bedwetting, whose suppression may be experienced as having the meaning of a threat of castration. Another element in the picture, one which "analysis shows us in a shadowy way", is that the overhearing of parental copulation may set up in the infant boy his first sexual excitation, which may act as a starting point for his whole sexual development. [S.E. 19: 250–51] However, as such observations are unlikely to be of universal occurrence, the question of "primal phantasies" arises, that is, infantile unconscious phantasies whose origins possible lie partly in what "were once real occurrences in the primeval times of the human family" [S.E. 16: 371]. Whatever the nature of the specific stimulus, under the influence of his burgeoning sexual desires the little boy "tries to seduce [his mother] by showing her the male organ", and she comes to understand that "his sexual excitation relates to herself". [S.E. 23: 189] Her response is to threaten him with castration, but "strange to say" the threats in themselves are insufficient for the purpose of restraining his advances. It is not until the boy has a view of the genital region of a little girl that the threat of castration takes its deferred effect, and he comes under the influence of the castration complex, having experienced "the severest trauma of his life".[13] [S.E. 23: 189]

The Oedipus complex had offered the child two possibilities of satisfaction, in accordance with his "bisexual constitution": "He could put himself in his father's place . . . and have intercourse with his mother as his father did, or he might want to take the place of his mother and be loved by his father, in which case his mother would become superfluous." [S.E. 19: 176] But his acceptance of the possibility of castration leads him to recognise that both entail the loss of his penis, the former "as a resulting punishment", the latter "as a precondition". Out of this situation "a conflict is bound to arise between his narcissistic interest in that part of his body and the libidinal cathexis of his parental objects." [S.E. 19: 176] The first of these normally triumphs: the child's ego turns away from the Oedipus complex, which is either repressed, or, ideally, abolished. In the latter case the complex "is literally smashed to pieces by the shock of threatened castration. Its libidinal cathexes are abandoned, desexualised and in part sublimated; its objects are incorporated into the ego, where they form the nucleus of the super-ego. . . . in ideal cases the Oedipus complex exists no longer, even in the unconscious; the super-ego has become its heir." [S.E. 19: 257] With the suppression of the Oedipus complex around the age of five comes the onset of the "latency period", after which there follows a lull in sexual activities. The complete organisation of the sexual function is only achieved at puberty.

This account essentially constitutes Freud's ideas on the sexual development of young male children. Notwithstanding the sup-

---

[13]These latter notions have their origins in Freud's analysis of Little Hans many years before, and first appeared in this generalised form in his paper "The Dissolution of the Oedipus Complex" in 1924, shortly after he had revised the case history in preparation for the complete edition of his works, published that same year. On the basis of an imaginary incident described by the boy involving his own and his mother's sexual organs and reported by the father (who throughout the "treatment" had blatantly prompted him to talk about such sexual matters), Freud inferred a "masturbatory phantasy" in relation to the boy's mother and concluded that the "treat of castration" made by his mother some fifteen months before "was now having a deferred effect on him". [S.E. 10: 32, 120] It is remarkable that inferences made on such a flimsy foundation (and clearly deriving from preconceived ideas) should become the prototypic model for his generalised expositions, remaining essentially unchanged for thirty years. (He does allow for a slight modification in a 1923 footnote to the Little Hans case history, where he writes that, given his finding of "the invariable presence of the castration complex" in analysed adults, he was driven to assume that in the absence of an overt threat children "construct this danger for themselves out of the slightest hints. . . ." [S.E. 10: 8n] This ties in with his conjecture elsewhere "that a phylogenetic memory trace [from the prehistory of the primal family] may contribute to the extraordinarily terrifying effect of the [castration] threat". [S.E. 23: 190n])

posed clinical evidence deriving from the Little Hans analysis, it is difficult to regard it as other than largely a figment of an extraordinarily colourful imagination. Not for the first time Freud erected a speculative (and more than a little far-fetched) theory on the flimsiest of foundations and became utterly convinced of its validity. In his view its central core represented a profound insight of universal significance. In his final summing-up in *An Outline of Psychoanalysis* he affirmed that "if psychoanalysis could boast of no other achievement than the discovery of the repressed Oedipus complex, that alone would give it a claim to be included among the precious new acquisitions of mankind". [S.E. 23: 192–93]

CHAPTER NINE

Popular Expositions

It is not difficult to recognise that Freud's "findings" in the papers on female sexuality are little more than highly imaginative speculations which bear only a tenuous relation to clinical observations, whatever his assertions to the contrary. Though true of most of his writings, this fact is usually less obvious and is sometimes only revealed by a detailed investigation of his claims. A feature of his more popular expositions is the brilliance of the presentation which camouflages both the doubtful nature of many of the supposed clinical observations and the flaws in the theoretical arguments. To illustrate this we shall select some passages from these works and subject them to the kind of close scrutiny that we have found to be absolutely essential when reading anything by Freud. The first of these will be from *The Question of Lay Analysis* (1926), described by James Strachey as the very best of the author's shorter general expositions of psychoanalysis.

The work is subtitled "Conversations with an Impartial Person" and is cast in the form of a dialogue between Freud and an imaginary intelligent layperson. After an account of some of the basic concepts of psychoanalysis, the author describes his therapeutic aim as being to seek out the repressions which have been set up and to urge the ego to correct them with the aid of the analyst. This leads into the very early years of childhood, to the situations of conflict from that time which have been forgotten. The path to these early conflicts is indicated by the patient's symptoms, dreams, and free associations, which, however, have to be interpreted, or translated, by the analyst because they have assumed forms that are "strange to our comprehension". If the repressed material can be reproduced in his memory, "his compliance will be brilliantly rewarded". [S.E. 20: 205]

There follows some entertaining repartee with the imaginary Impartial Person as Freud introduces his ideas on the sexual life of young children. He informs him that there is much that is unexpected about the manifestations of a child's early period of sexuality. For instance, it is surprising to hear how often little boys are afraid of being eaten up by their father (and also to realise that this relates to their sexual life). Equally surprising is that male children suffer from a fear of being robbed of their sexual organ by their father, and that this fear of castration has a powerful influence on their future development. [211]

Freud now gives a brief summary of the Oedipus theory and its ramifications, after which we are told that as a rule the child's sexual wishes "culminate in the intention to bear, or in some indefinable way, to procreate a baby. Boys, too, in their ignorance, do not exclude themselves from the wish to bear a baby." [213]

At this point Freud more directly addresses his impartial listener, voicing rhetorical surprise that he has remained silent in the face of being informed that "a child's first choice of an object . . . is an incestuous one". His listener, not unreasonably, responds by asking Freud what certainty he can offer for such findings, to which the latter replies: "It is based on direct observations. . . . We had begun by inferring the content of sexual childhood from the analysis of adults. . . . Afterwards, we undertook analyses on children themselves, and it was no small triumph when we were thus able to confirm in them everything we had been able to divine. . . ." [213–14]

One feels that a better informed impartial person might well have interrupted Freud's exposition here to say "Not quite everything!", for his assertion a short time before that the first object of a girl's love is her father [212] had been repudiated by Freud himself the previous year in his paper "On the Anatomical Distinction Between the Sexes". [S.E. 19: 251] However, in the absence of this challenge, he is able to reiterate that "we have become quite generally convinced from the direct analytic examination of children that we were right in our interpretation of what adults told us about their childhood". In addition, in some cases there was "irrefutable evidence" to confirm some of the events from childhood which had been reconstructed from the material of the analyses. [S.E. 20: 216]

It is of interest to consider the contents of the above passages in light of what we have already discovered about the author. There is no doubt that the presentation is brilliant and persuasive. Perhaps most persuasive of all is the way that he not only presents the ideas as confirmed facts, but also indicates the means by which they have been verified. However, we have learned not to take anything Freud says on trust, least of all when he is at his most emphatic. We shall therefore take one of his assertions about which we are in a position to obtain further information and examine it in some detail.

Among the "phenomena of sexual life" adduced in his account Freud reports that "often little boys are afraid of being eaten up by their father". [S.E. 20: 211] Since he alludes to this elsewhere in his writing [S.E. 21: 237], it is of interest to see on what evidence he bases his assertion. The information is contained in the paper *Inhibitions, Symptoms and Anxiety*, also published in 1926. In the course of a discussion involving three cases concerned with infantile animal phobias, Freud relates the latter to the idea of the child being devoured by its father. He tells us that "analytic observation" supplies the information which enables him to understand how this idea, which occurs in mythology, can become the subject of a phobia. [S.E. 20: 105] Though he does not explicitly direct attention to the notion in the first of the cases referred to, that of Little Hans, it is implicit in his identification of the latter's father with a horse the boy is afraid will bite him.[1] The evidence cited to indicate the role of the horse as father-substitute is that Hans had seen a horse fall down, and had also seen a playmate, with whom he was playing at horses, fall down and hurt himself. Analysis justified the inference that he had had a wishful impulse that his father should fall down and hurt himself as his playmate and the horse had done. [S.E. 20: 101–02] In the case history itself the inferred horse/father identification is supported by associating the horse's blinkers and muzzle with the father's eyeglasses and moustache. [S.E. 10: 42][2] These examples are representative of the calibre of the analytic evidence adduced in support of the identification, which was indispensable for Freud's explanation of the phobia in terms of his preconceived thesis of Oedipal hostility to the father.

Of the other two cases, one was a young American, who did not, in fact, develop an animal phobia. But, Freud informs us, it is precisely because of this omission that his case helps to throw light upon the other two, though how it does this remains obscure in the few sentences devoted to it: "As a child he has been sexually excited by a fantastic children's story which had been read aloud to him about an Arab chief who pursued a 'gingerbread man' so as to eat him up. He identified himself with this edible person, and the Arab chief was easily recognisable as a father-substitute. This phantasy formed the earliest substratum of his auto-erotic phantasies." [S.E. 20: 104–05] The reader is left to take on trust Freud's statements that the boy had been "sexually excited" by the gingerbread man story and that the Arab chief was easily recognisable as a father-substitute.

---

[1]The inference that the boy was afraid his father would bite him is stated explicitly in the case history. [S.E. 10: 50n]

[2]Freud reports that when he asked the boy directly if his horses wore eyeglasses he said no. He also reports asking whether the muzzle meant a moustache, but gives no indication of the reply, merely adding that he then "disclosed" to the boy that he was afraid of his father. [S.E. 10: 42]

The main line of evidence comes from the Wolf Man case, from which, Freud tells us, he was able to learn about the origin of another animal phobia. In this instance the animal was a wolf, and it too had the significance of a father-substitute. He reports that following a dream the patient had had in boyhood he had developed a fear of being devoured by a wolf, adding that it appeared at least highly probable that the father of his patient used, when playing with him, to pretend to be a wolf and jokingly threaten to gobble him up. After a brief reference to mythological parallels, he observes that the idea of being devoured by the father is so strange that it is hard to credit its existence in a child. However, "analytic observation" shows that the idea in fact "gives expression, in a form that has undergone regressive degradation, to a passive, tender impulse to be loved by him in a genital-erotic sense". [S.E. 20: 105] (This impulse was expressed more succinctly in the Wolf Man paper itself as "the wish to be copulated with by his father". [S.E. 17: 46]) Freud assures us that further investigation of the case history leaves no doubt of the correctness of that explanation. There follows a somewhat technical psychoanalytic discussion, which leads eventually to the conclusion that the phobia originated from the fear of castration, the latter having undergone a process of "oral regression" in the course of being repressed. [S.E. 20: 108]

Now, this whole argument ultimately depends on the boy's fear of his father being transformed into a fear of a wolf (the wolf being a father-substitute), precipitated by the father's playful threats to "gobble him up" [S.E. 20: 104]. Let us take each of these factors in turn to assess their validity.

As far as the boy's fear of his father is concerned, there is no substantive evidence it existed. Freud himself initially described the relationship as "a very affectionate one" [S.E. 17: 17], a statement confirmed by the Wolf Man in his memoirs, where he tells us that as a young boy he "dearly loved and admired" his father [Gardiner 1972: 8]. The repeated assertion in the case history that in infancy the patient harboured an unconscious fear of his father is pure surmise, postulated as a necessary concomitant of the theory of the castration complex. The paucity of direct evidence for the alleged fear is such that Freud had to appeal to "man's prehistory", asserting that "heredity triumphed over accidental experience" to induce fear of the "terrifying figure that threatened him with castration". [S.E. 17: 86] There are also doubts, as we have already noted, as to whether the boy suffered from a wolf phobia. The only relevant reference in the Wolf Man's memoirs is to a single occasion when his sister played a trick on him involving a menacing picture of the wolf in the fairy tale of "Little Red Riding Hood", about which he says: "Probably the cause of the outburst of rage was not so much my fear of the wolf as my disappointment and anger at Anna for teasing me." [Gardiner 1972: 7] Given Freud's propensity to transmute his data for analytic ends it is very possible that he turned this one incident into a recurrent event for his own purposes [S.E. 17: 16, 29–30; 20: 126], and in the 1926 paper it has become a "terror of being devoured" by a wolf [S.E. 20: 106]. As for playful threats by his father to "gobble him up", the notion comes entirely from Freud himself. In the case history he merely says "it is possible that during the patient's earlier years" his father may have made such threats in fun; in other words, it is pure surmise on Freud's part. [S.E. 17: 32] Finally, the identification of the father with a wolf again solely emanated from Freud, on the basis of his interpretation of the wolf-dream as a "primal scene" of parental sexual intercourse. He makes the claim in the case history that the Wolf Man "thought that the posture of the wolf in [the] picture might have reminded him of that of his father during the constructed primal scene" [S.E. 17: 39], but since the scene was a construction, not a memory, these are not words to be taken seriously.

It is clear that not only Freud's claim that often little boys are afraid of being eaten up by their father, but the whole edifice of his theory of childhood animal phobias in which this notion plays a role, rests on data which are largely erroneous, or at best unsubstantiated inferences. This serves to demonstrate that there is every reason to regard his "findings of analytic research" with considerable scepticism, however persuasively they are presented in his general expositions of psychoanalysis.

Another illustration of this occurs in relation to his claim in *The Question of Lay Analysis* that "in the mental life of children today we can still detect the same archaic factors which were once dominant generally in the primeval days of human civilisation". [S.E. 20: 212] This notion is addressed in more detail in the *Introductory Lectures on Pyschoanalysis* in the context of what are described as "primal phantasies" of childhood, in which "the individual reaches beyond his own experience into primeval experience". Freud suggests that "all the things that are told to us today in analysis as phantasy . . . were once real occurrences in the primeval times of the human family", and adds that he has "repeatedly been led to suspect that the psychology of the neuroses has stored up in it more of the antiquities of human development than any other source". [S.E. 16: 371] This is certainly an interesting piece of speculation, but the fact that the "phantasies" in question ("the seduction of children, the inflaming of sexual excitement by observing parental intercourse, the threat of castration") are in reality very largely nothing more than constructions or inferences originating in Freud's own mind effectively reduces the whole passage to the category of nonsense.[3]

Introductory Lectures on Psychoanalysis

With the quotation from *Introductory Lectures* we shall now turn to that work, in which Freud's ideas are presented on a more extensive scale. The book originated in a series of lectures delivered at the University of Vienna from 1915 to 1917, and, as appropriate for such material, the style is popular and entertaining, and also deliberately provocative. In his introduction Freud starts by telling his audience how difficult it is to form a judgement of psychoanalysis, and that the whole trend of their previous education and all their habits of thought are bound to make them into opponents of psychoanalysis. On these grounds he says, "I seriously advise you not to join my audience a second time" [S.E. 15: 15]—but perhaps he did not mean it *too* seriously. The main aim of the introduction seems to be to capture his audience's attention by making his subject sound both daring and outrageous. He warns that if one of them was inclined to enter into a permanent relationship with psychoanalysis, he would find himself in a society which regarded him with distrust and hostility. A little later he informs them that "two of the hypotheses of psychoanalysis are an insult to the entire world and have earned its dislike". [21] After this build-up it comes as something of an anticlimax to learn that the first "insult" is that "psychoanalysis declares that mental processes are in themselves unconscious and that of all mental life it is only certain individual acts and portions that are conscious". He adds that in maintaining that there is unconscious thinking and unapprehended willing psychoanalysis has "frivolously forfeited the sympathy of every friend of sober scientific thought, and laid itself open to the suspicion of being a fantastic esoteric doctrine eager to make mysteries and fish in troubled waters". [22] To read this passage one would never guess that, as Lancelot Whyte writes in *The Unconscious Before Freud*, "the general conception of unconscious processes was . . . topical around 1800, and fashionable around 1870–1880" [Whyte 1960: 169], nor that both Schopenhauer and Nietzsche had

---

[3]This is not to say, of course, that the seduction of children does not occur, but Freud is not referring here to actual occurrences but to supposed unconscious phantasies whose contents are divined by interpreting dreams and somatic symptoms.

long before stressed the unconscious sources of human behaviour [Sulloway 1979, 467]. In fact, the passage could well give the impression that Freud himself had discovered the concept of unconscious processes (a notion described by Sulloway as a myth), whereas the truth is that Breuer was able to write in *Studies on Hysteria* (1895) that "it hardly seems necessary any longer to argue in favour of the existence of current ideas that are unconscious or subconscious. They are among the commonest facts of everyday life." [S.E. 2: 222][4]

Nevertheless, according to Freud the "intellectual prejudice" against this idea, and the "aesthetic and moral" prejudice against the sexual element in psychoanalysis, are "kept in existence by emotional forces and the struggle against them is hard". [S.E. 15: 21] This sexual element, the second piece of audacity on the part of psychoanalysis, consists of the thesis that instinctual sexual impulses play an extremely large role in the causation of nervous diseases, and in cultural and social creations. He goes on to imply that it is the assertion of the general importance of sexuality in human affairs, rather than his specific extreme postulates, which is the source of the resistance to psychoanalytic contentions. However, his perceptions in this regard are more than a little faulty. In his comprehensive review of the literature, Ellenberger observes that "nothing is more remote from the truth than the usual assumption that Freud was the first to introduce novel sexual theories when anything sexual was taboo". [Ellenberger 1970: 545] Krafft-Ebing's book on sexual pathology of 1886 was a great success with the lay public in Vienna, and this was followed by other highly successful books dealing with sexual matters. Indeed, Ellenberger writes, the contemporary psychiatrists Aschaffenburgh, Löwenfeld, and Freidländer explained the success of Freud's sexual theories by the fact that they fell on fertile ground in Vienna. In his discussion of this same issue, Cioffi cites from the literature of the late 1800s examples of notions similar to those being advanced by Freud, and observes that the latter's ideas were very much part of the intellectual climate of the period. He adds pertinently that in reviewing adverse criticism in the psychiatric literature it should be kept in mind that Freud did not *publicly* repudiate his seduction theory for some years after he had abandoned it. [Cioffi 1973: 2–7] Much opposition was in fact predicated on his propensity for *exclusively* sexual explanations; as Moll wrote at the time: "Even

---

[4]James Strachey notes that the views of Freud's immediate teachers were governed by those of J.F. Herbart, in whose psychological system the notion of unconscious mental process played an essential part. [S.E. 14: 162]

the opponents [of psychoanalysis] do not deny that there are sexual processes in childhood. . . . What the critics deny is that much of what Freud interprets as sexual has anything whatsoever to do with sexuality." [Sulloway 1979: 472][5]

However, on the basis of his doubtful contentions, Freud tells his audience that society "disputes the truths of psychoanalysis with logical and factual arguments; but these arise from emotional sources and it maintains these objections as prejudices, against every attempt to counter them". He, however, unlike his opponents, has "no tendentious aim in view" and "merely wished to give expression to a matter of fact. . . ." [S.E. 15: 23–24] Arguments such as these can only be described as sophistry of a high order, and no doubt at this stage he is already well on the way to winning over his innocent audience to the "truths" of psychoanalysis.

Freudian Slips

The next part of the book is devoted to the discussion of what are translated into English as "parapraxes", by which are meant slips of the tongue and other equivalent occurrences. Freud's technique consists of tracking down the supposed unconscious determinant by encouraging the analysee through a series of associations, commencing from the slip, until an appropriate idea emerges. The flaw in Freud's argument is that it is dependent on the presupposition that with the tracing of a series of *associations* he has necessarily found an *explanation* for a phenomenon. But the fact that such a procedure may lead to a specific idea does not show that the latter was the *source* of the slip. Sebastiano Timpanaro has demonstrated this in his book *The Freudian Slip* in which he takes Freud's account of the *aliquis* incident in *The Psychopathology of Everyday Life* and subjects it to a rigorous examination. [Timpanaro (1976) 1985: 29–48] The episode in question is the one where an acquaintance reportedly made an error in quoting a line from Virgil, and Freud infers from a chain of associations that at the root of the misquotation lay the acquaintance's anxiety that he may have made a ladyfriend pregnant. Timpanaro takes every word in the quotation not utilised by Freud (because they had been correctly recalled)

---

[5]In this context Cioffi draws attention to the fact that even while Freud's followers were asserting that much opposition to psychoanalysis stemmed from a revulsion against the emphasis on sexuality, some critics were complaining that mere rationality was powerless against doctrines so alluring!

and demonstrates that if *any one of them* had been the subject of a misquotation it would still be possible by the same technique to plausibly relate it to the disturbing worry in the mind of the acquaintance. As Timpanaro writes, "by passing through so wide a range of transitions, one can reach a single point of arrival from any point of departure whatever". [43] If there is a particular problem pressing on the mind of the analysee, it is scarcely surprising that ideas relating to the matter of concern should arise in the course of the associative procedure. But this does not necessarily mean that the presence in the mind of the problem in question is in any sense a *cause* of the error.[6]

Freud attempts to deal with a similar criticism in regard to his application of the analytic technique to number associations in a footnote added to *Psychopathology* in 1920. He refers to experiments performed by Rudolph Schneider in which the latter observed that numbers arbitrarily presented to subjects led by means of the associative technique to an apparent determinant in precisely the same way as numbers arising spontaneously in the mind of the subject. Schneider concludes that the emergence of supposed determining associations from spontaneously occurring numbers does not in any way prove that these numbers originated from the thoughts arrived at by analysis. In his response Freud argues that Schneider's results tell us nothing more about the origin of numbers (or words) which emerge spontaneously than was known before. The spontaneous ideas may be undetermined, or may have been determined by the thoughts arrived at by analysis, or even by thoughts not disclosed in the analysis. In analytic practice, he tells us, "we proceed on the presupposition that the second [of these possibilities] meets the facts and that in the majority of instances use can be made of it". [S.E. 6: 250–51n] But this response completely fails to get to grips with Schneider's (and Timpanaro's) challenge, and, as the last sentence indicates, essentially begs the question.[7]

---

[6]Macmillan notes that this objection has been made since at least 1912 (F.L. Wells) and has never received an adequate response. The *aliquis* example was criticised in similar terms to the above in 1922 by Tannenbaum. [Macmillan 1991: 554, 555–56] (The above critique of Freud's methodology remains valid regardless of whether the *aliquis* episode actually occurred as he describes it.)

[7]Freud writes that a critical examination of the problem and with it a justification of the psychoanalytic technique of association lie outside the scope of his book, a rather odd declaration in respect to a work whose whole argument is premissed on this technique. In fact, he nowhere adequately confronts this issue, and relies instead on the persuasiveness of his dictum that "applications of analysis are always confirmations of it" [S.E. 22: 146].

Another significant point in Timpanaro's book is taken up by John Forrester in *Language and the Origins of Psychoanalysis*. Timpanaro has demonstrated that many of the slips recorded in *The Psychopathology of Everyday Life* require an unconscious passage from a word in one language to a related word in another, and finds this highly implausible. But Forrester notes that "Freud's argument seems to go one step further and demands a knowledge of *etymologies* of words, both in foreign and native tongues". [Forrester 1980: 91] One can only feel that in such instances Freud is reaching ever higher levels of implausibility. He is also effectively demonstrating once again that what he is presenting as *unconscious* processes in the mind of the person concerned are frequently *conscious* processes in his own mind.

Early in the section on parapraxes in *Introductory Lectures* Freud meticulously prepares the way for the introduction of his technique. After giving a few examples of the type of occurrence he is about to explain, he suggests that we "call in someone who knows nothing of psychoanalysis, and ask him how he explains such occurrences. His first reply will certainly be: 'Oh! that's not worth explaining: they're just small chance events.' What does the fellow mean by this? Is he maintaining that there are occurrences, however small, which drop out of the universal concatenation of events— occurrences which might just as well not happen as happen? If anyone makes a breach of this kind in the determinism of natural events at a single point, it means that he has thrown overboard the whole *Weltanschauung* [world-view] of science. . . . I think our friend will hesitate to draw the logical conclusion from his first reply; he will change his mind and say that after all when he comes to study these things he can find explanations of them." [S.E. 15: 27–28]

In this passage Freud effectively confronts his audience with the stark choice of joining the ranks of the irrational, who reject scientific modes of thought, or accepting his ideas; for when Freud talks of "explanations" he means interpretations of the kind his techniques give rise to. He utilises this stratagem a little later when he deals with his imaginary interlocutor's objection that the explanation provided by the subject, arrived at by the associative method, is not conclusive. By way of analogy he instances the case of someone who has undertaken the chemical analysis of a substance and arrived at the weight of a component part of it, pointing out that inferences drawn from this result would not be criticised by another chemist on the ground that the isolated substance might equally have had some other weight. Yet, he argues, when faced with the psychical fact of a particular thought occurring in the mind of a subject, his interlocutor will not allow this fact's validity, on account of the mistaken illusion that there is such a thing as psychical freedom: something else might have occurred to the subject. [S.E. 15: 48–49] But the analogy is more than a little dubious, presupposing as it does that a thought arrived at by the associative technique is as predetermined (and by implication as repeatable) as a result arrived at by chemical analysis. However, the ground having been prepared by the assertion that reservations in regard to the principle of absolute psychical determinism reflect unscientific modes of thought, the analogy may suffice to persuade his audience that he has adequately rebutted the objection in question.

As Timpanaro points out, one reason why Freud's analyses often seem compelling is that he has an explanation of parapraxes, whereas the person confronted with the technique has none. We saw an example of this earlier when Freud asked his imaginary interlocutor how he explains such occurrences. Not *having* an alternative explanation, he can only reply that it is all a matter of chance, and of course Freud has no difficulty in demolishing such a feeble response. The persuasiveness of his procedure is further enhanced by the implicit utilisation of his precept, enunciated elsewhere, that "applications of analysis are always confirmations of it as well". [S.E. 22: 146] Thus, after having demonstrated his method a number of times he asks rhetorically: "Is this the explanation of *all* cases of slips of the tongue? I am very much inclined to think so, and my reason is that every time one investigates an instance of a slip of the tongue an explanation of this kind is forthcoming." [S.E. 15: 44] Again, a few lines later, in response to the question of whether his view can be extended to other sorts of parapraxis he affirms: "You will be able to convince yourselves of this when we come to examine instances of slips of the pen, bungled actions, and so on." [45] In other words, applications of analysis are synonymous with confirmations.

Almost inevitably when dealing with objections to his technique, Freud brings up the notion of "resistance": "Am I too mistrustful, however, if I suspect that at the very moment at which psychoanalysis makes its appearance before you, resistance to it simultaneously raises its head?" [48] From then on any challenge to his approach is liable to be treated the same way: "You will break off at that, but only to take up your resistance again at another point." [49]

Another favourite device occurs a little later. Freud acknowledges that his imaginary interlocutor has a good point and proceeds to answer it. The reader needs to be concentrating hard not to be deceived by his disarmingly persuasive presentation of his rebuttal.

The issue concerns the disregarding by Freud of a subject's hypothetical emotionally motivated rejection of a proposed analytic
explanation. He addresses his interlocutor as follows:

> Now, however, you think you have me at your mercy. "So that's
> your technique", I hear you say, "When a person who has made a
> slip of the tongue says something about it that suits you, you
> pronounce him to be the final authority on the subject. 'He says
> so himself!' But when what he says doesn't suit your book, then
> all at once you say he's of no importance—there's no need to
> believe him."
>
> That is quite true. But I can put a similar case to you in which
> the same monstrous event occurs. When someone charged with
> an offence confesses his deed to the judge, the judge believes his
> confession; but if he denies it, the judge does not believe him. If it
> were otherwise, there would be no administration of justice, and
> in spite of occasional errors we must allow that the system works.
> [50]

But the analogy is misleading. In the case when Freud proposes
an analytic explanation, the analysee may acknowledge the idea
arrived at by analysis, and with it the notion that it is the source of
the slip, because he has no alternative explanation for the slip.[8]
There is no analogous reason in respect to the confession of a
defendant, so the justification offered here for counting the at-
testation by the subject as corroboration is unsound. Moreover, if
we are to entertain the analogy, there are numerous reasons why an
innocent person might confess to a crime he did not commit. If we
disregard the obfuscatory analogy, it is clear that Freud has by no
means justified his position. It is little wonder that he now moves on
quickly, and momentarily seems to be changing the subject as a
diversion just when it seems the sceptic might be on the verge of
spotting the fallacy in his reply. For his adversary challenges him:
"Are you a judge, then? And is a person who has made a slip of the
tongue brought up before you on a charge? So making a slip of the
tongue is an offence, is it?" [50]

Freud's response is surprisingly weak, given that the sceptic is
his own puppet and that he therefore controls all the strings in this
imaginary confrontation: "Perhaps we need not reject the comparison. But I would ask you to observe what profound differences
of opinion we have reached after a little investigation of what
seemed such innocent problems concerning the parapraxes—dif-

---

[8]Timpanaro points out that when Freud speaks of a subject's admission of the
sense of a parapraxis he conflates the acknowledgement of the inferred idea and
the acceptance that the idea is the source of the slip. [Timpanaro (1976) 1985: 55]

ferences which at the moment we see no possible way of smoothing over". [50]

However, he has not yet finished: "I propose a provisional compromise on the basis of the analogy with the judge and the defendant. I suggest that you shall grant me that there can be no doubt of a parapraxis having a sense if the subject admits it himself. *I* will admit in return that we cannot arrive at a direct proof of the suspected sense if the subject refuses us information, and equally, of course, if he is not at hand to give us information." [50]

Quite what place this kind of bartering has in a serious intellectual debate is not entirely clear. Be that as it may, it is a device which is calculated to win over his audience, for it may well induce any waverers to grant his basic contentions. In all likelihood they will by now be ready to give assent without demur to the superficially plausible notion that analytic explanations are validated when the subject "admits" the sense of a parapraxis, while perhaps not noticing that his concession amounts to little more than the acknowledgement of a self-evident fact, that there cannot be direct confirmation (in the analytic sense) of an analytic inference in this context if there is no information available from the subject. This latter constraint counts for little in practice, for in the very next paragraph he explains how "as a rule" in such circumstances "confirmation" of an analytic interpretation may still be found, namely, "by examining the psychical situation". [50] The plausibility and coherence of the examples which follow are likely to be sufficient to induce conviction that he has made his case for extending the application of analytic explanations to virtually all instances of parapraxes.[9]

Prior to the section in which he resorts to utilising circumstantial evidence, Freud prepares the ground with an impressive passage in which he points out that it is a mistake to suppose that science consists entirely of strictly proven theses; "only a disposition with a passion for authority" would raise such a demand. For the most part scientific assertions are promoted to some particular degree of probability. [51] Though no doubt persuasive to his audience, this plea loses much of its force in the context of a theory resting on questionable and untested presuppositions. It is also pertinent to

---

[9]To take issue with Freud's approach is not to argue that disturbing thoughts are *never* a contributory factor in, for instance, slips of the tongue or lapses of memory, only that analytic-style explanations are appropriate far less frequently than he supposes. Timpanaro's critique comprehensively exposes the weaknesses in Freud's arguments in relation to unintended errors in speech and print while acquainting the reader with alternative explanations of specific cases.

note that the impression of moderation conveyed by the passage is scarcely congruent with the actuality of his customary approach. More representative of the latter is the liberal employment of assertions of "irrefutable evidence" [S.E. 20: 216], "unimpeachable facts" [S.E. 17: 102], and of propositions demonstrated "beyond a shadow of doubt" [S.E. 20: 106], in relation to analytically inferred theses concerning which tentativeness and scientific reticence would be far more appropriate. That these expressions more accurately convey his characteristic attitude is indicated by words he addressed to his colleague Ferenczi in 1913: "We possess the truth. I am as sure of it as fifteen years ago." [Brome 1984: 132]

Freudian Fantasies

Following the section on parapraxes, Freud presents his theory of dream interpretation, and we shall examine this subject in some detail in the next chapter. The third and last section of *Introductory Lectures* is devoted to an exposition of the general psychoanalytic theory of the neuroses. Some of the essential elements constituting this theory will be considered in a discussion of Freud's basic concepts later in this book; for the moment we shall only examine passages which further illustrate the doubtful nature of fundamental psychoanalytic presuppositions.

Freud's first task in this final section of the book is to convince his audience that psychoanalysis has succeeded in explaining the formation of neurotic symptoms. For this purpose he proceeds in a similar fashion as with parapraxes: he shows that "symptoms have a sense". [S.E. 16: 269] He does this by interpreting clinical material and products of the analysis in terms consistent with his theories and then claiming that his surmises represent descriptions of processes occurring in his patients' minds which are transformed into the symptoms in question. One of the cases which he uses to exemplify his procedure is that of a young woman who felt constrained to perform an obsessional ritual arranging of various items in her bedroom every night before she was able to sleep. [264-69] In order to enable her to understand her complaint, Freud writes, he "was obliged to give the girl hints and propose interpretations". [266] Evidently he was successful in this endeavour, for he reports that "one day . . . she suddenly understood the meaning" behind one particular rule when she observed that "the pillow . . . had always been a woman to her and that the upright wooden back [of the bed] a man". [267-68] Freud is able to take this further, for "if the pillow was a woman, then the shaking of the eiderdown till all the feathers were at the bottom and caused a swelling . . . meant making a woman pregnant". By way of multifarious interpretations of like kind he arrives at the conclusion that "the girl was in the grip of an erotic attachment to her father whose beginnings went back to her childhood" [269]: the meaning of the ceremonial was that she was "endeavouring to put herself in her mother's place". [299]

Later in the book Freud refers back to this case as one of two by means of which he has demonstrated that "it is quite generally the case that analysis allows us to arrive at the intention of neurotic symptoms". The analysis of these cases, we are told, "initiated us into these patients' most intimate sexual life". Moreover, "every other case that we submit to analysis would show us the same thing", namely, that the symptoms serve the intention of "the satisfaction of sexual wishes" that have been frustrated. [298–99] It is quite extraordinary that Freud seems to have been unable to perceive the circularity of this argument. By reading sexual connotations into each and every aspect of a case he invariably derives an explanation of symptoms consistent with his sexual theories. Notwithstanding the almost embarrassingly obvious fallacy inherent in such a procedure, he then proceeds to utilise "discoveries" arrived at in this fashion in the further development of his ideas.

In his discussion of the case of the young woman, following the interpretation of an obsessional placing of a particular pillow diamond-wise in line with her head as representing her "playing the man and replacing the male organ by her head" (the pillow representing "the open female genitals"), Freud writes: "Wild thoughts, you will say, to be running through an unmarried girl's head. But you must not forget that I did not make these things but only interpreted them." [268] Only a recognition of the extent of Freud's capacity for self-deception restrains one from describing his words here as disingenuous. Nevertheless, in a later chapter he seems to deliberately utilise obfuscation for persuasive purposes in his presentation of what is essentially the same notion in a different context. The passage in question is the one briefly referred to at the beginning of the last chapter, in which he tells the reader that the unconscious infantile phantasies uncovered by the analysis of symptoms frequently turn out not to be manifestations of actual infantile experiences. [S.E. 16: 376] Early in the discussion he associates this uncertainty in regard to unconscious phantasies with a supposedly analogous observation, that isolated childhood memories sometimes turn out to be false, or a mixture of truth and falsehood. He then notes that "responsibility for this unexpected disappointment lies, not with analysis, but in some way with the patients". [367] In this way he subtly endeavours to gain credence for the notion of unconscious phantasies by implying that, having a characteristic in common with memories, they are essentially similar mental processes, and are just as real. In the following paragraph his discussion of unconscious phantasies draws the unwary reader further into his web of obfuscation: "We are tempted to feel offended at the patient's having taken up our time with invented stories. . . . When he brings up the material which leads from behind his symptoms to the wishful situations modelled on his infantile experiences, we are in doubt to begin with whether we are dealing with reality or phantasies. . . . [H]e is now engaged in bringing to light the phantasies with which he has disguised the history of his childhood. . . . It remains a fact [*sic*] that the patient has created these phantasies for himself. . ." [378]

By the time the naive reader has finished the brilliant exposition in this chapter he may well believe there is a substantive basis for presuming the existence of unconscious phantasies of the kind envisaged by Freud. But any critical scrutiny of the theory presented in the chapter in question, especially if based on knowledge of its application in the case histories, can only reveal that behind the obfuscation the contents of the postulated unconscious phantasies are surmises which derive *entirely* from Freud's own imagination. Yet in such expositions not only does he not confess this frankly and unequivocally, on the contrary, as the above quotations show, he all too often strives to create the false impression that the patients are in some way directly responsible for them. It is hardly surprising that the unsuspecting reader may well end up enmeshed in the web of Freudian sophistry.

The Art of Persuasion

In the remaining pages of this chapter we shall examine further examples of Freud's sophistry, for it is the brilliance of his performance at this art that is one reason why, on a superficial reading, the lectures carry such conviction. The main feature of these passages is that they are based on half-truths or worse, and generally present both the author and psychoanalysis in terms which one finds hard to reconcile with the evidence which we have ascertained in this study. For someone who has seen this evidence it is almost sufficient merely to read the passages in question to recognise the hollowness of their pretensions, so the next example, taken from the beginning of Lecture 16, "Psychoanalysis and Psychiatry", will be summarised with the minimum of comment.

Freud starts by reminding his audience that when he had introduced his ideas to them about parapraxes and dreams he had "set great store on never taking a step without remaining in agreement" with their judgement. He had discussed a great deal with them and "gave way" to their objections, recognising their "'common sense' as a deciding factor". But this will not be possible with regard to the phenomena of neuroses, for they lack familiarity with the subject matter. [S.E. 16: 243]

However, he does not propose to give the audience dogmatic lectures; he wishes to stimulate thought and upset prejudices, not to arouse conviction. If they are lacking in knowledge of the material and so unable to form a judgement, they should neither believe nor reject, but listen and allow what is said to work on them. The only person who has a right to conviction was someone like himself who has "worked for many years at the same material" and has "the same new and surprising experiences". [243–44]

Freud emphasises that the psychoanalytic view is not a speculative system. On the contrary it is empirical—"either the direct expression of observations or the outcome of a process of working them over". He can assert without boasting that "these observations are the result of particularly hard, concentrated and deep-going work", something which his opponents were unwilling to take into account; for they apparently believe that what was at issue were merely "subjectively determined notions to which someone else might oppose others of his own choice". This behaviour of his opponents is not entirely intelligible to him. However, he will in the course of his lectures indulge in very little controversy, especially with individuals, for he has never been convinced by the maxim that "strife is the father of all things". This saying, he believes, is derived from the Greek sophists and is at fault, like them, through overvaluing dialectics. It seems to him, on the contrary, "that what is known as scientific controversy is on the whole quite unproductive, apart from the fact that it is almost always conducted on highly personal lines". Up to a few years previously he has been able to boast that he had only once engaged in a regular scientific dispute—with Löwenfeld—and it had ended in them becoming friends, which they have remained to this day. [244–45]

If his audience concludes that a rejection of all written discussion suggests a high degree of inaccessibility to objections, they should realise that when one has arrived at a conviction after such hard work one has "acquired a certain right to retain that conviction with some tenacity". It also needs to be pointed out that in the course of his work he has modified his views on "a few important points" and replaced them by fresh ones. And "in each case,

of course, [he has] made this publicly known". But the outcome of
this frankness was that some people continue to criticise him for
hypotheses which have long ceased to have the same meaning for
him, while others reproach him precisely for these changes and regard him as untrustworthy on account of them. In the face of these
contradictory objections by critics one can only behave in accordance with one's own judgement. But "in regard to *fundamental*
discoveries" he has "hitherto found nothing to alter". [245–46]

Having learned a great deal about the reality of Freud's professional life and work, one feels almost compelled to admire the
rhetoric of this passage, the product of a consummate performer.
Something of its masterly nature can be seen from the first
paragraph, where he makes it appear that his audience had made a
significant contribution to the ideas put forward in the earlier
lectures, and that he had even abided by its judgements, an
assertion which, if examined, can scarcely be taken seriously. However, the *impression* created is of an open-minded investigator who
is more concerned with ascertaining the truth than with the propagation of his own theories.

The whole passage is full of worthy sentiments which contrast
sharply with what we have discovered about his actual practice.[10]
Consider, for instance, the last paragraph, in which he commends
his own "frankness" about publicly announcing a change of view on
an important point. An editor's footnote points out that the chief
change in Freud's views up to that date had been "his abandoning
the theory of the purely traumatic causation of the neuroses and his
insistence instead on the importance of the innate instinctual forces
and on the great part played by phantasies". [246n] We have
already noted that Freud's first public intimation of his change of
views in this regard came some eight years after he had privately
informed Fliess that he no longer believed in his seduction theory,
and was a good deal less than frank, and that his first retraction
without equivocation came nine years later, behaviour hardly in
accord with his self-presentation.[11]

---

[10]There is, however, one sentence which we can accept as an accurate description of his technique: "You should listen and allow what I tell you to work on
you." [243]

[11]In the preface to the Second Edition of *The Interpretation of Dreams* (1908)
there occurs a particularly audacious statement along similar lines: "Anyone who is
acquainted with my other writings (on the aetiology and mechanism of the psychoneuroses) will know that I have never put forward inconclusive opinions as though
they were established facts. . . ." [S.E. 4: xxv] It was, of course, in regard to precisely the subject mentioned (the aetiology of the neuroses) that he had proclaimed
a "source of the Nile" discovery some twelve years previously, only to repudiate it
(privately) eighteen months later.

To analyse the whole passage at length would only mean repeating much that has already been written in relation to Freud's persuasive presentations earlier in this chapter. One would hope by now that the reader is conversant enough with both Freud's practice and with his literary talents to recognise the questionable nature of much of the content of those paragraphs. It is absolutely characteristic of the author that he should criticise the Greek sophists while in the very act of practising the art with which their name has become associated.

Freud gives another impressive performance throughout the penultimate chapter of *New Introductory Lectures on Psychoanalysis*, published in 1933. In the opening paragraphs of that chapter, entitled "Explanations, Applications and Orientations", he criticises authors, and "conversationalists" at social gatherings, for attacking psychoanalysis while remaining in ignorance of its theory and practice. He continues:

> But you may raise the question of why these people—both the ones who write books and the conversationalists—behave so badly; and you may incline to the view that the responsibility for this lies not only on them but also on psychoanalysis. I think so too. What you come upon as prejudice in literature and society is an after-effect of an earlier judgement—the judgement, namely, that was formed upon the young psychoanalysis by the representatives of official science. I once complained of this in a historical account I wrote, and I shall not do so again—perhaps that once was too often—but it is a fact that there was no violation of logic, and no violation of propriety and good taste, to which the scientific opponents of psychoanalysis did not give way at that time. The situation recalled what was actually put in practice in the Middle Ages when an evil-doer, or even a mere political opponent, was put in the pillory and given over to maltreatment by the mob. You may not realise clearly, perhaps, how far upwards in our society mob characteristics extend, and what misconduct people will be guilty of when they feel themselves part of a crowd and relieved of personal responsibility. At the beginning of that time I was more or less alone and I soon saw that there was no future in polemics but that it was equally senseless to lament and to invoke the help of kindlier spirits, for there were not courts to which such appeals could be made. So I took another road. I made a first application of psychoanalysis by explaining to myself that this behaviour of the crowd was a manifestation of the same resistance which I had to struggle against in individual patients. I refrained from polemics myself and influenced my adherents, when little by little they appeared, in the same direction. This procedure was the right one. The interdict which lay upon psychoanalysis in those days has been

lifted since then. But, just as an abandoned faith survives as a
superstition, just as a theory which has been given up by science
continues to exist as a popular belief, so the original outlawing of
psychoanalysis by scientific circles persists today in the facetious
contempt of the laymen who write books or make conversation.
So this will no longer surprise you. [S.E. 22: 137–38]

Early in this paragraph he says of the "judgement . . . formed
upon the young psychoanalysis by the representatives of science"
that he "once complained of this in a historical account" and will
"not do so again". He then proceeds to do precisely that, depicting
himself as the man of reason and principle, standing alone against
the mob, steadfastly refusing to compromise on his adherence to
the truth. One is almost dazzled by the halo. But the account is a
gross distortion of the facts. Sulloway describes the supposed hostile manner in which Freud's ideas were initially received as "one of
the most well-entrenched legends" of psychoanalytic history, and
documents the "blatant contradictions between the actual historical
facts and the traditional account of Freud's reception". [Sulloway
1979: 448, 452] Freud claims that there were no lengths to which his
scientific opponents would not go to pillory him. It would be nearer
the truth to say that there were few lengths to which he himself
would not go in his misrepresentation of those critics who challenged the validity of the claims of psychoanalysis. In his *History* he
asserts that it had "never occurred to [him] to pour contempt upon
opponents of psychoanalysis merely because they were opponents"
[S.E. 14: 38–39], whereas the truth is that he neglected few opportunities to deride his scientific critics, for instance in his *Autobiographical Study* berating them for "the degree of arrogance they
displayed, for their conscienceless contempt of logic, and for the
coarseness and bad taste of their attacks" [S.E. 20: 49]. In fact,
most critics treated Freud with considerable respect [Kiell 1988],
not untypical being Janet's call at a meeting of the Paris Psychotherapy Society on 16 June 1914 for a just appreciation of the
merits of the work of Freud and his school, whatever their errors
and exaggerations. [Ellenberger 1970: 821] But Freud was never
able to distinguish between criticisms and "attacks", and regarded
anybody who disputed his "findings" as an enemy.[12] So it was even
in the case of friends and colleagues, starting with Breuer and
Fliess, continuing through to Adler and Jung and beyond as each of

---

[12]As early as 1885 he had referred to Albrecht Erlenmeyer, who with some justification criticised Freud's indiscriminate advocacy of cocaine, as one of his "enemies". [Jones 1953: 103]

them in turn took issue with one or another of his extreme theories. Unfortunately, it was his testimony alone which became widely disseminated, to the extent that the grossly distorted picture he presented of the early years of psychoanalysis attained the status of historical fact. Only in recent times have the researches of Freud scholars resulted in the balance being redressed by the publication of more accurate accounts of the events in question. What still remains to be accomplished is a wider recognition of the rather more subtle ways that he misled his readers in his popular works.

Dreams

Dreams play an essential role in psychoanalysis, and Freud's theories in this field have proved to be very influential in spite of the many cogent critiques which have exposed their weaknesses. The reasons for examining them here are twofold: first, to illustrate that these weaknesses are an inherent part of pcsychoanalytic theory in general; second, to provide further demonstrations that it is Freud's interpretations (not, as he claimed, the dreams themselves) which are wish-fulfilments, invariably providing him with corroborations for one or another psychoanalytic theory.

Freud's method rests essentially on the basis of two techniques, free association and symbolic interpretation, together with his fundamental premiss of psychical determinism. He reiterates the latter in the sixth lecture of *Introductory Lectures,* where he discusses "The Premises and Technique of Interpretation": "Once before I ventured to tell you that you nourish a deeply rooted faith in undetermined psychical events and in free will, but that is quite unscientific and must yield to the demand of a determinism whose rule extends over mental life." [S.E. 15: 106] To induce his readers to accept the point of view expressed in the latter part of this sentence, Freud makes the assertion that to do otherwise would be "unscientific". He adopts a more sophisticated approach in the opening chapter of *New Introductory Lectures,* entitled "Revision of the Theory of Dreams". To illustrate the subtle means by which he draws his readers into an implicit acceptance of his basic premiss it is worth quoting the passage in full:

> Let us suppose, then, that someone—a patient in analysis, for instance—tells us one of his dreams. We shall assume that in this way he is making us one of the communications to which he has pledged himself by the fact of having started an analytic treatment. It is, to be sure, a communication made by inappropriate means, for dreams are not in themselves social utterances, not a means of giving information. Nor, indeed, do we understand what the dreamer was trying to say to us, and he himself is equally in the dark. And now we have to make a quick decision. On the one hand, the dream may be, as non-analytic doctors assure us, a sign that the dreamer has slept badly, that not every part of his brain

has come to rest equally, that some areas of it, under the influence of unknown stimuli, endeavoured to go on working but were only able to do so in a very incomplete fashion. If that is the case, we shall be right to concern ourselves no further with the product of a nocturnal disturbance which has no psychical value: for what could we expect to derive from investigating it that would be of use for our purposes? Or on the other hand—but it is plain that we have from the first decided otherwise. We have—quite arbitrarily, it must be admitted—made the assumption, adopted as a postulate, that even this unintelligible dream must be a fully valid psychical act, with sense and worth, which we can use in analysis like any other communication. Only the outcome of our experiment can show whether we are right. If we succeed in turning the dream into an utterance of value of that kind, we shall evidently have a prospect of learning something new and of receiving communications of a sort which would otherwise be inaccessible to us. [S.E. 22: 8–9]

Now in this passage Freud is using a device we have come across before. He presents us with stark alternatives: "On the one hand", we may accept a simple physical explanation of dreams that has nothing to say about the specific contents of a dream, which therefore remain a complete mystery. Or, "on the other hand", in contrast to this obviously unsatisfactory position, we may make "the assumption, adopted as a postulate", that a "dream must be a fully valid psychical act, with sense and worth". Given the choice of these two alternatives, there is little doubt which the reader is likely to prefer. But of course it is possible to hold the view that the contents of a dream are not entirely meaningless without being committed to Freud's more extreme formulation that it is a fully decipherable communication, and further, to believe that there is a great deal about dreaming which we simply do not yet understand. The fault with Freud's method of presentation is not that he is postulating a particular theory which happens to be rather audacious, but that he is attempting to induce acceptance of his ideas by dubious intellectual means. True, he disarmingly admits that his basic postulate is quite arbitrary, but this will count for little when he develops the subject further; for, as he says a little later about his technique of dream interpretation, it will make a "vivid impression on you". [10] So having carried the reader to the point of at least a tentative acceptance of the basic premiss, he now relies on an argument with which we have become familiar to do the rest. If, by means of his interpretive technique, he can succeed in translating dreams into apparently coherent and intelligible communications, he will have justified the basic premiss. In other words, by applying his procedure to a large number of cases he hopes to induce the reader to accept the validity of both his technique and his fundamental postulate. But all he is really doing is demonstrating his belief in the same fallacious argument we have met before, that "applications of analysis are always confirmations of it as well".

In the course of the discussion, Freud distinguishes between "the text of the dream or the *manifest* dream" and "what we are looking for, what we suspect, so to say, of lying behind the dream . . . the *latent* dream thoughts". [10] How he proposes to unveil the latter is explained as follows:

The dreamer is asked to divert his attention from the dream as a whole onto the separate portions of its content and to report everything that occurs to him in relation to each of these portions. These associations may be memories from the day before, or from times long past, reflections, discussions, and so on. The listener will begin to notice that the associations "throw a surprising light on all the different parts of the dream, fill in the gaps between them, and make their strange juxtapositions intelligible. . . . The dream is seen to be an abbreviated selection from the associations . . . made . . . according to rules that we have not yet understood. . . . There can be no doubt that by our technique we have got hold of something for which the dream is a substitute. . . ." It should be understood, however, that the associations are not yet the latent dream-thoughts. "On the one hand, the associations give us far more than we need for formulating the latent dream-thoughts. . . . On the other hand, an association often comes to a stop precisely before the genuine dream-thought. . . ." At this point the physician intervenes to fill in the missing gaps and to make explicit what the associations have only touched upon. The reader may feel that this sounds as though "we allowed our ingenuity and caprice to play with the material", but he has "only to carry out a dream-analysis" himself or "study a good account of one in our literature" to be "convinced of the cogent manner in which interpretive work like this proceeds". [11–12]

Before we examine Freud's procedure, we should note that he again emphasises that conviction will come from following through an actual detailed dream-analysis. In other words, it is the internal consistency and coherence of the interpretation which is effectively to be the final criterion of the validity of the technique, an argument already demonstrated to be seriously flawed. In addition, the method by which the coherence is to be obtained is questionable: "At that point we intervene on our own; we fill in the hints, draw undeniable [*sic*] conclusions, and give explicit utterance to what the patient has only touched on in his associations." [12] The examples we have seen of the conclusions arrived at in the dream analyses in the Wolf Man and Dora case histories hardly engender confidence in the legitimacy of the procedure which Freud is seeking to justify.

The Technique of Interpretation

It will be convenient to deal separately with the two strands which together constitute Freud's technique of dream interpretation. First, then, we shall consider the method of free association. In his *Introductory Lectures* Freud adopts a somewhat extreme position: "If you think it is arbitrary to assume that the first thing that occurs to the dreamer is bound to bring what we are looking for or to lead us to it, if you think what occurs to him might be anything in the world and might have no connection with what we are looking for, and that it is only exhibiting my trust in Providence if I expect something different—then you are making a great mistake. . . ." Referring back to an example of an association to a parapraxis he asserts: "It can be proved that the idea produced by the man was not arbitrary nor indeterminable nor unconnected with what we were looking for." [S.E. 15: 106] However, by the time he wrote *New Introductory Lectures* he had modified his position, in that he no longer assumes that the *first* association is necessarily significant: "At some points the associations are given without hesitation and the first or second idea that occurs to the patient brings an explanation. At other points there is a stoppage and the patient hesitates before bringing out an association, and, if so, we often have to listen to a long chain of ideas before receiving anything that helps us to understand the dream." [S.E. 22: 13]

Joseph Wortis, who undertook an analysis with Freud in 1934, describes his own experience as follows: "So far as analytic procedure is concerned, I did not find that letting the subject find his own associations to a dream was always observed. I would often give a whole series of associations to a dream symbol, for example, and he would wait until he found an association which would fit into his scheme of interpretation and pick it up like a detective at a line-up who waits until he sees his man." [Clark 1980: 121] Now, since we have seen that Freud frequently has preconceived notions about what he expects to find, the results of this procedure in practice are liable to be considerably more doubtful than his theoretical presentation might lead us to believe. But even if it were otherwise, that is, even if the clinical application were more in line with theory, the latter would still be open to a serious objection. This has been expressed by Wittgenstein in the following terms:

I have been going through Freud's *Interpretation of Dreams . . .* and it has made me feel how much this whole way of thinking wants combatting. . . .

The fact is that whenever you are preoccupied with something, with some trouble or with some problem which is a big thing in your life—as sex is, for instance—then no matter what you start from, the association will lead finally and inevitably back to that same theme. Freud remarks on how, after the analysis of it, the dream appears so very logical. And of course it does.

You could start with any of the objects on this table—which certainly are not put there through your dream activity—and you could find that they all could be connected in a pattern like that; and the pattern would be logical in the same way.

One may be able to discover certain things about oneself by this sort of free association, but it does not explain why the dream occurred. [Wittgenstein 1966: 50–51]

This critique is essentially the same as Timpanaro's of Freud's method of analysis of slips of the tongue. Both critics point out that the associative technique may well lead an interpreter from the original material to a problem of major concern for the person involved, but that it says very little about that material, and quite possibly contributes nothing to an understanding of why or how it arose. In other words, this aspect of Freud's theory of dream interpretation rests on the same unsound argument as his explanation of slips of the tongue so cogently criticised by Timpanaro.

It is interesting to note that an objection similar to that put by Wittgenstein is posed by Freud himself in *Introductory Lectures,* as from a sceptical reader: "We quite expect that what occurs to the dreamer in response to the dream-element will turn out to be determined by one of the dreamer's complexes, but what good does that do us? This does not lead us to an understanding of dreams but . . . to a knowledge of these so-called complexes. But what have they got to do with dreams?"[13][S.E. 15: 109]

Freud's answer is not very convincing. He argues that the dream-element which evokes the association "is itself derived from the dreamer's mental life, from sources unknown to him, and may therefore very easily itself be a 'derivative of the complex'. It is therefore not precisely fantastic to suppose that the further associations linked to the dream-elements will be determined by the same complex as that of the element itself and will lead to its discovery." [110] But this simply begs the question. The whole argument de-

---

[13]A criticism along these lines had been made by F. L. Wells a few years previously. [Macmillan 1991: 554]

pends entirely on Freud's *belief* (i.e., assumption) that the dream-element "may . . . very easily" be a derivative of an underlying complex—which is, of course, the very point at issue.

Freud now resorts to a favourite device: he produces two examples of supposedly analogous cases, involving the forgetting of proper names, to support his case. The reader may be so dazzled by the virtuosity displayed in these two instances that he may fail to appreciate that they only function as genuine analogies if one assumes what Freud is attempting to justify. He concludes from his examples that "the associations to the dream-element will be determined both by the dream-element and also by the unconscious genuine thing behind it" [112], seemingly not noticing that this is no more than his challenger is saying; the question at issue is whether the *dream-element* is determined by the underlying complex. Only the brilliance of his presentation obscures the fact that he has failed to provide a convincing argument to support his postulate.

It seems likely that Freud was well aware of the weakness of his *theoretical* case (no doubt he would argue that it works in practice), since he had to resort to such rather feeble expressions as "may therefore very easily . . . be" and "not precisely fantastic to suppose". Nevertheless, in the opening paragraph of the next chapter he characteristically asserts without qualification that "we have achieved . . . a conception of the nature of dream-elements . . . that they are ungenuine things, substitutes for something else that is unknown to the dreamer (like the purpose of a parapraxis). . . ." [113] There is little doubt that Freud's liberal use of such confident assertions tends to convey to the reader the impression that a strong case has been presented, albeit that (as here) a close scrutiny not infrequently reveals major flaws in his argument.

We may conclude, then, that in the hands of a skilled analyst, and used with discrimination, the method of free association may direct attention to problems of concern to a patient, though it is doubtful whether it tells us much about his dreams or their origins. When employed by an interpreter with strong preconceptions about what he expects to find, however, the technique is easily abused and may well produce results of dubious worth. This is exemplified by many of Freud's own interpretations, some of which we shall shortly be examining.

Before doing so it is essential to consider the second major element in Freud's theory of dream interpretation, that of representation by symbols.[14] He introduces the subject in *Introductory Lectures* in the context of those dream-elements in response to which no association occurs to the dreamer, arguing that it is justified "to interpret these 'mute' dream-elements ourselves" since "we are forced to recognise" that whenever we do so "we arrive at a satisfactory sense for the dream". [S.E. 15: 150] Throughout the many pages devoted to this topic it is impossible to find any convincing explanation of how he arrives at specific symbolic interpretations. Although he criticises other approaches for being arbitrary, one looks in vain for any evidence that his own method avoids being open to the same charge. True, he does raise, on our behalf, the question of "how we in fact come to know the meaning of these dream-symbols", the answer being that "we learn it . . . from fairy tales and myths, from buffoonery and jokes, from folklore" and so on [158–59], but since elsewhere he tells us that the meaning of "products of ethnic imagination such as myths and fairy tales" can be understood by applying "the psychoanalytic views derived from dreams" [S.E. 13: 185], this really leaves us none the wiser.[15] At the end of the discourse it is clear that in spite of his attempt to obscure the fact, his symbolic translations *are* essentially arbitrary, except insofar as they must fit in with his sexual theories. The real justification in any specific case is the argument from coherence, and the supposition that "an accumulation of many similar cases eventually gives the necessary certainty to what began as a timid experiment". [S.E. 15: 150]

The Decoding of Dreams

It is now time to examine some examples of dream interpretation, of which there are an astonishingly large number in *The Interpretation of Dreams,* the contents of which increased considerably through its many editions. Generally it will be necessary to paraphrase the accounts, and we shall start by describing an interpretation reported by Freud which he commends specifically for the way it illustrates the technique of symbolic translation.[16]

---

[14]Although symbolic interpretation of dreams is popularly associated with Freud, it has of course, as Freud himself points out, been practised from the earliest times.

[15]The fact that a limited number of sexual symbols are common currency in everyday discourse does not validate the indiscriminate and tendentious utilisation of symbolic translation to be found in Freudian dream analysis. Nor should criticism of Freud's excesses in this regard be taken to imply a denial that dreams may involve some symbolic representation.

[16]Freud reports that the dream and its associations were recorded in English in a paper by Alfred Robitsek in 1912.

The dreamer was a girl who was engaged to be married, and her dream as she described it was: *I arrange the centre of a table with flowers for a birthday.* This immediately translates as "an expression of her bridal wishes: the table with its floral centre-piece symbolised herself and her genitals; she represented her wishes for the future as fulfilled, for her thoughts were already occupied with the birth of a baby; so her marriage lay a long way behind her." Further discussion led directly to numerous associations of the same nature. The flowers were "lilies of the valley, violets or pinks or carnations." The lily is a popular symbol of chastity, and a valley is a frequent female symbol in dreams, so she was expressing "the preciousness of her virginity". The fact that they were "expensive flowers" expressed "her expectation that her husband would know how to appreciate its value". [S.E. 5: 175]

Violets suggested an unconscious link with the French word *viol*, "rape", and as an association the dreamer gave the word "violate", indicating her thoughts on the violence of defloration, and possibly also a masochistic trait in her character. Pinks were also called "carnations" by the dreamer, and she associated them with "colour"; but then she confessed that what had occurred to her had in actuality been "incarnation", which relates to "carnal". Her lack of straight-forwardness showed that it was at this point that resistance was greatest, and corresponded to the fact that this was where the symbolism was most clear and that "the struggle between libido and its repression was at its most intense in relation to this phallic theme". [375]

We are next told that "the birthday for which she was preparing in the dream meant, no doubt, the birth of a baby. She was identifying herself with her *fiancé,* and was representing him as 'arranging' her for a birth—that is, copulating with her. The latent dream thought may have run: 'If I were he I wouldn't wait—I would deflower my *fiancé* without asking her leave—I would use violence." [376]

Further interpretations, such as that velvet and moss were "a clear indication of a reference to pubic hair", culminate in the conclusion that the dream "gave expression to thoughts of which the girl was scarcely aware in her waking life—thoughts concerned with sensual love and its organs". [377]

Given Freud's commendation we may take the above as representative of the analytic technique of symbolic interpretation, especially as it appears in a section with the sub-heading "Some Further Typical Dreams". Comment would seem to be superfluous, and it is left to the reader to decide whether the concluding interpretation, paraphased as "she was being 'arranged for a birthday'—that is, she was being copulated with", more likely reflects what is unconsciously in the mind of the girl or what is consciously in the mind of the interpreter.

It is worth emphasising again that even if the girl did have such thoughts in her mind—though in that case they might well be conscious rather than unconscious—it would still not tell us anything about the dream or its origins. For, as Wittgenstein argued, an arbitrary group of objects on a table might equally well be used, by means of the associative method, to lead back to something which is on the mind of the patient. But that would tell us nothing about how or why the objects arrived on the table, nor of course would it indicate there was any direct relationship between the objects and the girl's thoughts, and certainly not that the latter were *responsible* for the presence of the objects on the table.

The "confession" of the dreamer that in relation to pinks she had actually thought of "incarnation", with its association with "carnal", suggests a further point. Once an analysee realises that the therapist is anticipating sexual connotations, it becomes difficult for him or her *not* to think in such terms when being encouraged to free associate. In other words, the Freudian predilection for sexual associations almost inevitably results in what is effectively a self-fulfilling prophecy.

From a typical dream we now turn to one reported in *New Introductory Lectures,* which Freud describes as "a young girl's remarkable dream":

"She dreamt she came into a great hall and found someone in it sitting on a chair; this was repeated six or eight times or more, but each time it was her father." Freud informs us that, from accessory details in the interpretation, this room stood for the womb. The dream "then becomes equivalent to the phantasy, familiarly found in girls, of having met their father already during their intra-uterine life when he visited the womb while their mother was pregnant". [S.E. 22: 25]

Freud warns us not to be "confused by the fact that something is reversed in the dream—that her father's 'coming-in' is displaced on to herself". [25] Once again the reader should decide for himself which is the more remarkable, the dream itself or its interpretation.

Here is another "typical" example from *The Interpretation of Dreams,* including its preamble:

> I have already shown elsewhere that strikingly innocent dreams may embody crudely erotic wishes, and I could confirm this by many new instances. But it is also true that many dreams which appear to be *indifferent* and which one would not regard as in any respect peculiar lead back on analysis to wishful impulses which

are unmistakably sexual and often of an unexpected sort. Who,
for instance, would have suspected the presence of a sexual wish
in the following dream before it had been interpreted? The
dreamer gave this account of it: *Standing back a little behind two*
stately palaces was a little house with closed doors. My wife led
me along the piece of street up to the little house and pushed the
door open; I then slipped quickly and easily into the inside of a
court which rose in an incline. Anyone, however, who has had a
little experience in translating dreams will at once reflect that
penetrating into narrow spaces and opening closed doors are
among the commonest sexual symbols, and will easily perceive in
this dream a representation of an attempt at *coitus a tergo*
(between the two stately buttocks of the female body). The narrow passage rising in an incline stood, of course, for the vagina.
The assistance attributed by the dreamer to his wife forces us to
conclude that in reality it was only consideration for her that
restrained the dreamer from making attempts of this kind. It
turned out that on the dream-day a girl had come to live in the
dreamer's household who had attracted him and had given him
the impression that she would raise no great objections to an
approach of that kind. The little house between the two palaces
was a reminiscence of the Hradshin [Citadel] in Prague and was a
further reference to the same girl, who came from that place. [S.E.
5: 397]

The account follows immediately after a denial by Freud (inserted in 1919) that his dream interpretations are invariably of a
sexual nature: "The assertion that all dreams require a sexual
interpretation, against which critics rage so incessantly, occurs
nowhere in my *Interpretation of Dreams*. It is not to be found in
any of the numerous editions of this book and is in obvious
contradiction to other views expressed in it." [397]

Now, while there is no doubt that this statement is true, the fact
remains that a cursory examination of his dream interpretations is
sufficient to indicate that the overwhelming majority of his analyses
of other people's dreams have a strong sexual element. Many of the
analyses of his own dreams do not, but of these he tells us: "I am
obliged to add . . . that in scarcely any instance have I brought
forward the *complete* interpretation of one of my own dreams, as it
is known to me." [S.E. 4: 105n] With this proviso it would be fair to
say that the critics are essentially correct. Freud himself asserts that
"the more one is concerned with the solution of dreams, the more
one is driven to recognise that the majority of the dreams of adults
deal with sexual material and give expression to erotic wishes".
[S.E. 5: 396] He also states that "the very great majority of symbols
in dreams are sexual symbols" [S.E. 15: 153]; the list of items to be

interpreted as sexual symbols extends over four pages in *Intro-ductory Lectures* and over a similar number in *The Interpretation of Dreams*. In view of this it seems extraordinary that he should protest so vehemently against the assertions that psychoanalysis always looks for a sexual interpretation. (He complains about this in *Autobiographical Study, Introductory Lectures, New Introductory Lectures,* an encylopaedia article, and on two separate occasions in additions to the dream book. [S.E. 20: 46; 15: 192; 22: 8; 18: 252; 4: 160n; 5:397]) That he does so in the face of the fact that the assertion is substantially true suggests that his critics had touched on a sensitive area, with the implication that his predilection for sexual explanations was obsessional, as Jung has intimated. Should anyone still doubt this, he should consider the following dream and the analysis which follows:

A man dreamt as follows: *He saw two boys struggling—barrel-maker's boys, to judge by the implements lying around. One of the boys threw the other down; the boy on the ground had ear-rings with blue stones. He hurried towards the offender with his stick raised, to chastise him. The latter fled for protection to a woman, who was standing by a wooden fence, as though she was his mother. She was a woman of the working classes and her back was turned to the dreamer. At last she turned round and gave him a terrible look so that he ran off in terror. The red flesh of the lower lids of her eyes could be seen standing out.*

The dream had made copious use of trivial events of the previous day. He had in fact seen two boys in the street, one of whom threw the other down. When he hurried up to stop the fight they had both taken to their heels.—*Barrel-maker's boys.* This was only explained by a subsequent dream in which he used the phrase *'knocking the bottom out of a barrel'.*—From his experience he believed that *ear-rings with blue stones* were mostly worn by prostitutes. A line from a well-known piece of doggerel about *two boys* then occurred to him: 'The other boy was called Marie' (i.e., was a girl).—*The woman standing.* After the scene with the two boys he had gone for a walk along the bank of the Danube and had profited by the loneliness of the spot to micturate against *a wooden fence.* Further on, a respectably dressed elderly lady had smiled at him in a very friendly manner and had wanted to give him her visiting-card. Since the woman in the dream was standing in the same position as he had been in when he was micturating, it must have been a question of a micturating woman. This tallies with her terrible *look* and the *red flesh standing out,* which could only relate to the gaping of the genitals caused by stooping. This, seen in his childhood, reappeared in later memory as *'proud flesh'*—as a wound.

The dream combined two opportunities he had had as a little
boy of seeing little girls' genitals: when they were *thrown down*
and when they were *micturating. And from the other part of the
context it emerged that he had a recollection of being chastised* or
threatened by his father for the sexual curiosity he had evinced on
these occasions. [S.E. 4: 201]

Such detail as Freud gives of the process of interpretation of the
above dream suffices to make clear that whatever associations were
produced by the man, the prurient elements in the interpretation
are entirely the products of Freud's own mind.

Dreams and the Unconscious

Freud makes much of what can be learned from dreams, and tells
us that dream interpretation has "unequalled importance both for
the theory and the practice of analysis". [S.E. 20: 193] In *The
Interpretation of Dreams,* for instance, he writes that "our dreams
convince us" that "it is the fate of all of us . . . to direct our first
sexual impulse towards our mother and our first hatred and our
first murderous wish against our father". [S.E. 4: 262]

Let us examine the kind of evidence on which Freud bases such
statements. In the dream book, in the context of "typical dreams",
he says: "When I insist to one of my patients on the frequency of
Oedipus dreams, in which the dreamer has sexual intercourse with
his own mother, he often replies: 'I have no recollection of having
had any such dream'. Immediately afterwards, however, a memory
will emerge of some other inconspicuous and indifferent dream,
which the patient has dreamt repeatedly. Analysis then shows that
this is in fact a dream with the same content—once more an
Oedipus dream. I can say with certainty that *disguised* dreams of
sexual intercourse with the dreamer's mother are many times more
frequent than straightforward ones." [S.E. 5: 397–98]

Fortunately, in later editions Freud does not leave the subject
there but adds a footnote which furnishes an example of the
evidence on which he bases his claim. As a "typical example of a
disguised Oedipus dream of this kind" he appends the following:

A man dreamt that *he had a secret liaison with a lady whom
someone else wanted to marry. He was worried in case this other
man might discover the liaison and the proposed marriage come
to nothing. He therefore behaved in a very affectionate way to the
man. He embraced him and kissed him.* [S.E. 5: 398–99n]

Freud observes that in his actual life the dreamer had a secret liaison with a married woman, and suspected that her husband may have noticed something. The husband's life was threatened by illness, and the dreamer had the intention of marrying the widow after his death. This situation "placed the dreamer in the con-stellation of the Oedipus dream", for "his wish was capable of killing the man in order to get the woman as his wife". However, the dream expressed the wish in a "hypocritically distorted form". The dreamer made out that someone else wanted to marry her, which corresponded to his own secret intention, and his hostile wishes towards her husband "were concealed behind demonstrations of affection which were derived from his memory of his relations with his own father in childhood". [399n]

With interpretations of this order one can well imagine that Freud does indeed come across Oedipus dreams with remarkable frequency. He does not actually demonstrate that the dream was one "of sexual intercourse with the dreamer's mother", but we must presume he would regard such a comment as naive since he supposes he has revealed the true impulses behind the dream, and as these are Oedipal in nature, the rest follows.

In a passage in *Introductory Lectures* Freud describes some characteristics of the nightmare world of the unconscious hidden from us only by the distorting stratagems of the censorship:

> The ego, freed from all ethical bonds, also finds itself at one with all the demands of sexual desire, even those which have long been condemned by our aesthetic upbringing and those which contra-dict all the requirements of moral restraint. The desire for pleasure—the 'libido', as we call it—chooses its objects without inhibition, and by preference, indeed, the forbidden ones: not only other men's wives, but above all incestuous objects, objects sanctified by the common agreement of mankind, a man's mother and sister, a women's father and brothers. Lusts which we think of as remote from human nature show themselves strong enough to provoke dreams. Hatred, too, rages without restraint. Wishes for revenge and death directed against those who are nearest and dearest in our waking life, against the dreamer's parents, brothers and sisters, husband or wife, and his own children are nothing unusual. These censored wishes appear to rise up out of a positive Hell; after they have been interpreted when we are awake, no censorship of them seems to us too severe. [S.E. 15: 142–43]

Reading a passage like this would in itself, one feels, be sufficient to give many people nightmares. However, it should be kept in mind that all these horrors are inferred by Freud from dreams generally no more sinister than the ones we have already examined in this chapter. It is his extraordinarily versatile interpretive technique, together with aspects of his own personality, which are responsible for his finding in them the unrestrained passions he describes. Such passages tell us far more about the workings of Freud's own mind than about the contents of those of his patients.

Freud attempts to deal with criticisms of this nature in *Introductory Lectures,* when he writes: "One day the objective value of research into dreams seemed to be put in question by an observation that patients under analytic treatment arrange the content of their dreams in accordance with the favourite theories of their physicians—some dreaming predominantly of sexual instinctual impulses, others of the struggle for power and yet others even of rebirth (Stekel)." [S.E. 15: 237] His response to the challenge begins with a sentence of massive irrelevance: "The weight of this observation was, however, diminished by the reflection that human beings had dreams before there was any psychoanalytic treatment which could give those dreams a direction, and that people who are now under treatment used also to dream during the period before the treatment started." [238] The burden of the rest of his case is that whereas the physician may influence the dream material, the unconscious dream-wish is exempt from such influence. But his argument, as so often, begs the question, for it is based on the *assumption* that at the root of the dream material there lie specific unconscious impulses which are immutable.

However, if the criticism was put in the form reported by Freud, it may well have been meant to be taken ironically, for the more pertinent observation is that it is the analytic bias of the interpreter which makes the dream contents *appear* to be in accordance with his favourite theories. In other words, the method of analysis is so versatile that it can come up with virtually any interpretation to match the analyst's preconceptions, and is therefore inherently self-validating.[17] This is a criticism which undermines the whole technique which serves as a basis for Freud's theory of dreams, and one to which he nowhere gives a remotely adequate response.

The nearest he comes to dealing with it is in a passage in *The Interpretation of Dreams,* where he notes the objection that "the whole thing is completely arbitrary", that "we are merely exploiting chance connections in a manner which gives an effect of ingenuity", and that "in this way anyone who cares to take such useless pains

---

[17]Among Freud's interpretive rules, for instance, is one "according to which every element in a dream can . . . stand for its opposite just as easily as for itself". [S.E. 5: 471]

can worry out any interpretation he pleases from any dream". [S.E. 5: 527] He meets this objection by first appealing to the "impression" made by his interpretations and to the "surprising connections" which emerge, in other words, the familiar argument from coherence. [528] The main part of his case, however, is more theoretical. He maintains that it is demonstrably untrue that free association involves a purposeless stream of ideas, and that it can be shown that during that process "purposive ideas take charge and thereafter determine the course of the involuntary ideas". [528] He knows "for a fact" that purposive ideas underlie trains of thought in dreams as they do in hysteria and paranoia. If there appears to be no meaningful connection between successive associations, this is because of "the pressure of the censorship", which either conceals the link or distorts the thoughts so that "neither of them appears in its true shape". [529] But, of course, Freud's concept of the censorship implicitly assumes the absence of arbitrariness in mental life, so in effect his whole argument once again depends on the assumption of the very point at issue.

The Popularity of Freudian Dream Interpretation

The question which we must now address is, in view of its shortcomings, how is it that Freud's theory of dreams has proved to be so influential? The reasons are manifold, mostly relating to the manner of his presentation of his ideas in general, but in the case of his dream theory one particular factor predominates over and above the others. It is most easily identified by a reading of the description of the dream theory in one of the short expositions, of which *Five Lectures on Psychoanalysis* is an excellent example. The truth of the matter is that in Freud's hands it makes for a seductively plausible, even compelling, account, and at the same time the ideas are so attractive and intellectually exciting that it is almost impossible to resist. Where is there anything in any other theory or speculation about dreams to match the concept of the censorship, allowing only innocuous-seeming ideas to surface from the bubbling cauldron of unrestrained passions which lurk in the depths of the psyche? Who can resist a good story, and where is there a better story-teller than Freud? His artistic talents encompass almost all the devices in the story-teller's armoury. One has only to read the first chapter of *Introductory Lectures* to appreciate that one is in the presence of a literary craftsman, a master of the art of gaining and holding the attention of an audience. It requires a determinedly sceptical frame of mind, together with the patience necessary for subjecting the expositions to a close scrutiny, to avoid becoming enmeshed in the web of sophistry that Freud weaves around his ideas. In addition, in the case of his theory of dreams the reader may well feel that at least he has made some kind of sense out of the mysterious phenomenon of dreaming which has intrigued the human race for millenia.

Popular expositions of psychoanalysis such as *The Question of Lay Analysis* are brilliantly persuasive in the coherence of all their constituent parts and even the sceptical reader can scarcely fail to be impressed. One can only counter their effect by wrenching one's mind back to the reality that lies behind the facade, which is that the ideas are almost completely unsubstantiated and are frequently supported by false assertions and fallacious reasoning. As far as the theory of dreams is concerned, for instance, after reading a brief exposition one almost feels that it is a pity to spoil the story by pointing out that there is little empirical evidence to support it, and that it is almost entirely dependent on an interpretive technique which is seriously flawed. We have already quoted statements by Freud which indicate the importance he attached to his theory of dream interpretation. In fact, he regarded it as one of the indispensable foundations of his whole system of ideas. On the first page of *New Introductory Lectures* he writes that it played "the part of a shibboleth, the use of which decided who could become a follower of psychoanalysis. . . ." [S.E. 22: 7] Elsewhere he describes the study of dreams as "the most trustworthy method of investigating deep mental processes" [S.E. 18: 13], and in *Five Lectures* he is even more adamant: "The interpretation of dreams is in fact the royal road to a knowledge of the unconscious; it is the securest foundation of psychoanalysis. . . ." [S.E. 11 :33] Yet, as we have seen, the dream theory rests on the shifting sands of fallacious arguments and unsubstantiated assertions. In the words of Anthony Storr, it "cannot withstand critical scrutiny". [Storr 1989: 114][18]

It remains only to record Freud's own characteristically inflated view of *The Interpretation of Dreams,* as expressed in 1931 in the preface to the third (revised) English edition: "It contains, even according to my present-day judgement, the most valuable of all the discoveries it has been my good fortune to make. Insight such as this falls to one's lot but once in a lifetime." [S.E. 4: xxxii]

---

[18]In his detailed critique of the dream theory Clark Glymour describes Freud's method as "worthless", the objections to it "obvious", and the means by which he sought to induce acceptance of the method "the cheapest of rhetorical tricks". [Glymour 1983: 65]

Theoretical Revisions

The changes, sometimes radical, made by Freud to some of his theses at various times have been cited as testimony to his responsiveness to adverse empirical evidence. [Grünbaum 1984: 117] However, it has been argued earlier in this book that the specifically psychoanalytic theories, such as his notions of the instinctual sexual processes of infancy, for the most part bear only a tenuous relationship to his immediate clinical experience, in which case the latter is hardly likely to have made an appreciable contribution to modifications of what are essentially speculative ideas with minimal empirical support. This point will be amplified by reference to specific instances in the discussion which follows.

In the Dora case history Freud plays down the role of speculation in the development of his theories. He assures his readers that he approached the study of the psychoneuroses without preconceived ideas and proceeded to adjust his views "until they seem adapted for giving an account of the collection of facts which had been observed", and continues: "I take no pride in having avoided speculation; the material for my hypotheses was collected by the most extensive and laborious series of observations." [S.E. 7: 112–13] Now, as an account of his normal procedure, this can hardly be regarded as accurate. This is not a matter of reproaching him for retrospectively imposing an inductivist gloss on his methodology, but of recognising that his customary practice was to justify his conjectural notions by tendentiously interpreting material occurring in the analytic situation in such a way that it conformed to his theoretical preconceptions and then to present interpretations derived in this manner as confirmatory evidence. In Sulloway's words: "Time and time again, Freud saw in his patients what psychoanalytic theory led him to look for and then to interpret the way he did; and when the theory changed, so did the clinical findings." [Sulloway 1979: 498]

A typical example of Freud's methodology is to be found in the Dora case history, where he writes that according to a "rule" which he had "found confirmed over and over again by experience . . . a symptom signifies the representation—the realisation—of a phantasy with a sexual content". [S.E. 7: 46–47] Using this rule he pro-

ceeds to interpret Dora's symptoms in terms of supposed unconscious sexual phantasies which he himself has inferred—thus finding further confirmations for his theory. Again, on the basis of his
theoretical notions, he tells us that he expects to find "a fairly
strong homosexual predisposition" in neurotics, and that he had
"never yet come through a single psychoanalysis of a man or a
woman without having to take into account a very considerable
current of homosexuality". [60] With his versatile analytic technique he has no difficulty in interpreting certain aspects of his patient's behaviour as an indication of unconscious homosexual feelings, thereby extending his generalisation to one more case.

In the paper "My Views on the Part Played by Sexuality in the
Aetiology of the Neuroses" (1906) Freud claims that the fact that he
had modified his ideas on this subject was a "guarantee . . . that the
theory is nothing other than the product of continuous and ever
deeper-growing experience" for "what is born of speculation . . .
may easily spring into existence complete and thereafter remain
unchangeable". [S.E. 7: 271] But this argument is fallacious, since it
is perfectly feasible that a speculative theory might come to be
regarded as unsatisfactory and be modified in the light of further
speculations without there necessarily being any fresh data. This is
exemplified in this very paper when he writes concerning his
previous accounts of reports of infantile seductions that he has
since "learned to explain a number of phantasies of seduction as
attempts at warding off memories of the subject's *own* sexual
activity (infantile masturbation)". [274] Note that the clinical
material remains unchanged—he has simply *learned to explain* it in
different terms. True, he puts forward two ostensible reasons for
the change, but they are clearly no more than rationalisations: In
the earlier period "by chance" a disproportionately large number of
his patients had been seduced in childhood; and "further information now became available" indicating that some people who were
similarly abused had remained normal. [274, 276] The first is hardly
to be taken seriously, since for the most part the "seductions" were
his own inferences which he foisted on the patients. As for the
second, supposedly new and "unexpected", finding, we have already noted that he had acknowledged it and rebutted its significance in the 1896 papers nearly ten years earlier.[1]

---

[1]The widely held view that Freud's renunciation of the seduction theory can be
adequately explained on the basis of his acknowledgement of adverse clinical evidence does not withstand a close scrutiny of the actual circumstances of its abandonment as described in chapter 2. A more likely explanation is alluded to in that
chapter and summarised in chapter 4 in the context of his published reasons.

Changes of Theory

Throughout his career Freud developed, and occasionally revised, his ideas, but the rationale for the modifications was not generally any conflict with direct clinical observation. The revisions for the most part came about either as a result of the failure of his earlier theories to encompass satisfactorily the analytic material (consisting predominantly of conjectural notions), or they were simply a consequence of his ongoing speculative quest. This is illustrated by the following examples.

Freud's original view concerning the process by which anxiety is exhibited is expressed in a footnote added to *Three Essays* in 1920: "One of the most important results of psychoanalytic research is [the] discovery that neurotic anxiety arises out of libido, that it is the product of a transformation of it. . . ." [S.E. 7: 224n] But in *Inhibitions, Symptoms and Anxiety* (1926) he reports that an examination of phobias "fails to bear out" this assertion and "seems, rather, to contradict it directly". [S.E. 20: 109] In fact, he now states categorically that "Anxiety never arises from repressed libido"; instead he tells us that "it is always the ego's attitude of anxiety which is the primary thing and which sets repression going." [109] In other words, as he reiterates in *New Introductory Lectures* (1933), "anxiety makes repression and not, as we used to think, the other way round". [S.E. 22: 89]

How does Freud justify his change of position? The explanation is given in an addendum to the 1926 paper:

> The objection to this [original] view arose from our coming to regard the ego as the sole seat of anxiety. It was one of the results of the attempt at a structural division of the mental apparatus which I made in *The Ego and the Id*. Whereas the old view made it natural to suppose that anxiety arose from the libido belonging to the repressed instinctual impulses, the new one, on the contrary, made the ego the source of the anxiety. Thus it is a question of instinctual (id-) anxiety or ego-anxiety. Since the energy which the id employs is desexualized, the new view also tended to weaken the close connection between anxiety and libido. I hope I have at least succeeded in making the contradiction plain and in giving a clear idea of the point in doubt. [S.E. 20: 161]

Whether or not this *is* completely clear to the reader, one thing at least is apparent. Nowhere in the explanation is there any reference to direct clinical evidence; the change arises as a result of Freud finding a more satisfying way of incorporating anxiety into his theoretical structure in the light of his latest speculations. As he

writes in *New Introductory Lectures:* "With the thesis that the ego
is the sole seat of anxiety . . . we have established a new and stable
position from which a number of things take on a new aspect."
[S.E. 22: 85] It is true that the revision is ostensibly derived from his
analysis of phobias in the 1926 paper, but since this analysis
consists essentially of interpretations made on the basis of the
aforementioned theoretical innovations, this does not materially
change the situation. His central conclusion in the revised theory
that "the anxiety felt in animal phobias is the ego's fear of castration" [S.E. 20: 109] (rather than a consequence of the process of
repression) is, as he explains, derived from his analysis of the Wolf
Man's famous wolf-dream in terms of a primal scene of parental
sexual intercourse. The clinical material, it will be recalled, consists
of a dream in which a little boy wakes up at night to find himself
being stared at by a number of wolves in a tree. Freud's interpretation leads him to conclude that in infancy his patient's "wish to
be loved by his father" was repressed as a result of castration
anxiety, "for he thought that a relation of that sort presupposed a
sacrifice of his genitals". [108] The extent to which this conclusion
was dependent on tendentious interpretation is apparent from
Freud's assertion that it was a "triumph of repression" that the
resultant phobia "should no longer have contained any allusion to
castration". [108]

The assumption made in some quarters that Freud's revisions of
theory provide evidence of his responsiveness to adverse evidence is
not borne out in this instance. The "evidence" here is essentially an
analytic interpretation which bears so tenuous a connection to the
actual clinical material that it is difficult to conceive how the latter
can in any meaningful sense be legitimately described as furnishing
a refutation of the original theory of anxiety. Indeed, the same
clinical material (and even the same analytic interpretation!) was
the basis for the *affirmation* in the case history of the original view
that the boy's anxiety derived from the repression of homosexual
libido. [S.E. 17: 113] The fact that all data are theory laden does
not, of course, mean that all evidential claims merit equal respect.
This instance involves a clear case of the self-fulfilling use of theory
to generate a clinical finding to accord with a preconceived notion.[2]
Moreover, in 1920 Freud was still asserting categorically that
"psychoanalytic research" demonstrated that neurotic anxiety was
the result of the transformation of libido [S.E. 7: 224n], that is,

---

[2]The finding in question is the unconscious memory of the primal scene, the
analysis of which enabled Freud to derive explications consistent with each of two
mutually conflicting theoretical postulates.

several years after meeting with the clinical material which supposedly refuted this viewpoint. As he himself explains, the modification of theory was a consequence of speculative notions in regard to the structure of the mind which he started to develop in the early 1920s, rather than a response to adverse evidence as such. Having postulated in *The Ego and Id* (1923) that the ego is the actual seat of anxiety (rather than that the latter arose from repressed instinctual [id] impulses), he had little choice but to modify his earlier theory.

The second example of a theoretical revision relates to one of the fundamental notions of psychoanalysis. Following a reference to the Oedipus complex in his *History*, Freud writes: "The study of individual people had shown (and always will show) that the sexual complexes in their original sense are alive in them." [S.E. 14: 63] However, in "The Dissolution of the Oedipus Complex" (1924), after describing his latest view of the psychoanalytic process by which "the [male] child's ego turns away from the Oedipus complex", he reveals that "if it is ideally carried out" it results in the complete abolition of the complex. [S.E. 19: 176–77] Now this is a very important conclusion, for as he points out, it delineates the normal from the pathological, so the means by which he arrives at it is of some interest. His explanation of the process is as follows: "The object-cathexes[3] are given up and replaced by identifications. The authority of the father or the parents is introjected into the ego, and there it forms the nucleus of the super-ego, which takes over the severity of the father and perpetuates his prohibition against incest, and so secures the ego from the return of the libidinal object-cathexis. The libidinal trends belonging to the Oedipus complex are in part de-sexualised and sublimated . . . and in part inhibited in their aim and changed into impulses of affection." [176–77] Once again there is no reference to any specific clinical evidence which might have led to the change in his view. It clearly arises out of the new ideas he had recently developed about the structure of the mind in *The Ego and the Id*, and in this instance seems not to have even been necessitated by any theoretical difficulties in regard to his previous position.

The theoretical innovation that the Oedipus complex is completely abolished in normal (i.e., non-neurotic) men provides a good illustration of the fact that Freud's ideas derive essentially from subjective cogitation unfettered by direct clinical observation. In 1921, in his paper on "Group Psychology", having stated that the Oedipus complex succumbs to repression, he writes: "Psychoanaly-

---

[3]Libidinal attachments to the parents.

sis, which illuminates the depths of mental life, has no difficulty in showing that the sexual ties of the earliest years of childhood also persist, though repressed and unconscious. . . . It is quite certain that this [sexual] current is still there . . . and can always be cathected and put into activity again by means of regression." [S.E. 18: 138] Yet within three years this important psychoanalytic discovery is implicitly repudiated and fresh psychoanalytic research reveals that the Oedipus complex is not just repressed but is completely abolished in normal men, so that it "exists no longer, even in the unconscious". [S.E. 19: 257] Why has this significant theoretical change occurred? It is because Freud has alighted on the notion that the destruction of the Oedipus complex results in the formation of the super-ego, which, among other things, functions as the vehicle of conscience, and it now suits his purpose to consider that the instinctual impulses associated with the complex are subsumed into the super-ego.

Freud's change of view raises awkward questions which he made no attempt to deal with. In *Introductory Lectures* he writes that "analysis confirms all that the [Oedipus] legend describes", namely, that the male infant experiences hatred and death wishes directed towards the father and aims to possess his mother as a woman. [S.E. 16: 335] In adulthood, he tells us, these hostile and incestuous wishes have been abandoned as far as conscious life is concerned, but still prove (from the analysis of dreams) to be present at night-time and to be functioning in a certain sense. "Since, however, everyone, and not only neurotics, experiences these perverse, incestuous and murderous dreams, we may conclude that people who are normal today have passed along a path of development that has led through the perversions and object-cathexes of the Oedipus complex, that that is the path of normal development. . . ." [338] The question which remains unanswered is, how can these confident assertions be squared with his later equally confident assertion that deeper analysis shows that in normal (non-neurotic) men the Oedipus complex is not simply repressed, but ceases to exist completely, even in the unconscious? It is difficult not to conclude that with the latter contention Freud has undermined his own earlier analytic research, and in doing so cast doubt on the nature of the evidence for the existence of the infantile sexual processes he postulates and indeed on the analytic technique itself.

Equally revealing is a comment he makes in his paper "On Narcissism", completed in the spring of 1914. In the course of explaining the limitations of Adler's conception of the "masculine protest", he writes that he finds it impossible to place the genesis of neurosis upon the narrow base of the castration complex, and that he knows of cases of neurosis in which it plays no pathogenic part, and even fails to appear at all. [S.E. 14: 92–93] Now, this conflicts with his later view that the initiation of the complex is the greatest trauma of a boy's life, one which subsequently affects the whole of his relations with men and women in general, and in a footnote to the paragraph in question the editor notes that in 1926 this was drawn to Freud's attention. [93n] In his response he says he no longer recollects what he had in mind at the time, and that he could not now name any neurosis in which the complex is not to be met with. But of course he may find, or not find, anything he wishes, and who is to gainsay him, for the processes he describes are unconscious and to be revealed only by those initiated into the psychoanalytic method of divination.

We shall now examine one further example of a major revision of Freud's ideas, namely, the changes in his theory of instincts. This is based on a hydraulic model, as he explains in *Three Essays* with regard to his conception of libido. [S.E. 7: 168, 217] The latter is defined as a form of psychical energy, envisaged in quantitative terms, whose production, increase or diminution, distribution, and displacement affords the means of explaining psychosexual pheno-mena. Originally, as a working hypothesis, two classes of "primal instincts" were clearly distinguished, the ego or self-preservation instincts, and the libidinal or sexual instincts, out of the conflict of which neuroses were thought to arise. [S.E. 14: 124] Then, follow-ing the development of his theory of narcissism, Freud was led to conclude that the ego-instincts were themselves libidinal in nature (*Beyond the Pleasure Principle*, 1920). The distinction between the two sets of instincts was no longer to be regarded as "qualitative" but as "topographical". [S.E. 18: 51–52] In Freud's words: "The opposition between the ego-instincts and the sexual instincts was transformed into one between the ego-instincts and the object-instincts,[4] both of a libidinal nature. But in its place a fresh opposi-tion appeared between the libidinal (ego- and object-) instincts and others, which must be presumed to be present in the ego and which may perhaps actually be observed in the destructive instincts. Our speculations have transformed this opposition into one between the life instincts (Eros) and the death instincts." [61n]

The major innovation was the introduction of a death instinct, exhibited in the form of destructive or aggressive instincts. At the same time the previously conflicting sexual (libidinal) and ego (life preservative) instincts were subsumed into Eros ("the preserver of

---

[4]Libidinal energy attached to objects.

life" or the "life instincts"), and the repressive function of the ego-instincts was taken over by the super-ego. These are immense changes which quite clearly have little to do with direct clinical observation, but arose out of Freud's attempts to encompass fresh speculative material as his theories developed.

What is especially noteworthy about the course taken by Freud's theory of instincts is that the postulated entities and concepts become so plastic that it is difficult to imagine any psychological phenomenon which could not be "explained" in terms of them. We are told that the two classes of instincts may operate against, or combine with, each other, and that "this concurrent and mutually opposing action of the two basic instincts gives rise to the whole variegation of the phenomena of life". [S.E. 23: 149] In other words, they may be "fused, blended, and alloyed with each other" [S.E. 19: 41] in order to explain whatever needs explaining. Clearly, he has arrived at a formula which should prove capable of solving any problem with which he is likely to be faced.[5]

The Insubstantiality of Psychoanalytic Validation

The primary reason why it is possible for Freud to manipulate and modify his conceptual schemes almost at will is that his corroborations consist essentially of tendentious analytic interpretations, derived on the basis of the preconceived postulates, of whatever material arises in the clinical situation. We have seen this most clearly in respect to his theories of infantile sexuality: as he tells us himself, "the earliest experiences of childhood were not obtainable any longer as such, but were replaced in analysis by transferences and dreams". [S.E. 4: 184] These latter productions, of course, have to be translated; hence he is always able to adduce material to support his speculative notions.

---

[5]The above comments in regard to Freud's theory of instincts should not be taken to imply a criticism of his willingness to speculate in what was a largely unexplored field, but as a further illustration of the fact that Freudian concepts tend to be almost infinitely malleable. Just how much this is so can be seen from the fact that at one stage he was prepared "to include the so-called self-preservation instincts of the ego among the death instincts". [S.E. 18: 53] In the words of the eminent psychologist William McDougall: "Freud does not scruple to change his most fundamental propositions, and to pull them about in a way which, if they were the foundations of a logically constructed system, would bring the whole structure tumbling upon this mighty Samson and his devoted followers." [McDougall 1936: 56]

An example of such a notion which has in the past gained wide acceptance is that of the latency period, an idea which Freud acknowledges to have originated with Fliess. [S.E. 7: 178n] Freud postulates that the very early manifestations of infantile sexuality (oral and anal erotism), the evidence for which he supposedly "found from the study of neurotic disorders" [233], blossoms into the phallic phase between the ages of two and five, after which sexual development is interrupted by a period of "latency" lasting until the onset of puberty. In the case of boys the latency period is ushered in by the castration complex, which inhibits the Oedipal sexual desires of the phallic phase. But all this is essentially pure speculation, unsupported by substantive evidence. Significantly, Jung's reading of the situation is rather different: the early "pre-sexual stage", characterised almost exclusively by the functions of nutrition and growth, is followed, from about the third to fifth year, by the prepubertal period. The first signs of interests and activities which may fairly be called sexual, though "still having the infantile characteristics of harmlessness and naïveté", occur with the onset of the prepubertal stage, during which the "germination" of sexuality takes place. [Jung 1961: 117] In fact Jung writes in regard to what he describes as the "peculiar doctrine of the so-called 'period of latency'" that what Freud "calls a disappearance is nothing other than the *real beginning of sexuality*". [164–65][6]

Evidence of the tenuousness of the relation between Freud's theories and the real world is not difficult to find. For instance, the fact that the erroneous notion that the first attachment of an infant girl is to the father persisted for so long in psychoanalytic theory demonstrates to what extent the latter depends on theoretical speculation rather than on observations, for one must presume that the majority of analysts did know the true situation (certainly those with children could hardly fail to be aware of it) but so trapped were they in their theoretical structures that they were apparently unable to recognise that their *genuine* knowledge contradicted the theory.

An occurrence in the history of the psychoanalytic movement which is equally revealing relates to the exposition by Otto Rank of his theory of the birth trauma. The analyst Edward Glover has referred to "the rapidity with which some analysts were able to discover 'birth traumas' in all their patients for some time after Rank first published his book on the *Trauma of Birth,* and before it was officially exploded". [Glover 1931: 399] (By the latter Glover

---

[6]In regard to the infantile stages of psychosexual development posited by Freud and his claim that they relate to adult personality traits, Macmillan writes that in the light of the lack of evidential support these hypotheses "deserve as much (or as little) consideration as any other idle speculation". [Macmillan 1991: 539]

presumably means Freud's eventual discounting of Rank's theory.)
Ernest Jones reports that "for some weeks [Freud] had tried to
apply Rank's theory in his daily work by interpreting the associations wherever possible in terms of birth, but he got no response
from his patients, nor had the interpretations any other effect on
them. Ferenczi, on the other hand, had had wonderful results by
applying the same method and could not do without it in a single
case." [Jones 1957: 71]

It is instructive to contrast Freud's attitude towards a scientific
evaluation of Rank's theory compared to that towards similar
proposals made with regard to his own theories. In his paper
Inhibitions, Symptoms and Anxiety he writes in criticism of Rank:
"No body of evidence has been collected to show that difficult and
protracted birth does in fact coincide with the development of a
neurosis, or even that children so born exhibit the phenomena of
early infantile apprehensiveness more strongly and over a longer
period than other children. . . . It should be one of the advantages of
Rank's aetiological theory that it postulates a factor whose existence can be verified by observation. And so long as no such attempt
at verification has been made it is impossible to assess the theory's
value." [S.E. 20: 152] However, this exemplary stance in favour of a
genuinely scientific method of evaluation is not maintained when
his own theories are at issue. In response to the results of some
experimental research which were communicated to him by the
American psychologist Saul Rosenzweig he wrote: "I have examined your experimental studies for the verification of psychoanalytic propositions with interest. I cannot put much value on
such confirmations because the abundance of reliable observations
on which these propositions rest makes them independent of experimental verification." [Rosenzweig 1986: 36–37] The latter sentence is a remarkable declaration to come from someone working in
a field of scientific enquiry. If, however, we restate it in terms of
what we have seen to be the reality of Freud's methods, that is, if we
replace the phrase "abundance of reliable observations" by "abundance of interpretations", it can be seen to reflect the true situation:
that for the most part his psychoanalytic propositions are indeed
"independent of experimental verification".[7]

---

[7]When, in 1937, under the auspices of the United States National Research
Council, Rosenzweig offered honorary editorships of a prospective journal to be
devoted to research in psychopathology to a number of eminent figures, including
Janet, McDougall, Bleuler, Meyer, and Freud, the latter alone declined, giving as
his reason: "Within the scope of my orientation, I cannot see that there is a need to
create a special journal just for *experimental* research in psychopathology."
[Rosenzweig 1986: 39]

Just how much this is so is apparent from a passage in *Introductory Lectures* in which Freud comments on phantasies of being seduced in childhood supposedly found by analysis. He states that such occurrences may in some instances be real memories; however, "if in the case of girls who produce such an event in the story of their childhood their father figures fairly regularly as the seducer, there can be no doubt either of the imaginary nature of the accusation or of the motive that led to it".[8] He then tells us that whether "they have occurred in reality" or "they are put together from hints and supplemented by phantasy . . . the outcome is the same, and up to the present we have not succeeded in pointing to any difference in the consequences". [S.E. 16: 370] In other words he is saying that the detectable effect on a child is no different whether it has actually been sexually abused by a relative or whether it has only retrospectively imagined that the experience occurred. This remarkable assertion is explicable only if one is prepared to enter the esoteric world of psychoanalysis. Freud expresses the position in the following terms: "Sometimes, then, symptoms represent events which really took place and to which we may attribute an influence on the fixation of the libido, and sometimes they represent phantasies of the patient's which are not of course suited to playing an aetiological role." [367] A little later he affirms: "The phantasies possess *psychical* as contrasted with *material* reality, and we gradually learn to understand that *in the world of the neuroses it is psychical reality which is the decisive kind.*" [368][9]

All this might have some semblance of plausibility were it not for our knowledge of the methods by which Freud infers the existence of the supposed phantasies. In this same section he refers to "occurrences which recur again and again in the youthful history of neurotics", and specifically to "a few of particular importance", namely, "observation of parental intercourse, seduction by an adult and threat of being castrated". Of the first of these he notes that "it is perfectly possible for a child . . . to be a witness of the sexual act

---

[8]The motive he gives on this occasion is that the child spares herself "shame about masturbation by retrospectively phantasying a desired object into these earliest times".

[9]This basic postulate of psychoanalysis is in fact an inevitable consequence of Freud's method of interpreting symptoms and dreams, for he has *no way* of distinguishing whether a conjectured unconscious process represents a phantasy or a memory. By another of his brilliant *tours de force* he converts this serious shortcoming of his technique into a virtue, and utilises it to proclaim a fundamental new principle. Henceforth it will not *matter* that he cannot distinguish phantasies from memories.

between his parents or other grown-up people", but he adds that if "the intercourse is described in the most minute details, which would be difficult to observe, or if, as happens most frequently, it turns out to have been intercourse from behind, *more ferarum* [in the manner of animals], there can be no remaining doubt that the phantasy is based on an observation of intercourse between animals (such as dogs) and its motive was the child's unsatisfied scopophilia during puberty". [368–69] Now, this idea comes from the Wolf Man case history, and the only evidence for the existence of the supposed phantasy in that case is the wolf-dream and related associations. In other words, there is *no* serious evidence for the existence of any such phantasy, which was a product of Freud's own imagination. Similarly for the next example he gives: "The extreme achievement on these lines is a phantasy of observing parental intercourse while one is still an unborn baby in the womb." Fortunately, he provides us with an illustration of how he arrives at his knowledge of this type of phantasy. In *The Interpretation of Dreams,* in a passage dating from 1909, he reports "the dream of a young man who, in his imagination, had taken advantage of an inter-uterine opportunity of watching his parents copulating":

> He was in a deep pit with a window in it like the one in the Semmering Tunnel. At first he saw an empty landscape through the window, but then invented a picture to fit the space, which immediately appeared and filled in the gap. The picture represented a field which was being ploughed up deeply by some implement; and the fresh air, together with the idea of hard work which accompanied the scene, and the blue-black clods of earth, produced a lovely impression. He then went on further and saw a book upon education open in front of him . . . and was surprised that so much attention was devoted in it to the sexual feelings (of children); and this led him to think of me. [S.E. 5: 399–400]

With the reference to himself Freud ends the dream account without further comment. Such then is the kind of material upon which he infers the existence of unconscious phantasies, and it is on the basis of these ideas that he makes the claim that the outcome of events even as traumatic as childhood sexual abuse by adults cannot be distinguished from cases where there were only phantasies of such events. In other words, because his conceptual scheme, in which phantasy and reality are equivalent, leads him to such a conclusion, then for Freud it is so. There is no need for any other investigation to check this conclusion, for as he stated in his response to Rosenzweig, psychoanalytic findings are "independent of experimental verification".[10]

Part of the diffculty in assessing Freud's work is that it is hard to believe that his confident statements can really be based on such flimsy evidence. One feels there *must* be more to it than this. But over and over again a close scrutiny shows that if one delves beneath the extravagant claims and the masterful use of language, the ideas rest not on the foundations of empirical observation, but on little more than the speculations of an extraordinarily imaginative mind. There is no genuine evidence for the existence of unconscious phantasies of the kind posited by Freud, and one is left wondering which is the more remarkable, the brilliant stroke that enabled him to rise virtually unscathed out of the potentially disastrous demise of the infantile seduction theory, or the extent to which he was able to deceive so many people into believing that he had made important discoveries based on his clinical experiences.

That is not to say that there were no critics at the time who clearly recognised the fundamental flaws in Freud's work. In articles published in 1908 the brilliant writer and satirist Karl Kraus pointed out that it is impossible to demonstrate that any psychoanalytic pronouncement is false. [Szasz 1977: 29] In 1912 the eminent neurologist and sexologist Albert Moll wrote: "Freud endeavours to establish his theory by the aid of psychoanalysis. But this involves so many arbitrary interpretations that it is impossible to speak of proof in any strict sense of the term." [Sulloway 1979: 471][11] From Freud's own writings we may also deduce that there were others who voiced the same view, for he writes in his *Autobiographical Study* that "my opponents regarded psychoanalysis as a product of my speculative imagination and were unwilling to believe in the long, patient and unbiased work which had gone into its making", adding that they believed that "analysis had nothing to do with observation or experience". [S.E. 20: 50] So clearly there were some who recognised that the emperor had no clothes (or at least very few) in spite of all his claims to the contrary. Yet somehow with the passage of time these cogent criticisms ceased to

[10]In his discussion in *Introductory Lectures* Freud writes that "it has still to be explained why the same phantasies with the same content are created on every occasion", speculating they may be "a phylogenetic endowment". [S.E. 16: 370] Such is his remarkable capacity for self-deception that he fails to realise that the uniformity of content is a consequence of the versatility of the analytic technique which in his hands invariably produces tendentious interpretations that are consistent with his theoretical postulates.

[11]Moll also made the following perceptive observation: "The impression created in my mind is that the theory of Freud and his followers suffices to account for the case histories, not that the clinical histories suffice to prove the truth of the theory." [Sulloway 1979: 470]

have much influence, and the largely uncorroborated postulates of psychoanalysis became widely accepted. Why this should have happened will be considered in the remaining chapters of this book.

CHAPTER TWELVE

Techniques of Persuasion

The question which must now be addressed is how it came about that a theoretical system that rests largely on false claims and fallacious arguments could gain such widespread influence. Undoubtedly the many misleading assertions and occasional dubious practices to be found in Freud's works have contributed to this, but essentially the answer may be divided into two almost distinct components which together have proved to be formidable combination.[1] Throughout his writings extensive use is made of some general psychological concepts, such as repression, resistance, and other unconscious processes, which have become common currency in psychotherapy. In fact, nowadays this aspect of his work is probably regarded as his most enduring contribution to our understanding of the human mind, and a discussion and evaluation of his use of these concepts will be undertaken in the next chapter. The other part of the answer we have already drawn attention to, and it relates to the form rather than the content of his writings. Freud was not only a brilliant writer, he was also a superb propagandist, and in his works he utilised a number of devices which have less to do with legitimate argument than with the art of persuading people to accept propositions for which there is a paucity of genuine evidence. They occur throughout his writings, but for the most part they are to be found in the general expositions, the works by means of which his theories have become widely disseminated. In this chapter we shall present examples of some of these techniques of persuasion.

Analytic Inferences as "Findings"
A major factor contributing to the persuasive power of Freud's writings is his oft-repeated claim that he is only communicating material based on clinical observations. The constant repetition of

---

[1] Ernest Gellner's book *The Psychoanalytic Movement* [1985] provides a sociological and philosophical account of the reasons for the widespread acceptance of psychoanalytic ideas.

this assertion, and the frequent references to his "findings" and "discoveries", inevitably creates in the mind of the reader a feeling that there must be at least *some* substance to it; but as we have seen, there is generally very little in the way of genuine clinical evidence to substantiate it. Consider, for example, this assertion in *An Auto-biographical Study* concerning his "surprising discoveries as to the sexuality of children . . . made in the first instance through the analysis of adults": "Later (from about 1908 onwards) it became possible to confirm them fully and in every detail by direct observations upon children." [S.E. 20: 39] When we look for the *evidence* on which he bases this claim we find, as usual, that we have nothing other than his own word that his discoveries have been so confirmed. The only information available relates to the date 1908 mentioned by Freud, for that was the year of the analysis of Little Hans, and without doubt this is the intended reference. But a reading of the Little Hans paper reveals that the relevant findings are, almost invariably, nothing more than tendentious interpretations. The claim that this paper contains confirmatory evidence of the kind of infantile sexuality postulated by Freud does not stand up to close scrutiny, yet it comprises virtually all there is in his writings on which we are able to assess his assertions concerning the results of direct observations on children.[2]

Elsewhere he does reveal the true story, as for instance in his paper "Remembering, Repeating and Working-Through" (1914), where on the subject of certain "experiences which occurred in very early childhood" he writes that "one gains a knowledge of them through dreams and one is obliged to believe in them on the most compelling evidence provided by the fabric of the neurosis." [S.E. 12: 419] This is further confirmation that the alleged data of psychoanalysis are obtained by interpretation and not by observation, as he so frequently claims.

The ubiquitous use of expressions such as "findings of analytic research" obscures the fact that what are being presented are generally no more than inferences and interpretations. Similarly, when Freud writes "analytic research shows", or "analysis confirms", he is generally alluding to nothing more substantive than

---

[2]Two further points are worth making in regard to the assertion quoted above from the *Autobiographical Study*. First, in the same year that Freud wrote that his discoveries concerning the sexuality of children had been confirmed "in every detail", he announced that the infant girl's first libidinal attachment was to her mother and not to her father, as he had previously maintained. Second, his scarcely credible claim to have confirmed a complex theory relating to human beings in *every* detail becomes intelligible once one appreciates that his analytic technique can be used to validate virtually any theory he posits.

analytic inferences and speculations. Thus we are told that "psycho-analysis has brought to light" the wishes and developments of early childhood [S.E. 13: 189], and specifically that "analysis leaves us in no doubt" that the child's wishes in relation to its opposite-sex parent are incestuous in nature [S.E. 20: 213]. Such passages serve to create the impression of a well-grounded body of knowledge rather than of the speculative and often doubtful inferences which comprise the bulk of the findings of psychoanalysis.

Rebuttals to Criticism

Freud himself was well aware of the many criticisms and reservations concerning both his technique and his theories, and he occasionally alludes to these in his expositions. In doing so he contrives to create the impression that they have been squarely confronted and adequately countered, when in fact, as we have seen, this is often not the case. Not infrequently his response implicitly assumes the point at issue and has only the *appearance* of being an answer to the objection put forward. In such cases the weakness of his argument may be camouflaged by the use of two favourite devices. One of these is to buttress his position by presenting an analogy, though the only legitimate use of analogies is to *clarify* a point being made, not to provide supposed evidence for its validity. Then the reader is likely to be inundated with repetitions of the procedure he is attempting to justify, the purpose of which is to induce a sense of conviction rather than to persuade by force of argument. Even though he may not have satisfactorily dealt with a specific criticism, his presentation is so brilliant that he generally manages to convey the impression that he has done so, and he proceeds as if the objection has been decisively rebutted. Invariably he gives a convincing display of seriously considering the objections he has, with apparent scrupulousness, presented to his readers before they are inevitably dispatched and he emerges triumphant.

Some examples of this practice have already been described in the two previous chapters, and we shall now examine one or two more. The first, taken from *Introductory Lectures*, occurs when he is endeavouring to counter the criticism that "a number of the solutions to which we find ourselves driven in interpreting dreams seem to be forced, artificial, dragged in by the hair of their head—arbitrary, that is. . . ." [S.E. 15: 232] His response is to argue that it is all a matter of "displacement", by means of which the dream-censorship creates "substitute structures". These are not easily recognised as such, being connected with the genuine thing by "the strangest, most unusual, external associations". [233] But these things are *meant* to be hidden. In a similar way spies and smugglers attempt to evade frontier controls by hiding forbidden things in places where they decidedly do not belong; for instance, between the double soles of their boots. If they are secreted there "it will certainly be possible to call them 'far-fetched', but it is also true that a great deal will have been found". [234]

Freud can scarcely be said to have dealt with the challenge, for by falling back on his description of how the dream-censorship substitutes the manifest dream content in place of the latent dream elements he is evading the point at issue; it is the interpretations conjectured *by the analyst* on the basis of the manifest dream (the "substitute structure") which are being judged to be forced and artificial, and he fails to produce compelling arguments to justify the adducing of these seemingly arbitrary interpretations. His analogy comparing evasion of frontier controls with the censorship is equally question-begging, but serves to divert attention from his failure to confront the real issue. He follows this with several entertaining examples of interpretations, culminating in one "of historic impor-tance" involving a dream of Alexander the Great when he was laying siege to the city of Tyre. Alexander dreamt that he saw a dancing satyr, and this was interpreted by dividing the word *satyros* into *sa Turos* ("thine is Tyre"), signifying that he would triumph over the city. Encouraged by this interpretation, Alexander was led to continue the siege and eventually captured Tyre. Freud concludes by assuring us that "the interpretation, which has a sufficiently artificial appearance, was undoubtedly the right one" [236], seemingly obliv-ious to the more probable explanation that the artificial appearance is due to the fact that Aristander, the dream interpreter, contrived to ensure that his interpretation would be such as to be favourably received by his master. However, his stream of ingenious interpreta-tions may well have succeeded in persuading the reader he has made out a plausible case when in fact he has not genuinely confronted the actual criticism he is purporting to answer.

The next example, demonstrating his use of analogy, comes from the section dealing with death-wishes in *The Interpretation of Dreams*. He has previously asserted that all dreams involving the death of a loved one indicate a death wish directed towards that person if the dreamer experiences grief. This necessitates that he explain the anomaly of "a repressed wish entirely eluding censor-ship and passing into the dream without modification". [S.E. 4: 266] He proposes as part of the explanation the unlikely notion that the wish is so heinous that "the dream-censorship is not armed to meet such a monstrosity". If this suggestion stood alone, its improbability would, one hopes, be apparent in the light of the function of the censorship, but he adds: "just as Solon's penal code contained no punishment for parricide". This serves to provide a cloak of plausibility to his proposal, though of course it is quite irrelevant and inappropriate in this context. However, he also calls to his aid another of his imaginative flights, for the other part of his explanation is that "the repressed and unsuspected wish is particularly often met half way by a residue from the previous day in the form of a *worry* about the safety of the person concerned. This worry can only make its way into the dream by availing itself of the corresponding wish; while the wish can disguise itself behind the worry that has become active during the day." [226–67]

We shall refrain from commenting on these sentences, which purport to be part of the explanation of how the wish evaded the censorship, and note only that this passage constitutes Freud's answer to what he describes as "a riddle perfectly capable of solution". [267] So he has managed, with the aid of a smokescreen in the form of an inappropriate analogy, to create the impression that his improbable explanation is at least plausible, which enables him to claim that he has satisfactorily dealt with the difficulty.

An indication that Freud's custom of presenting objections to his ideas is not quite the scrupulous practice it appears at first sight is the fact that two of the points against the seduction theory which he raised and supposedly rebutted in "The Aetiology of Hysteria" in 1896 [S.E. 3: 207, 209] he later himself used as reasons for his withdrawal from the theory.[3] It would seem that the practice owes at least as much to its effectiveness as a disarming persuasive device as to its intellectual value.[4]

Polarised Presentations

Another device to which we have drawn attention is the presentation of an argument in oversimplified, polarised terms in such a way that the reader may be ensnared into concurring with Freud's

---

[3]These are that it was improbable that perversions against small children were widespread enough to account for the frequency of the occurrence of hysteria, and that there were people who had been sexually abused as children who nevertheless had remained normal in adulthood. [Masson 1985: 264; S.E. 7: 190, 276]

[4]When he presents objections to his theories Freud has nothing to lose and everything to gain. Nothing to lose, because if he does not someone else will (and probably already has); everything to gain, because it enables him to pose as a person open to argument while his brilliant rhetorical skills ensure that his ideas always appear to emerge unscathed, albeit that a close scrutiny of his case frequently reveals serious weaknesses.

view in preference to an unacceptable alternative. Perhaps the best example is one we have already examined from the beginning of the section on parapraxes in *Introductory Lectures*, where pure chance is counterposed to Freud's own version of strict psychical determinism in such a way as to create the impression that to oppose his ideas is effectively to throw overboard the whole scientific world-view. [S.E. 15: 28] Naturally, few would be willing to take such a step, and the unwary reader may find himself acquiescing to a proposition about which he would otherwise have serious reservations were the arguments presented less tendentiously. In similar fashion, the contention that dreams are "psychical acts possessing meaning and purpose" is juxtaposed with the notion that they are "purely somatic phenomena, without meaning or significance". [S.E. 13: 169] We are then assured "there is no half-way house between these two views of dreams", thereby disposing of the possibility of a more complex explanation. He uses the same device to manipulate his audience into accepting the dubious proposition that because organs other than the genitals *may* be used for sexual stimulation it necessarily follows that *all* sensual pleasure derived from them is essentially sexual in nature. [S.E. 16: 323–24] In the course of his argument he juxtaposes this view, in relation to the behaviour of young children, against one he imputes to his audience, that of the sexual purity of children. Since few of the audience, by that time at least, are likely to hold such a naive view, they may easily fall victim to Freud's sophistry. The device is also used in regard to symbolism in dreams, where the impression is created that to challenge his specific use of symbols is effectively to deny the significance of symbols in human affairs generally. [S.E. 15: 152] By such means he contrives to induce his readers to accept ideas and procedures which have by no means been adequately justified. Once such an acceptance has been obtained, as Freud himself writes, "the different theses of psychoanalysis are so intimately connected that conviction can easily be carried over from a single point to a larger part of the whole. It might be said of psychoanalysis that if anyone holds out a little finger to it it quickly grasps his whole hand." [S.E. 15: 193] It would be difficult to conceive of a more pertinent warning of the pitfalls that await the unwary when reading Freud's popular expositions.

Therapeutic Claims

In the course of his expositions Freud frequently makes claims of therapeutic success, and these serve to lend plausibility to his analyses when they might otherwise be dismissed as far-fetched.5. For instance, he sometimes asserts that specific symptoms disappeared when the patient accepted his interpretation of them [S.E. 16: 266, 280], and these claims without doubt add to the persuasive power of his writings, but such evidence as exists suggests that they should be viewed with considerable scepticism. For example, in the Wolf Man case history, regarding the patient's intestinal trouble he writes that "in the course of the work his bowel began, like a hysterically affected organ, to 'join in the conversation', and in a few weeks' time recovered its normal functions" [S.E. 17:76], yet the Wolf Man denied that this was true. But even if Freud's claims are taken at their face value, it does not follow, as he implies, that the correctness of his interpretations is demonstrated by the disappearance of the symptoms. [S.E. 5: 528] Analysts from schools which differ considerably from Freud's in their interpretations also have such therapeutic successes to their credit, and behaviour therapists claim high success rates in relation to symptom removal. Clearly, the explanation for the analytic cures has to be sought in something other than the validity of the specific interpretations, and in all probability owes a great deal to suggestion.

Claims to Scientific Status

Freud was anxious to claim for psychoanalysis the prestige associated with science, and on occasion he specifically compares his methods to those of physics or astronomy. [S.E. 20: 57-58; 14: 77; 23: 158–59] For example, in *An Outline of Psychoanalysis* he writes that "the hypothesis we have adopted of a psychical apparatus extended in space, expediently put together, developed by the exigencies of life, which gives rise to the phenomena of consciousness only at one point and under certain conditions . . . has put us in a position to establish psychology on foundations similar to those of any other science, such, for instance, as physics". He goes on to say in regard to his "technical methods of filling up the gaps in the phenomena of our consciousness" that "we make use of these methods just as a physicist makes use of experiment". [S.E. 23: 196–97] Although there is, of course, little in common between the tendentious interpretations utilised to validate psychoanalytic notions and the experiments devised by physicists to test their theories, such

5In *Introductory Lectures* he claims that "the thesis that symptoms disappear when we have made their unconscious predeterminants conscious" has "been confirmed by all subsequent research". [S.E. 16: 280] No evidence is provided in support of this categorical assertion.

assertions may convey an impression of scientific rigour to those unversed in the realities of his methods.

It is of interest to examine the rest of his argument in this particular passage, where he goes on to acknowledge the criticism made in regard to the "inferences and interpolations" obtained by his "technical methods" that there is often a "lack of agreement among analysts". We are told that "the novelty of the problem is to blame for this—that is to say, a lack of training". But it also appears that there is in addition "a special factor inherent in the subject itself" which makes it in this respect "unlike physics", namely, that "we are not always concerned with things which can only arouse a cool scientific interest". By way of example he puts forward the case of "a woman analyst who has not been sufficiently convinced of the intensity of her own wish for a penis" and who consequently "fails to attach proper importance to that factor in her patients". But he reassures us that "such sources of error, arising from the personal equation, have no great importance in the long run", and goes on to compare the situation with that of the early development of the microscope. [197]

This passage illustrates a number of Freud's devices in a short space: First the claim that the methods of psychoanalysis are on a par with those of physics, the implication being that they have the potential to give results of corresponding reliability. This is followed by the acknowledgement of a criticism that potentially undercuts this contention, to which he responds with an argument which actually evades the issue. Finally, he provides two more analogies, one a reference to the "personal equation" (a technical term used in astronomy) and the other relating to problems associated with the development of the microscope, neither of which is genuinely comparable to the situation under discussion. The whole passage is characteristic of his ability to give a doubtful proposition the appearance of plausibility.

Overstatement

Another feature of Freud's writings to which we have already drawn attention is his tendency to make assertions in excessively emphatic terms, the effect of which is to create an impression in the reader's mind that he is being presented with well-founded statements of fact, even when they are in reality no more than speculative notions. His works abound with references to his "findings" and "discoveries", for which there is "irrefutable evidence", or which have been "confirmed" with "certainty", or to the "last degree of certainty", or "with a certainty beyond all doubt". [S.E. 20: 216; 19: 208; 22: 87; 4: 257] Consider, for example, a section in the paper "The Claims of Psychoanalysis to Scientific Interest" (1913). In it we are told that his theories of dream interpretation have been *"confirmed"*; that psychoanalysis has *"demonstrated"* that all dreams have a meaning; that the psychological process of dream-work has enabled us to *"find* that there is a censorship", and *"forces on us irresistibly* a view of mental life which appears to decide the most controversial problems of psychology"; that psychoanalysis has "put into our hands the *key* to all the riddles of the psychology of the neuroses", and *"shown"* that hysterical attacks "are mimetic representations of scenes . . . with which the patient's imagination is [unconsciously] occupied"; and that "it was nothing less than a *triumph"* when "psychoanalytic research . . . *succeeded in showing"* that all obsessive acts [of an obsessional neurosis] have a meaning. Notwithstanding this list, "the number of psychoanalytic *findings* . . . of importance for general psychology is too great" for Freud to enumerate in the paper. [S.E. 13: 167–175; emphases added.]

An extreme example of this practice occurs in a passage in the Wolf Man paper, in which he makes the claim that "scenes [phantasies] of observing parental intercourse, of being seduced in childhood, and of being threatened with castration are unquestionably an inherited endowment, a phylogenetic heritage. . . ." [S.E. 17: 97] The overstatement here is clear enough, but elsewhere, when the assertion is more plausible, such a confident tone may well influence the reader to accept something too readily when it should at least be subjected to a close scrutiny. Consider, for instance, the following example from the section in *The Interpretation of Dreams* where he is purporting to demonstrate that some dreams indicate the dreamer's desire for the death of a loved relative. We are told that "the death-wish against parents dates back to earliest childhood" and that "this supposition is confirmed with a certainty beyond all doubt in the case of psychoneurotics when they are subjected to analysis." [S.E. 4: 257] This formulation gives the impression that the matter is beyond dispute, but when we turn to the evidence he presents in support of such a categorical assertion we find ourselves back in the familiar realms of interpretation: "We learn [from analysis] that a child's sexual wishes . . . awaken very early, and that a girl's first affection is for her father and a boy's first childish desires are for his mother". Consequently "the father becomes a disturbing rival to the boy and the mother to the girl", and "such feelings can lead to a death-wish". [257] By way of direct evidence an eight-year-old girl is quoted as saying, on an occasion when her mother was called away from the table, "I'm

going to be Mummy now. Do you want some more greens, Karl?
Well help yourself, then!" In the case of a boy, on the hypothetical
assumption that he is "allowed to sleep beside his mother when his
father is away from home", it seems "he may easily begin to form a
wish that his father should *always* be away", and "one obvious way
of attaining this wish would be if his father were dead". But such
observations "do not carry such complete conviction as is forced
upon the physician by psychoanalyses of adult neurotics. In the
latter case dreams of the sort we are considering are introduced into
the analysis in such a context that it is impossible to avoid
interpreting them as *wishful* dreams." [258] In other words there is
in actuality very little in the way of confirmatory evidence, other
than analytic interpretation buttressed by the argument from
coherence, and we must not allow ourselves to be unduly influenced
by the fact that Freud *tells* us that it is impossible not to interpret
the dreams as evidence of death wishes, another example of his
cavalier use of overstatement designed to create a false impression
of certitude where none actually exists.[6]

Occasionally Freud states that he himself has been surprised by
his findings, which serves to maintain the illusion that he has made
genuine discoveries rather than put forward the results of his
speculative theorising. For instance, in *New Introductory Lectures*
he writes that his investigations led to the "surprising" discovery
that infant girls have "a fear of being murdered or poisoned by their
mother" [S.E. 22: 120], and again, it was "a surprise to learn from
analyses that girls hold their mother responsible for their lack of a
penis" [124]. In similar fashion, in *Introductory Lectures* he describes certain symbolic translations as being "contrary to our expectations", although it is clear from examples of their use that they
are essentially his own conjectures. [S.E. 15: 157] Elsewhere he
writes that "psychoanalysis has shown us, to our growing astonishment, the enormously important part played by what is
known as the 'Oedipus complex' . . . in the mental life of human

---

[6]In his later writings, as we have seen, Freud claimed direct confirmation of
Oedipal impulses from the analyses of young children. In his discussion of Little
Hans in *Inhibitions, Symptoms and Anxiety* he writes he has been able "to
establish with certainty" that a hostile wish against the boy's father had been
repressed, but when he adduces "proof of this" it turns out merely that "analysis
justified the inference" of a wishful impulse that his father should be hurt. [S.E. 10:
102] Equally dubious is his tendentious inference from another episode that Hans
wanted his father out of the way, tantamount, we are told, to an intention of
putting one's father out of the way oneself, and thus "tantamount . . . to the
murderous impulse of the Oedipus complex". [102]

beings". [S.E. 19: 208] He is surely unique among researchers in voicing surprise at the results of his own speculative theorising, and in doing so contrives to create the false impression that they are genuine discoveries.

Shifting Ground

Cioffi has pointed out in relation to the seduction theory papers that when Freud wishes to strengthen his case for the reality of the supposed infantile sexual scenes he suggests his patients recalled and recounted them, whereas when he is concerned to forestall the charge of naively accepting hysterical fabrications he emphasises that the patients have no feeling of recollecting the scenes. [Cioffi 1984] This utilisation of shifts of position to suit his current argument occurs elsewhere in his writings, as we have had occasion to note. For instance, when he wishes to convey the impression that his assertions in regard to the sexual lives of infants would be virtually self-evident were it not for psychical resistances, he says that is remarkable that they have hitherto been overlooked. [S.E. 19: 18; 19: 220; 20: 39] At other times, when concerned to emphasis the power of the analytic method, he writes that such discoveries can only be made by those trained in the technique. [S.E. 7: 133; 17: 107] Again, in the Little Hans case history, where the extent to which the boy was presented with analytic ideas could not be concealed, he acknowledges that "a psychoanalysis is not an impartial scientific investigation, but a therapeutic measure"; its essence is "not to prove anything, but merely to alter something". [S.E. 10: 104] Subsequently, concerned to elevate the status of psychoanalysis, he insists that it is a scientific discipline, and retrospectively claims that the findings of the Little Hans analysis were confirmations of his sexual theories. [S.E. 20: 39] And one final example. In a lecture presented in 1904, anxious to impress the physicians to whom the address was given, he asserts that he has been able to elaborate and test his therapeutic method only on very severe (in fact "the severest") cases, and that his material (on the basis of which he had supposedly developed the foundational psychoanalytic theories of male sexuality) "consisted entirely" of such extreme cases. [S.E. 7: 263] However, much later, when presenting his theories of female sexuality, in a context in which he is anxious to assert the universality of his ideas, he is at pains to emphasise the *lack* of severity of his cases. It is, he writes, because the people upon whom his investigations have been carried out were by no means seriously abnormal that he thinks his conclusions regarding the development of females in general deserving of belief. [S.E. 22: 121][7]

Resistances to Psychoanalysis

Freud never tired of repeating the now notorious contention that the opposition to psychoanalysis stemmed from "resistances" which "were not of an intellectual kind but arose from emotional sources". [S.E. 19: 221][8] In *New Introductory Lectures* he says of the scientific opponents of psychoanalysis that their opposition was "a manifestation of the same resistance which I had to struggle against in individual patients". [S.E. 22: 138] Again, in *Five Lectures on Psychoanalysis* we are told that "resistance finds it easy to disguise itself as an intellectual rejection. . . . We often become aware in our opponents, just as we do in our patients, that their power of judgement is very noticeably influenced affectively in the sense of being diminished". [S.E. 11: 39] The implication of these passages is clearly that the opposition to his ideas was not worthy of serious consideration, for as he says in his *History*, "psychoanalytic theory enabled me to understand this attitude in my contemporaries and see it as a necessary consequence of fundamental analytical premisses". [S.E. 14: 23]

He went even further in an article published in a scientific journal in 1913, arguing that the fact that there was opposition to the theses of psychoanalysis was in itself an indication of its validity: "But anyone who respects the rule that scientific judgement should not be influenced by emotional attitudes . . . will regard the resistances to it as actual evidence in favour of the correctness of its assertions." [S.E. 13: 180] It is but a short step to the final stage, as expressed in *An Outline of Psychoanalysis*, of repudiating all necessity for answering criticisms: "The teachings of psychoanalysis are based on an incalculable number of observations and experi-

---

[7]It is, of course, possible that the later, more carefully selected, cases were less severe than the earlier ones (though it should be recalled that Clark has expressed doubts about Freud's claims in regard to the latter). The point at issue here is that if it is necessary for justifying the universality of Freud's theories of female sexuality that the cases analysed be not too severe, can he also claim general validity for his theories of male sexuality if, as he asserts, the cases from the study of which the latter were supposedly developed were of great severity?

[8]This was a particularly successful device when adduced in relation to opposition to his sexual theories, so much so that his contention that such opposition stemmed from irrational sources, rather from reasonable objections to his extreme theories, as was frequently the case, became widely accepted.

ences, and only someone who has repeated those observations on himself and on others is in a position to arrive at a judgement of his own upon it." [S.E. 23: 144] This statement encapsulates the fallacy inherent in Freud's system, for effectively he is asserting the circular argument that only someone who has *accepted* the premises of psychoanalysis (since this is necessary in order to make the required "observations") is able to make a just evaluation of it.

Self-Presentation

Another feature of Freud's writings is his technique of self-presentation. For example, in *The Question of Lay Analysis* he chides his more extreme colleagues for "all the mischief some analysts have done with the interpretation of dreams" [S.E. 20: 193], and generally conveys the impression of a moderate figure (in contrast to his opponents), presenting his method in exemplary terms, even sometimes confessing his own surprise at his findings. Elsewhere he describes how he stood aside from the controversies around psychoanalysis, resolving "not to answer [his] opponents", and using his influence "to restrain others from polemics". [S.E. 14: 39] One almost feels it would be the height of bad taste to doubt his statements describing his obviously well-validated findings of analysis, coming as they do from such a modest and charming gentleman. This aspect of his writings was remarked upon by Wittgenstein in a letter to a friend: "I, too, was greatly impressed when I first read Freud. He's extraordinary—of course he is full of fishy thinking and his charm and the charm of his subject is so great that you may easily be fooled." [Malcolm 1984: 100]

Although at times Freud expressed a modest assessment of his talents, he had no such reservations concerning his achievements. On more than one occasion, by direct implication, he cast himself as equivalent in his field to Copernicus and Darwin. For instance, in the paper "Resistances to Psychoanalysis" (1925) he writes that the psychoanalytic formulation of the unconscious was "the *psychological* blow to men's narcissism", comparable to "the *biological* blow delivered by the theory of descent [of Darwin] and the earlier *cosmological* blow aimed at it by the discovery of Copernicus". [S.E. 19: 221][9] The same comparison is made in *Introductory*

---

[9]In this same paper, after declaring that "men in the mass behaved to psychoanalysis in precisely the same way as individual neurotics under treatment for their disorders", he modestly confesses that "it was no small thing to have the whole human race as one's patient". [S.E. 19: 221]

Lectures, where he credits psychoanalysis with the responsibility for the "third and most wounding blow" to "human megalomania", the previous two having been delivered by Copernicus and Darwin. [S.E. 16: 285] As Freud himself declared in his *History* that he was "the true originator of all that is particularly characteristic in [psychoanalysis]" [S.E. 14: 8], and that it was his creation, the implication that his position is alongside the other two great figures is clear enough. In similar fashion, in *An Outline of Psychoanalysis* he describes his "discovery of the repressed Oedipus complex" as justifying a claim to include psychoanalysis "among the precious new acquisitions of mankind". [S.E. 23: 192–93] Such grossly exaggerated valuations of his theories, further disseminated by his adherents, have undoubtedly played their part in inducing many people to overestimate both his achievements and his stature.

Attention has frequently been drawn to Freud's exceptional literary gifts, but perhaps less often to his mastery of the art of rhetoric. In regard to the latter Mahony observes:

> I am ever struck by the early Freud's written endorsement of hypnosis and enthusiastic description of its cures as compared with his subsequent scepticism about that means and its achievements. Similar argumentative methodology, processive style, and assured tone actually bear much of the brunt of the persuasive force for the "truths" of Freud's changing and contradictory theories. In short, a comprehensive work remains to be done on Freud's methods of persuasive expression; one would have to separate his theses from their purported demonstration, follow the rhetorical argumentation behind that "demonstration", and finally compare the rhetorical scaffolding of Freud's subsequent retractions. [Mahony 1984: 160][10]

It is difficult to conceive of a more cogent testimony to the fact that Freud's powerfully persuasive writings have the capacity to induce wide acceptance of propositions which on close examination prove to be fallacious.

---

[10]It is only fair to add that Mahony's view is very different from the one expressed here, since he believes that even Freud's disavowed early writings "have a perennial validity". [160]

The Basic Concepts
of Psychoanalysis

In an article published in an encyclopaedia in 1923 Freud lists unconscious mental processes, the theory of resistances and repression, and the appreciation of the importance of sexuality and of the Oedipus complex as constituting the foundations of psychoanalytic theory. [S.E. 18: 247] Of these the sexual theories have already been discussed, and the remaining ones will be examined in the following pages. First, however, we shall consider the question of Freud's precursors, not in order to imply that he directly utilised their ideas, but to illuminate the historical and cultural background out of which his theoretical formulations developed. All aspiring innovators have significant predecessors, but in relation to Freud's conceptions the full range of antecedents is extraordinarily large, and the extent to which these have been effectively obliterated in psychoanalytic mythology is perhaps without precedent.

The most fundamental of the ideas utilised by Freud is that of unconscious mental processes. We have already noted that the impression is conveyed in his writings that he was the first investigator to recognise the significance of such processes in mental life, and that in *Introductory Lectures* he described the notion as one of the "hypotheses of psychoanalysis" [S.E. 15: 21]. Again, in an article written for a scientific journal in 1913 he claimed "the setting up of the hypothesis of unconscious mental activities" as one of the "psychoanalytic contributions to psychology". [S.E. 13: 178] At other times, as in the paper "A Difficulty in the Path of Psychoanalysis" (1917) he does give credit for the idea to "famous philosophers" such as Schopenhauer [S.E. 14: 143], though he insists that only psychoanalysis has truly demonstrated their existence, a claim which we shall examine—and find wanting—in the next chapter. What he fails to acknowledge at any time is that, as Whyte [1960] and Ellenberger [1979] have shown, the concept was common currency at the time he started using it; as we have noted, his older colleague and mentor, Josef Breuer, observed in *Studies on Hysteria* in 1895 that it was no longer even necessary to argue in favour of the notion of unconscious ideas since they were among

the commonest facts of everyday life. In fact, it was an essential
element of Breuer's theoretical ideas, as of those of many other
investigators, Binet and Janet among them. (The distinctive way the
concept is used in psychoanalysis will be considered in the next
chapter.)

That there is still a widespread misconception with regard to
Freud's supposed pioneering role in formulating the notion of
unconscious ideas is indicated by the statement by Hofstadter and
Dennett in *The Mind's I* (1981) that "when Freud initially hypothe-
sized the existence of *un*conscious mental processes, his proposal
met widely with stark denial and incomprehension". [1981: 12] Yet
in his book *The Origins of Concepts in Human Behaviour* (1977)
Mark Altschule writes: "It is difficult—or perhaps impossible—to
find a nineteenth-century psychologist or medical psychologist who
did not recognize unconscious cerebration as not only real but of
the highest importance." With respect to the claims of psychoanalysis he notes: "As all students of dogma know, a struggling new
dogma may gain adherents by unscrupulously claiming as its own
ideas already known but not definitely attached to any currently
recognized personality. Hence, it is to be expected that the disciples
of Freud, Jung, and others should claim the discovery of the unconscious." [Altschule 1977: 199]

The idea of unconscious processes as conceived in the field of
pathological psychology arose in conjunction with the concept of
repression, the theory of which Freud describes as "the cornerstone
on which the whole structure of psychoanalysis rests". [S.E. 14: 16]
In his *Autobiographical Study* he writes that "it was a novelty and
nothing like it had ever before been recognised in mental life". [S.E.
20: 30] Yet eleven years earlier he had himself written in his *History*,
with reference to a passage in Schopenhauer's *World as Will and
Idea*, that "what he says there about the struggle against accepting a
distressing piece of reality coincides with my concept of repression
so completely that once again I owe the chance of making a discovery to my not being well-read". [S.E. 14: 15] In the same work
he claims: "The theory of repression quite certainly came to me
independently of any other source; I know of no outside impression
which might have suggested it to me. . . ." [15] However, against
this categorical assertion must be placed a passage in *Studies on
Hysteria* which he and Breuer published in 1895, i.e., at the very
beginnings of psychoanalysis. There Breuer writes of "the wealth of
thoughts which have been fended off and repressed from consciousness but not suppressed. In one way or another there comes
into existence a region of mental life—sometimes poor in ideas
and rudimentary, sometimes more or less on a par with waking

thought—our knowledge of which we owe, above all, to Binet and Janet." [S.E. 2: 349][1]

Ellenberger observes that "a feature of the Freudian legend is the blotting out of the greatest part of the scientific and cultural context in which psychoanalysis developed, hence the theme of absolute originality of the achievements, in which the hero is credited with the achievements of his predecessors, associates, disciples, rivals and contemporaries. . . . The current legend . . . attributes to Freud much of what belongs, notably, to Herbart, Fechner, Nietzsche, Meynert, Benedikt and Janet, and overlooks the work of previous explorers of the unconscious, dreams and sexual pathology.[2] Much of what is credited to Freud was diffuse current lore, and his role was to crystalise these ideas and give them an original shape." In his survey of the historical background to the concepts customarily associated with psychoanalysis he notes that "there is hardly a single concept of Freud or Jung that has not been anticipated by the philosophy of nature and Romantic medicine". [Ellenberger 1970: 547] (Iago Galdston also notes that "the components of [Freud's] meta-psychology . . . were already known, and defined, in many respects in superior ways, in Romantic Medicine. That includes his dream interpretation, the Unconscious, repression, the Id, Ego and Super-Ego, the concepts of Eros and Thanatos, and much else besides." [Cioffi 1973: 116])[3]

---

[1]It might be argued that Freud's claim of originality in *An Autobiographical Study* related to his own *specific* theory, but it would still remain true that his assertion that nothing like it had ever before been recognised is grossly misleading. Jones acknowledges Johann Herbart as an example of a predecessor whose writings, as we shall see below, were known to Freud and who included a rather similar concept of repression in his psychological system.

[2]Of the names mentioned here Freud acknowledged the influence of only one. In *An Autobiographical Study* he writes: "I was always open to the ideas of G. T. Fechner and have followed that thinker upon many important points." [S.E. 20: 59]

[3]In this context it is interesting to note that in *Hysteria* (1965) Ilza Veith writes: "This review of the writings that constitute the history of hysteria has brought to the author's attention an amazing amount of anticipation, and actual formulation of many of the ideas traditionally believed to have originated in the mind of Sigmund Freud." [Veith 1965: ix] As we have seen, in some instances much of the responsibility for this widespread misconception can be laid directly at the door of Freud himself. A further example occurs in relation to his ideas on childhood sexuality, which he describes as "a subject the very existence of which had scarcely been suspected previously" [S.E. 18: 243], one "that had hitherto been fundamentally overlooked by science". [S.E. 19: 197] Yet Stephen Kern concludes from a study of the literature of the period prior to 1900 that "almost every element of Freud's theory of child sexuality was exactly anticipated, or in some way implied or suggested, before him". [Kern 1973: 137] An example of a misconception propagated by one

The most notable precursors of Freud are Schopenhauer and Nietzsche. According to Ellenberger: "The similarities between certain essential teachings of Schopenhauer and Freud have been shown by Cassirer, Scheler, and particularly by Thomas Mann. Mann, who during his youth had been deeply immersed in the metaphysics of Schopenhauer, declares that, while becoming acquainted with Freud's psychoanalysis, he was 'filled with a sense of recognition and familiarity'. He felt that Freud's description of the id and ego was 'to a hair' Schopenhauer's description of the will and the intellect, translated from metaphysics into psychology. Dream psychology, the great importance given to sexuality and the whole complexus of thought 'is a philosophical anticipation of analytic conceptions, to a quite astonishing extent'." [Ellenberger 1970: 209]

In his book *The Philosophy of Schopenhauer*, Bryan Magee notes that the philosopher argued that not only are most of our thoughts and feelings unknown to us, but that the reason for this is a process of repression which is itself unconscious. After presenting Schopenhauer's views in some detail, Magee observes that the remarkable passages he has summarised constitute "an unmistakably clear and explicit exposition of an idea now generally credited to Freud, who was not yet born". [Magee 1983: 132–33]

With regard to Nietzsche, Ellenberger summarises the writings of Alwin Mittasch and Ludwig Klages, who have demonstrated the numerous ways in which the philosopher anticipated Freud. He conceived the notion of dammed-up psychic energy which could be transferred from one instinct to another, leading him to consider the human mind as a system of drives. He also asserted that man is a self-deceiving being, who is constantly deceiving his fellow men. The unconscious he viewed as an area of confused thoughts, emotions, and instincts, and at the same time an area of re-enactment of past stages of the individual and of the species, and dreams as a re-enactment of fragments of our own past and the past of mankind. [Ellenberger 1970: 273]

---

of Freud's disciples occurs in relation to the technique of free association. Strachey writes that Freud abandoned the use of hypnotic suggestion and "replaced it by an entirely fresh instrument, which was later known as 'free association'", and he goes on to describe it as an "unheard-of" technique. [Freud 1962: 18] However, Altschule quotes a passage from a paper published in the journal *Brain* by Galton in 1879 in which the latter discusses the method of free association and states that an understanding of the process showed how "the phenomenon of a long-forgotten scene, suddenly starting into consciousness, admitted in many cases of being explained". [Altschule 1977: 140] It is known that Freud subscribed to *Brain* at the time when the paper appeared; Altschule states (without giving any reference) that he translated that very paper into German for the use of physicians and medical students.

The concept of sublimation was applied by Nietzsche to both the sexual and aggressive instincts, and he asserted that "Good actions are sublimated evil ones". He also observed that "the degree and quality of a person's sexuality finds it way into the topmost reaches of his spirit". [274]

The process of repression was also described by Nietzsche, though he gave it the name "inhibition". As an example of its workings he wrote: "I have done it, says my memory. I cannot have done it, says my pride and remains inexorable. Finally the memory gives way." [274]

In his *Autobiographical Study* Freud denies that these two great predecessors had any influence on the development of his own ideas: "The large extent to which psychoanalysis coincides with the philosophy of Schopenhauer—not only did he assert the dominance of the emotions and the supreme importance of sexuality but he was even aware of the mechanism of repression—is not to be traced to my acquaintance with his teaching. I read Schopenhauer very late in my life. Nietzsche, another philosopher whose guesses and intuitions often agree in the most astonishing way with the laborious findings of psychoanalysis, was for a long time avoided by me on that very account; I was less concerned with priority than with keeping my mind unembarrassed." [S.E. 20: 59] However, the ideas of the two philosophers in question were widely debated within late nineteenth-century intellectual circles, and Freud could scarcely have avoided encountering them; in fact, it is known that he had been an active member of a student society in which their views were avidly discussed. As Sulloway observes: "It is simply inconceivable that Freud, who was a member of the Reading Society for five years, was as totally uninfluenced by Schopenhauer and Nietzsche as he liked to think. The point to be emphasised here, however, is not so much that these two philosophers *did* influence Freud—especially since that influence is difficult to trace in any detail—but rather that Freud was so vehement in repeatedly denying that he could possibly have drawn anything from their work. How revealing it is to hear him say, for example, that his occasional attempts at reading Nietzsche were always 'smothered by an excess of interest'!" [Sulloway 1979: 468] Ellenberger in fact goes as far as to assert: "For those acquainted with both Nietzsche and Freud, the similarity of their thought is so obvious that there can be no question about the former's influence over the latter." [Ellenberger 1970: 276]

A more direct influence may have been exerted by Johann Herbart, who developed his own conception of a dynamic unconscious. Jones reports the research of a Polish psychologist, Luise

von Karpinska, who first called attention to the resemblance between some of Freud's fundamental ideas and those promulgated
by Herbart seventy years previously. As Jones recounts it, Herbart
conceives of unconscious mental processes as being dominated by a
constant conflict, and mental life as dualistic, as did Freud. An idea
is described as being *verdrängt* [repressed] when it is unable to
reach consciousness because of some opposing idea or when it is
driven out of consciousness by one. Two thresholds in the mind are
posited, corresponding to Freud's two censorships. At one of them
an inhibited idea is rendered inactive and can enter consciousness
only when the inhibition is lifted. (This corresponds to Freud's
preconscious.) At the other threshold wholly repressed ideas are
still in a state of rebellious activity directed against those in consciousness and succeed in producing indirect effects. (This parallels
Freud's unconscious.)

Little wonder that Jones remarks that "all this is very interesting" and goes on to describe other parallels with Freud's ideas.
Moreover, he reports another "remarkably interesting fact", that in
Freud's last year at the gymnasium there was in use a textbook
which "may be described as a compendium of the Herbartian psychology". [Jones 1953: 407-410]

Resistance

It is evident, then, that most of the major psychological concepts
utilised by Freud were by no means original, and to evaluate his
unique contribution we must look to his novel development and
applications of these concepts. Without doubt he has done more
than any other person to try to formulate and elucidate the precise
workings of psychological processes such as repression, defence,
sublimation, and so on, and has thereby brought them to the attention of both professionals and the lay public. His expositions include many passages containing genuine insights, but they are
weakened by implausible applications and the knowledge that his
propositions all too easily lend themselves to facile and tendentious
modes of discourse. This is well illustrated by his treatment of the
concepts of resistance and repression.

He introduces the notion of resistance in characteristically
brilliant fashion in *Introductory Lectures*, and then goes on to warn
that it may take many forms and that consequently the doctor must
be distrustful and remain on his guard against it. In psychoanalytic
therapy, as with dream analysis, the patient is instructed to put

himself in a state of quiet, unreflecting self-observation, and to report whatever internal perceptions he is able to make—feelings,
thoughts, memories—in the order in which they occur to him. No
selection whatsoever is to be made among these associations on the
grounds of their being too disagreeable, unimportant, irrelevant, or
nonsensical, and he must leave aside any criticism of what he finds,
whatever shape that criticism may take. It is known from the technique of dream interpretation that the associations giving rise to
such doubts and objections are precisely the ones which invariably
contain the material which leads to the uncovering of the unconscious. [S.E. 16: 286–87]

After describing some of the ways in which the patient attempts
to circumvent the provisions of the technique of free association,
Freud writes that "in the end, through resolution and perseverance,
we succeed in extorting a certain amount of obedience to the fundamental technical rule from the resistance—which thereupon jumps
over to another sphere". So "it now appears as an *intellectual* resistance, it fights by means of arguments and exploits all the difficulties and improbabilities which normal but uninstructed thinking
finds in the theories of analysis. It is now our fate to hear from this
single voice all the criticisms and objections which assail our ears in
a chorus in the scientific literature of the subject." [289] But "intellectual resistances are not the worst: one always remains superior to
them." [290] More difficult to overcome is the patient's propensity
to repeat attitudes and emotional impulses from his early life which
can be used as a resistance against the doctor and the treatment by
what is known as "transference". However, resistances of this kind
should not be simply condemned, for they include much of the most
important material from the patient's past and bring it back in so
convincing a fashion that they become some of the best supports of
the analysis if they are dealt with skilfully. The character traits
mobilised for fighting against the alterations being sought were
formed in relation to the determinants of the neurosis and in
reaction against its demands. It is the overcoming of these resistances which is the essential function of analysis, and this is the only
part of the work which gives assurance that something has been
achieved with the patient.

Finally in this catalogue of the forms and methods of the resistance we are told that the patient uses as reasons for slackening his
effort "all the chance events that occur during his analysis . . . every
diversion outside the analysis, every comment by a person of authority in his environment who is hostile to analysis, any chance
organic illness . . . and, even, indeed, every improvement in his
condition". [291]

Freud's exposition conveys the psychoanalytic view of resistance
with great clarity. Before we examine it critically in the light of his
actual practice, it is of interest to note that, as elsewhere in his
popular writings, he anticipates some possible objections himself,
suggesting that "we should do well to find room for a cautious
doubt whether we have not been too light-heartedly assuming resistances. Perhaps there really are cases of neurosis in which associations fail for other reasons, perhaps the arguments against our
hypotheses really deserve to have their content examined, and
perhaps we are doing patients an injustice in so conveniently setting
aside their intellectual criticisms as resistance." [292] In response to
these reservations he writes:

> But, Gentlemen, we did not arrive at this judgement lightly. We
> have had occasion to observe all these critical patients at the
> moment of the emergence of a resistance and after its disap-
> pearance. For resistance is constantly altering its intensity during
> the course of a treatment; it always increases when we are ap-
> proaching a new topic, it is at its most intense while we are at the
> climax of dealing with that topic, and it dies away when the topic
> has been disposed of. . . . If we are on the point of bringing a
> specially distressing piece of unconscious material to his con-
> sciousness, [the patient] is extremely critical; he may previously
> have understood and accepted a great deal, but now it is just as
> though those acquisitions have been swept away. . . . But if we
> succeed in helping him to overcome this new resistance, he recovers
> his insight and understanding. Thus his critical faculty is not an
> independent function, to be respected as such, it is the tool of his
> emotional attitudes and is directed by his resistance. [292–93]

Now, though much of Freud's exposition shows genuine psychological insight, there are two major flaws in it. One of these he
attempts to deal with in the above passage, in which he seeks to
dispose of the suggestion that the patient's objections to his ideas
may have some substance and cannot therefore simply be dismissed
as resistance. But his description of the course of such incidents in
analysis is consistent with a genuine intellectual objection being
proposed against one of his implausible interpretations and then
being overcome by the force of his arguments and personality.
Philip Rieff describes such an episode from the Dora case history
thus: "Dora expressed disbelief, Freud applauds his own persis-
tence; he speaks of using facts against the patient and reports how
he overwhelmed Dora with interpretations, pounding away at her
argument, until 'Dora disputed the facts no longer'." [Rieff 1959:
82] Though he undoubtedly moderated this aggressive approach in
his later analyses, we know that he almost invariably treated opposition to his interpretations as expressions of resistance. In dealing

with reservations raised in regard to his ideas on slips of the tongue in *Introductory Lectures*, he asks his audience: "Am I too mistrustful, however, if I suspect that at the very moment at which psychoanalysis makes its appearance before you resistance to it simultaneously raises its head?" [S.E. 15: 48] He reminds us of this excessive mistrust of *any* opposition to his ideas when he associates the patient's intellectual resistance with "all the criticisms and objections which assail our ears in a chorus in the scientific literature of the subject". Freud himself presents a perfect illustration of a major limitation of his analytic technique: that its validity is seriously reduced, or even nullified, if the therapist has excessively strong preconceptions of what he expects to find. There is no doubt that Freud regarded Dora's "usual contradictions" [S.E. 7: 108–09] to his far-fetched and tendentious interpretations as resistance on her part, yet reading the paper one can only commend her emotional and intellectual integrity (and courage) in rejecting them in the face of her therapist's powerful personality. The technique demands a considerably greater degree of open-mindedness on the part of the therapist than Freud was capable of .

The other major objection is more basic. Freud assumes an all-pervading psychical determinism, so that every single aspect of the patient's behaviour is regarded as having a meaning which can be interpreted in psychoanalytic terms. Such an attitude tends to reduce the notion of unconscious mental processes to a simplistic concept of an independent entity labelled "the Unconscious" which may be used to explain each and every situation the analyst feels called upon to make intelligible. Even when applied with considerably more discrimination than was the case with Freud, this almost inevitably lends itself to facile interpretations, and given the many years of training in the analytic approach undergone by the analyst he is all too likely to regard reasonable scepticism towards these interpretations as resistance.[4]

Repression

Closely related to resistance is the concept of repression, which Freud describes as a pathogenic process by means of which the re-

---

[4]That such an attitude is an occupational hazard of psychoanalysis is indicated by the words of Edward Glover, former Director of Research at the London Institute of Psychoanalysis, in regard to training analyses. He writes that it is difficult for a trainee analyst to defend his scientific integrity against his analyst's theory and practice, for "according to his analyst the candidate's objections to interpretations rate as 'resistances'". [Glover 1952: 403]

sistance prevents certain mental events entering into consciousness, resulting in the formation of symptoms. He goes on to describe the process in terms of a spatial analogy in which a "watchman" presides at the threshold between a large entrance hall (the system of the unconscious) and a small drawing-room (in which consciousness resides). The function of the watchman is to control the passage of mental impulses trying to cross the threshold from the unconscious to the conscious system. An impulse may be turned away at the threshold, or pushed back after it has entered the drawing-room. Impulses from the unconscious which are turned back by the watchman are described as repressed. However, those allowed to cross the threshold do not necessarily become conscious on that account; they may remain in the system of the *preconscious*. The action of the watchman corresponds to the resistance encountered when efforts are made to lift the repression by means of analytic treatment. [S.E. 16: 295–96]

At this point Freud breaks off to suggest that it will be said that these ideas "are both crude and fantastic and quite impermissible in a scientific account". He acknowledges they are crude, and even that they are "incorrect", but says he already has something better to take their place. They should be regarded as "preliminary working hypotheses", helping to make his observations intelligible. [296]

Nevertheless he insists that the conceptions of "the two rooms, the watchman at the threshold between them and consciousness as a spectator at the end of the second room must . . . be very far-reaching approximations to the real facts". [296] These hypotheses of the two systems and their relation to each other and to consciousness find support from the observation that "the watchman between the unconscious and the preconscious is nothing else than the *censorship*, to which, as we found, the form taken by the manifest dream is subject". [297] There follows a brief description of the role of the censorship in his dream theory, from which he concludes: "Our hypothesis about the structure of the mental apparatus, which allows us to understand the formation alike of dreams and of neurotic symptoms, has an incontrovertible claim to being taken into account in regard to normal mental life as well." [297–98][5]

---

[5]In his paper "The Unconscious" (1915) Freud posits the existence of two censors. When unconscious impulses are turned back at the threshold with the preconscious system, derivatives of these impulses can circumnavigate the censorship and reach a certain intensity of cathexis in the preconscious. If this intensity is exceeded and the impulses try to force themselves into consciousness they are recognised as derivatives of the unconscious and are repressed afresh at the new frontier of censorship, between the preconscious and the conscious systems. Freud writes that "in psychoanalytic treatment the existence of the second censorship . . . is proved beyond question". [S.E. 14: 193]

We must not, of course, be unduly impressed by Freud's use of the word "incontrovertible", since his justification for his ideas on the structure of the mental apparatus invokes an equally speculative entity, the censorship from his dream theory. What he has in mind by his "something better" to replace these notions is not immediately apparent. Possibly he is referring to the ideas he eventually introduced in 1923 in *The Ego and the Id* and developed further in *New Introductory Lectures* (1933). Without entering into the extremely involved (not to say confused) speculations in those works, we may say that the mental apparatus is divided into three regions designated as the ego, the super-ego, and the id. (The notions of the conscious, preconscious, and the unconscious are retained but do not correlate in any simple way with the newly defined entities.) The ego is described as the "coherent organisation of mental processes" to which "consciousness is attached" [S.E. 19: 17]; it controls the discharge of excitations into the external world. The super-ego is "a special agency in the ego . . . which represents demands of a restrictive and rejecting character." [S.E. 22: 69] Repression is the work of this super-ego, "carried out either by itself or by the ego in obedience to its orders". [69] The id (so named after a suggestion of Groddeck, but originating with Nietzsche[6]) is a mental region consisting exclusively of "instinctual cathexes seeking discharge". [73] It is characterised as "the dark, inaccessible part of our personality", a "cauldron full of seething excitations". [73] It might be said that "the ego stands for reason and good sense while the id stands for the untamed passions". [76]

The interrelation between these entities is by no means clear. At one time the super-ego is described as "a grade in the ego, a differentiation within the ego" [S.E. 19: 28], but on a later occasion we are told that "the super-ego merges into the id" [S.E. 22: 79]. Again, though the ego is envisaged as "a portion of the id" [76], the latter is also described as a "mental region that is foreign to the ego" [72], and indeed "alien" to it.[7] It is not surprising to find that Freud

---

[6]In *An Outline of Psychoanalysis* Freud writes "we give the name of 'id'" to "everything that is inherited, that is present at birth. . . ." [S.E. 23: 145] According to William McDougall this is precisely the sense in which it was used by Nietzsche. [McDougall 1936: 61]

[7]That Freud himself seems confused about the respective functions of the ego and the id can be seen from the following. Prior to the introduction of the id into his writings he had stated that "the ego is the true and original reservoir of libido, and it is only from that reservoir that libido is extended on to objects". [S.E. 18: 51–52] Then in *The Ego and the Id* he designates "the id as the great reservoir of libido" [S.E. 19: 30n], asserting that it "sends part of this libido out into erotic object-cathexes" [46]. However, in later writings, without any explanation, he

himself describes his discussion of the subject in *New Introductory Lectures* as "exacting and not, perhaps, very illuminating". [79] He observes that the ego's "three tyrannical masters are the external world, the super-ego and the id" [77], but since this is saying little more than that man's consciousness is governed by his environment, his conscience, and his innate instincts, it is hardly a great revelation. As Farrell writes in relation to later developments along these lines: "Ego-psychology seems to be primarily a way of talking, from which it is difficult to extract confirmable generalisations. In consequence of this, perhaps, it has not been of much heuristic value in psychology, however stimulating it may have been to analysts themselves." [Farrell 1981: 171]

To the criticism that his "ego-psychology comes down to nothing more than taking commonly used abstractions literally and in a crude sense, and transforming them from concepts to things—by which not much would be gained", Freud responds:

> To this I would reply that in ego-psychology it will be difficult to escape what is universally known; it will rather be a question of new ways of looking at things and new ways of arranging them than of new discoveries. So hold to your contemptuous criticism for the time being and await further explanations. The facts of pathology give our efforts a background that you would look for in vain in popular psychology. So I will proceed. [S.E. 22: 60]

Now here of course we have Freud's familiar device of raising a valid criticism and appearing to give some semblance of a satisfactory response when in fact he has not dealt with the real issue. If we take it that his newly formulated entities are the "something better" to take the place of the old ones, they are open to the same criticisms as the latter. Not only are they speculations of a kind not amenable to empirical validation, their functions are so imprecisely delineated that they can be employed in almost arbitrary fashion to provide support for virtually any theoretical formulation. Their advantage from Freud's point of view is the versatility of the functions they may perform and the explanations they may furnish, separately or in concert. McDougall summed up the fault in this kind of theorising when he observed that "if we allowed ourselves

---

reverts to his original view that "the ego is always the main reservoir of libido, from which libidinal cathexes of objects go out". [S.E. 22: 103] Strachey finds the inconsistency "disturbing" [S.E. 19: 64], but it seems of little consequence either way. As McDougall observes, Freud's writings on this subject resemble "a great tangle in which Freud lashes about like a great whale caught in a net of his own contriving". [McDougall 1936: 56]

the laxity of reasoning which is habitual to Freud and many of his disciples, and if we possessed his fertile ingenuity, there would be literally no limits to the possibilities of application of his principles". [McDougall 1936: 124]

The pertinence of this observation can be seen when we turn to examples of the way that Freud conceives of the process of repression in practice. In the paper on "Repression" (1915) he writes that "the mechanism of a repression becomes accessible to us only by our deducing that mechanism from the *outcome* of the repression". [S.E. 14: 154] To illustrate this he chooses "a well-analysed example of an animal phobia", that of the Wolf Man. [155] What is repressed in this instance is a libidinal attitude of the little boy towards his father, coupled with a fear of him. As a result of the repression there is substituted a fear of a wolf. In the more extensive *Inhibitions, Symptoms and Anxiety* (1924), where he tackles the problem of the mechanism of repression anew, the only direct clinical evidence he provides again relates to animal phobias, for "we understand them better than any other cases" [S.E. 20: 124]. In this revised explication he tells us in regard to the Wolf Man that the instinctual impulses which have been overtaken by repression are "sadistic aggressiveness towards the father and a tender passive attitude to him", the latter being the more important of the two. [106] Further technical discussion leads to the conclusion that the motive force of the repression was the castration complex: "it was from fear of being castrated . . . that the little Russian relinquished his wish to be loved by his father, for he thought that a relation of that sort presupposed a sacrifice of his genitals. . . ."[8] He goes on to explain that the affect of anxiety, which was the essence of the phobia, came not from the process of repression (i.e., not from the libidinal cathexes of the repressed impulses), but from the repressing agency itself: "The anxiety belonging to the animal phobia was an untransformed fear of castration." [108]

In the course of the discussion Freud informs us how he obtained "unmistakable proof that what repression overtook was [the boy's] passive tender attitude to his father": it was "the analysis of his wolf-dream" which revealed this crucial fact. [107] It will be recalled that the dream, involving wolves in a tree, was interpreted as representing a censored version of sexual intercourse between the

---

[8]It is explained in the Wolf Man paper that it was the activation by the wolf-dream of his earlier observation of his parents' sexual intercourse which gave the little boy "the conviction of the reality of castration" (for he had seen with his own eyes his mother's "wound"), and the understanding that it was "a necessary condition of intercourse with his father". [S.E. 17: 45–46]

boy's parents, and the fanciful nature of that reconstruction effectively renders Freud's explication of the process of repression bereft of substantive content. The flaw in his approach is that he is dependent for his knowledge of what has been repressed on his doubtful interpretive technique, and this in turn utilises such equally doubtful concepts as the castration complex. The above is a representative example of how he employs the concept of repression, and one must conclude that although he must be credited with popularising the notion, his application of it does little to advance our understanding of it as a psychological process.

The Transference

The encyclopaedia article listing the fundamental ideas which constitute the foundations of psychoanalytic theory also contains a section emphasising the importance of the "transference" between patient and analyst.[9] In order to fully appreciate this aspect of the therapeutic process which occurs during a psychoanalysis, it will be necessary to review briefly Freud's ideas on the way that neuroses arise. In *An Autobiographical Study* (1925) he recounts how investigation of the underlying causes of the neuroses had led to the discovery that they derive from experiences of early childhood relating to sexual excitations and the reactions against them. [S.E. 20: 33] These experiences, in the main, are not the result of accidental external events but arise from instinctual processes, most notably the Oedipal impulses. The castration complex, which arises as a direct consequence of the Oedipus complex, "is of the profoundest importance in the formation alike of character and of neuroses". [37]

It is important to appreciate that when Freud refers to experiences of early childhood in the context of the aetiology of the neuroses, he has in mind the kind of *psychical* experiences he postulates to occur in relation to the Oedipus complex. (In "A Short Account of Psychoanalysis" (1924) he states explicitly: "It became ever clearer that [the Oedipus complex] was the nucleus of every case of neurosis." [S.E. 19: 198. Also 21: 184; 22: 87]) It is the occurrence of impulses arising from the reactivation of these proc-

---

[9]Janet also recognised the importance of the *rapport*, involving sometimes powerful emotions directed towards the therapist, including psychological dependency, but his suggestions for handling it were rather different from Freud's. [Ellenberger 1970: 374]

esses in later life which Freud understands to underlie the development of neuroses in adulthood. In *An Autobiographical Study* the pathogenic process itself is described in the following way: An instinctual impulse arises in the subject's mind and is opposed by the ego. The normal solution to this conflict is that the instinct is repudiated and its cathexis of energy is withdrawn. In the neurotic solution the ego draws back on its first collision with the objectionable instinctual impulse; it debars it from access to consciousness and to direct motor discharge, so that the impulse retains its full cathexis of energy. Consequently the ego is obliged to protect itself against the constant threat of a renewed advance on the part of the repressed impulse by making a permanent expenditure of energy, thus impoverishing itself. The repressed impulse, now unconscious, is able to find means of discharge and of substitutive satisfaction by circuitous routes, giving rise to neurotic symptoms. [S.E. 20: 29–30]

In his last major work, *An Outline of Psychoanalysis*, Freud reiterates his view that "neuroses are acquired only in early childhood (up to the age of six)", and though he allows an aetiological role for certain accidental influences of childhood, such as sexual abuse by adults, he emphasises that it is in relation to the Oedipus complex that the origins of neuroses are to be found. [187][10] In the case of a boy the castration complex affects the whole of his relations with his father and mother and subsequently with men and women in general. [190] Equally profound are the effects of envy for the penis in the case of a girl; in fact her whole development is coloured by it. [193] The description of the pathological process is essentially the same as that in *An Autobiographical Study*, other than that the ego may be in conflict with demands from the external world as well as with instinctual impulses. The more extensive account in *The Question of Lay Analysis* (1926) is in the terminology of ego-psychology, which cannot disguise the fact that nothing essentially new is added to the postulated process, except that it is described in more impressive language.

We are now in a position to attempt to follow Freud's description of the "transference" between patient and analyst in the light of his views on the genesis of neuroses. He describes it as a special emotional relation that is regularly formed in the course of an analysis and which in the hands of the physician "becomes the most

---

[10]As Macmillan emphasises (and contrary to popular belief), "the further one goes in the development of Freud's theory [of neuroses] the larger is the importance of innate, hereditary factors and the smaller the role of the environment". [Macmillan 1991: 541]

powerful therapeutic instrument and plays a part scarcely to be overestimated in the dynamics of the process of cure". [S.E. 18: 247] As usual his theoretical view of the process is circumscribed by his psychoanalytic notions; he claims the development of such a relationship as "proof" that forces of a sexual nature lie behind the formation of neurotic symptoms, and contends that it "derives all of its characteristics from earlier erotic attitudes of the patient's which have become unconscious". Specifically, the attitudes which are "invariably acted out" in the transference "always have as their subject some portion of infantile sexual life—of the Oedipus complex, that is, and its derivatives". [S.E. 18: 18]

In detailing the process Freud writes that the patient sees the analyst as some important figure out of his childhood or past, and consequently transfers onto him his earlier feelings and reactions. The transference is ambivalent and involves both affectionate and hostile attitudes towards the analyst, who is generally put in the place of one or other of the patient's parents. If the attitude is positive, it serves the analytic situation. In place of the aim of becoming healthy and free from symptoms there emerges the aim of pleasing the analyst. The patient's "weak ego becomes strong. . . . he leaves off his symptoms and seems apparently to have recovered—merely for the sake of the analyst." If the patient puts the analyst in the place of his father (or mother) he gives him "the power which his super-ego exercises over his ego. . . . The new super-ego has the opportunity of a sort of *after-education* of the neurotic." However, the analyst must not misuse this influence to attempt to mould the patient in his own image. If he does, he will only be repeating a mistake of the parents, who crushed their child's independence by their influence, and he will only be replacing the child's earlier dependence by a new one. [S.E. 23: 174–75]

How the therapist utilises the transference for permanent improvement is, perhaps of necessity, left rather vague. With careful preparation the patient can be helped to learn from the feelings he experiences in this relationship. He is encouraged to collaborate in the intellectual work, though "as a rule we put off telling him of a construction or an explanation till he himself has so nearly arrived at it that only a single step remains to be taken, though that step is in fact the decisive synthesis". [178] The most important part of the analyst's task is to deal with the resistances as they arise. Rather surprisingly, Freud tells us that the outcome of the struggle between the ego and the resistances "is a matter of indifference". Whether it results in "the ego accepting . . . an instinctual demand which it has hitherto rejected, or whether it dismisses it once more, this time for good and all, . . . in either case a permanent danger has been disposed of, the compass of the ego has been extended and a wasteful expenditure of energy has been made unnecessary." [179]

The overcoming of resistances entails considerable time and trouble, but "brings about an advantageous alteration of the ego which it will maintain independently of the outcome of the transference and will hold good in life". At the same time the therapist works "at getting rid of the alteration of the ego which had been brought about under the influence of the unconscious", for "whenever we have been able to detect any of its derivatives in the ego we have pointed out their illegitimate origin and have instigated the ego to reject them." [179]

Freud summarises the therapeutic process as occurring in two phases. In the first "all the libido is forced from the symptoms into the transference and concentrated there". The second phase involves "the elimination of repression in this renewed conflict", a process made possible "by the alteration of the ego which is accomplished under the influence of the doctor's suggestion". The work of interpretation brings unconscious material to conscious awareness, thereby enlarging the ego and making it "conciliatory towards the libido and inclined to grant it some satisfaction". At the same time the ego's "repugnance to the claims of the libido is diminished by the possibility of disposing of a portion of it by sublimation". [S.E. 16: 455]

Divesting Freud's words of their psychoanalytic jargon, we might possibly paraphrase them by saying that the therapeutic aim is to make conscious the unconscious processes and motivations which have contributed to the problems the patient is experiencing and to encourage the patient to modify them. This, in principle, is unexceptionable, but in practice much depends on the subjective views of the analyst regarding the nature of these unconscious processes. It is difficult to have much confidence in the procedure when the interpretations and inferences utilised by the analyst are derived from psychoanalytic notions of the kind described in this book. Nor is confidence in the approach of Freud and his followers enhanced when we read that the two most refractory complexes are encountered by the analyst when he is "trying to persuade a woman to abandon her wish for a penis on the ground of its being unrealisable" or when he is "seeking to convince a man that a passive attitude to men does not always signify castration . . .", in which latter case the patient's transfer-resistances manifest themselves in his refusal "to subject himself to a father-substitute". [S.E. 23: 252][11]

---

[11]Current trends in psychoanalytic therapy do not engender any more confidence. As Morris Eagle has shown from a close examination of some major recent developments, they are at least as unsatisfactory as more traditional approaches in regard to theory and to therapeutic process and outcome. [Eagle 1983]

In his summing-up of the therapeutic process, Freud writes of
the analyst's role that "we serve the patient in various functions, as
an authority and a substitute for his parents, as a teacher and
educator". [S.E. 23: 181] The Wolf Man reports that Freud had
told him, "Don't criticise, don't reflect, don't look for contradictions, but accept what I tell you, and improvement will come by
itself" [Obholtzer 1982: 31], which hardly seems calculated to
promote the declared aim of strengthening the ego. That this is the
attitude that Freud expected from his patients is confirmed in *The
Question of Lay Analysis*, where we are told that "the neurotic sets
to work because he has faith in the analyst, and he believes him
because he acquires a special emotional attitude towards the figure
of the analyst". [S.E. 20: 224–25] The Wolf Man's analysis seems
not to have resulted in an increase in personal autonomy, for he
tells us: "Too strong a transference ends with your transferring to
individuals who replace Freud, as it were, and with your believing
them uncritically. And that happened to me, to a degree." [Obholt-
zer 1982: 31]

The Role of Suggestion

In *An Autobiographical Study* Freud acknowledges that in the
transference can be recognised the same dynamic factor that
hypnotists call "suggestibility", which is the agent of the hypnotic
rapport. [S.E. 20: 42] Nevertheless, he emphatically denies that
therapeutic success in psychoanalysis owes anything to direct suggestion, and when dealing with this issue he contrasts his technique
with hypnotism in cases where the latter is used to eliminate symptoms. However, he is on doubtful ground when he asserts that in
psychoanalysis the role of suggestion is limited to its acting "as a
motive force to induce the patient to overcome his resistances".
[S.E. 20: 225] This implies that, while it is granted that the authority
of the analyst induces the patient to accept his interpretations, the
therapeutic process consists essentially (and exclusively) of the
patient's working through of the material. But the nature and operation of suggestion is too complex to be disposed of so simply.
Suffice it to say here that suggestion can have effects on the
patient's symptoms without there necessarily being a direct attempt
to eliminate them by this means. Moreover, the faith that a patient
experiences in his therapist may have a positive influence on his
condition regardless of the validity of the therapist's theories. Freud
wishes us to believe that it is because the interpretations put
forward by the analyst and accepted by the patient are valid that

progress occurs during the course of the working-through, and that suggestion only assists in the first part of this process. However, were this the case it is difficult to see how different schools of psychotherapy, employing widely different approaches and postulates, have been able to claim therapeutic success. Insofar as these claims have validity, it seems likely that factors common to the different approaches, rather than specific analytic theories, are therapeutically significant. Of these, suggestion in a more or less direct form may well play an important part.

Freud deals with this issue in relation to the validity of psychoanalytic theory in *Introductory Lectures*, where he addresses the challenge that "the influencing of our patient may make the objective certainty of our findings doubtful", and that "what is advantageous to our therapy is damaging to our researches". If this point were justified "psychoanalysis would be nothing more than a particularly well-disguised and particularly effective form of suggestive treatment and we should have to attach little weight to all that it tells us about what influences our lives, the dynamics of the mind or the unconscious". In his response he writes that these accusations are contradicted more easily by an appeal to experience than by the help of theory: "Anyone who has himself carried out psychoanalysis will have been able to convince himself on countless occasions that it is impossible to make suggestions to a patient in that way." The doctor has no difficulty in making him a supporter of some particular theory, and thereby making him share some possible error of his own, but this only affects his intelligence, not his illness. "After all, his conflicts will only be successfully solved and his resistances overcome if the anticipatory ideas he is given tally with what is real in him. Whatever in the doctor's conjectures is inaccurate drops out in the course of the analysis; it has to be withdrawn and replaced by something more correct." [S.E. 16: 452]

Freud goes on to explain that the analyst endeavours "by a careful technique" to avoid the occurrence of "premature successes due to suggestion", though no harm is done if they do occur since he is not satisfied by a first success. It is the working through of the transference which brings about a fundamental change in the patient and a lasting therapeutic outcome, and it is this which marks the distinction between psychoanalysis and "purely suggestive therapy". [452–53]

Freud's argument, though superficially plausible, does not withstand close scrutiny. His description of the process of the working through of the transference and the resolving of the patient's neurotic resistances is impressive, but is not borne out by either the mediocre therapeutic record of psychoanalysis or an examination of his own case histories. In the latter it is only too evident that unsubstantiated conjectures, in general, do not necessarily drop out in the way he describes, but tend to remain incorporated in the structure of the interpretive narrative. In the passage under discussion Freud's argument that the therapeutic outcome will only be successful if the constructions and interpretations of the analyst "tally with what is real" in the patient begs the question, since it does not dispose of the challenge that psychoanalysis is simply a particularly subtle and complex form of suggestion and that any successes are due to this rather than to the authenticity of the psychoanalytic inferences.

Criticism of Freud's failure to allow for the more subtle effects of suggestion was made from the earliest days of psychoanalysis.[12] His denial that such effects in any way undermined his psychoanalytic claims even extended to the case of Little Hans, in spite of his frank acknowledgement that the boy had to be presented with the prerequisite thoughts and was otherwise manipulated by his father. [S.E. 10: 104] How weak and tendentious is his argument that suggestion was not a significant factor in that case is indicated by his curiously worded assertion that "the small patient gave evidence of enough independence to acquit him upon the charge of 'suggestion'". [105]

His sensitivity on this issue eventually provoked him into making a denial so categorical that it cannot possibly be true. In the paper "Constructions in Analysis" he writes: "The danger of our leading a patient astray by suggestion, by persuading him to accept things which we ourselves believe but which he ought not to, has certainly been enormously exaggerated. . . . I can assert without boasting that such an abuse of 'suggestion' has never occurred in my practice." [S.E. 23: 262] Clearly this is a pronouncement he is in no position to make with such absolute confidence; nor could an analyst of such perfection exist this side of heaven. That he should feel it necessary to make a claim of this nature leads to the suspicion that he was aware that suggestion might actually play a considerably greater role in analysis than he was prepared to admit.[13]

---

[12]For instance, in 1900 Robert Gaupp pointed out that suggestion, whether conscious or unconscious, can result in responses from a susceptible patient which fit in with the ideas held by the physician. He adds that this may be the reason why Freud's psychoanalyses "abound in materials which other researchers seek in vain". [Kiell 1988: 38]

[13]In fact, in his last major work, *An Outline of Psychoanalysis*, he concedes that "therapeutic successes that occurred under the sway of the positive transferences are open to the suspicion of being of a *suggestive* nature". [S.E. 23: 176]

As we have noted, the psychological processes discussed above constitute the basic essentials of psychoanalytic theory as enumerated by Freud in his 1923 article. However, before drawing any general conclusions, there remains to be considered the way in which the most fundamental of these, the theory of unconscious mental processes, is characteristically utilised in psychoanalysis, and this will be considered in the next chapter.

Final Estimations

In his *Outline of Abnormal Psychology* McDougall writes the following in relation to psychoanalytic theorising: "The world of concepts in which Freud conducts his tours of discovery is so fluid and shifting that it lends itself to every manipulation. Every emotion, and every sentiment, is ambivalent, is both itself and its opposite, and can be transmuted into something radically different; every sign and symbol and symptom can be interpreted in opposite ways." [McDougall 1926: 413] This is exemplified by a remarkable passage in *The Ego and the Id* in which Freud is attempting to find order in the intricacies arising from the conjunction of "the triangular character of the Oedipus situation and the constitutional bisexuality of each individual":

> Closer study usually discloses the *more complete* Oedipus complex, which is twofold, positive, and negative, and is due to the bisexuality originally present in children; that is to say, a boy has not merely an ambivalent attitude towards his father and an affectionate object-choice towards his mother, but at the same time he also behaves like a girl and displays an affectionate feminine attitude to his father and a corresponding jealousy and hostility towards his mother. [S.E. 19: 33]

And again:

> At the dissolution of the Oedipus complex the four trends of which it consists will group themselves in such a way as to produce a father-identification and a mother-identification. The father-identification will preserve the object-relation to the mother which belonged to the positive complex and will at the same time replace the object-relation to the father which belonged to the inverted complex; and the same will be true, *mutatis mutandis*, of the mother-identification. The relative intensity of the two identifications in any individual will reflect the preponderance in him of one or other of the two dispositions. [34]

With formulations such as these it is little wonder that Freud is able to explain virtually any behaviour by tendentious application of his conceptual schemes. The arbitrariness to which such a procedure lends itself is illustrated by the consideration of psychoana-

Seductive Mirage

lytic explications in regard to homosexuality. In his paper on "Group Psychology" (1921) Freud gives the following explanation of the "genesis of male homosexuality in a large class of cases":

> A young man has been unusually long and intensely fixated upon his mother in the sense of the Oedipus complex. But at last, after the end of puberty, the time comes for exchanging his mother for some other sexual object. Things take a sudden turn; the young man does not abandon his mother, but identifies with her; he transforms himself into her, and now looks about for objects which can replace his ego for him, and on which he can bestow such love and care as he has experienced from his mother." [S.E. 18: 108][1]

Elsewhere he provides other explanations of male homosexuality, opportunistically deriving them from theoretical formulations with which he is currently engaged. For instance, at the time of his involvement with Little Hans he invokes the castration complex, arguing that the conviction of little boys that their sister will develop a penis as she grows older may result in a fixated idea of "a woman with a penis" in some cases, so that in adulthood they will be unable to do without a penis in their sexual object. [S.E. 9: 216] On a later occasion, when he is beginning to develop his notion of narcissism, he writes that infant males pass through a stage when they take their own body as their love object, and that in some cases they may linger unusually long in this "half-way phase between auto-erotism and object-love". This has the consequence that they fail to emancipate themselves from the idea that the object of their choice must possess genitals like their own. [S.E. 12: 60–61] Should any of these explanations be regarded as inappropriate in specific instances, he can always fall back on his general pronouncement that "every human being oscillates all through his life between heterosexual and homosexual feelings, and any frustration or disappointment in the one direction is apt to drive him over into the other". [S.E. 12: 46]

What is problematic in regard to Freud's procedure is not that it can be conclusively shown that any of these explanations is necessarily in error, but that the flexibility of his conceptions enables him virtually at will to derive tendentious explications, largely unconstrained by empirical considerations, which he implicitly presents as corroborations of his basic theses. This is exemplified again by the

---

[1]Contrary to the above, in an earlier description of the same process Freud reports that in all cases examined it had been established that future male inverts pass through an intense but *short-lived* fixation to their mother. [S.E. 7: 145n]

way he deals with a difficulty arising in relation to traumatic neuroses such as occur in wartime.

His problem is that at first sight traumatic neuroses seem to defy his general sexual aetiology. However, he is able to circumvent this potential counter-example by drawing upon "two facts which have been stressed by psychoanalytic research", namely, that mechanical agitation is a source of sexual excitation, and that painful and feverish illnesses exercise a powerful effect on libido: "Thus, on the one hand, the mechanical violence of the trauma would liberate a quantity of sexual excitation, which owing to the lack of preparation for anxiety, would have a traumatic effect; but, on the other hand, the simultaneous physical injury, by calling for a narcissistic hypercathexis of the injured organ, would bind the excess of excitation." [S.E. 18: 33] On a later occasion he remarks that it is greatly to be regretted that not a single analysis of a traumatic neurosis is extant. However, he is at pains to emphasise that this expression of regret is "not because such an analysis would contradict the aetiological importance of sexuality": for "any such contradiction has long been disposed of by the introduction of the concept of narcissism, which brings the libidinal cathexis of the ego into line with the cathexes of objects and emphasises the libidinal character of the instinct of self-preservation". [S.E. 20: 129][2]

There are several points worth noting here. The first is that the technical terms may deceive those impressed by such language into thinking that Freud has said something meaningful. Then there is the fact that even in the absence of a single relevant case history Freud *knows* that he is going to be able to explain any such case with which he may be presented in the future, and it will be in terms he has already decided upon. Finally, the flexibility of his concepts and their modes of interaction ensure that even phenomena which at first sight contradict his theories pose no problem and that a psychoanalytic explanation will always be forthcoming.[3]

---

[2]In this same passage Freud also tentatively invokes the castration complex, as he does more explicitly in *The Ego and the Id*, where he writes that it is possible "to regard the fear of death . . . as a development of the fear of castration". [S.E. 19: 58]

[3]This is also exemplified in "A Case of Paranoia Running Counter to the Psychoanalytic Theory of the Disease". [S.E. 14: 261–272] Although this paper has been cited as illustrative of Freud's willingness to consider possible refutations of his theories, his analysis of the case rather demonstrates the reverse, in that it shows the ease with which he is able to manipulate his conceptual schemes to transform an apparent refutation into a confirmation.

The Workings of the Unconscious

The inexhaustible capacity of psychoanalysis to supply explanations for everything may make it superficially impressive, but in
reality it frequently reduces such explanations to the level of the
specious. Thus, to take a wide range of examples, agoraphobia in
women is found to derive from "the repression of the intention to
take the first man one meets in the street" [Masson 1985; 217–18],
the "deepest unconscious root of anti-semitism" from the castration
complex [S.E. 10: 36n], and early man's control of fire from the
renunciation of "the homosexually-tinged desire to put it out with a
stream of urine" [S.E. 22: 187].⁴ Even where an explanation may be
considered to have a certain plausibility, its value may be at least
partially vitiated by the indiscriminate manner in which it tends to
be applied. For instance, instead of facing up to the uncomfortable
implications of the fact that analytic therapy not infrequently fails
to achieve a successful outcome, Freud claims the difficulties in
such cases, as a generality, arise from an unconscious resistance
deriving from the patient's "powerful need for punishment which
we could only class with masochistic wishes". [S.E. 22: 108]⁵

Freud tells us that when a member of his family complains of
having bitten his tongue, pinched a finger, or the like, "he does not
get the sympathy he hopes for, but instead the question: 'Why did
you do that?'". [S.E. 6: 180] The implication in this is that accidents
are classable as "parapraxes" and generally have an unconscious
motivation. McDougall has indicted such a simplistic view of the
working of unconscious processes in the following terms:

> I accept without reserve the view that much mental activity is
> beyond the reach of our introspective efforts; and I have no seri-
> ous objection to the description of such activities as *unconscious*

---

⁴It is instructive to note that Freud writes that in deriving his explanation for
the early control of fire from myths he is only unravelling distortions "of the same
sort, and no worse than, those we acknowledge every day, when we reconstruct
from patients' dreams the repressed but extremely important experiences of their
childhood". [S.E. 22: 187]

⁵Just as Freud can explain why some people are resistant to the "truths" of psychoanalysis, he can also explain why some patients do not get well. In *Introductory
Lectures* he tells us that "most of the failures of [the] early years were due not to
the doctor's fault . . . but to unfavourable external conditions". [S.E. 16: 458]
Later, when more careful selection of patients reduced this factor, he has another
reason. Out of a sense of guilt the patient "refuses to give up the punishment of suffering". However Freud admits that it is "particularly difficult to convince the
patient that this motive lies behind his continuing to be ill". Instead "he holds fast
to the more obvious explanation that treatment by analysis is not the right remedy
for his case". [S.E. 19: 49–50]

(though I prefer to call them *subconscious*). but Freud and his disciples, most perversely as I think, have insisted on making an entity, *the Unconscious*, a quasi-personification of all unconscious activities. This, it may be said, is a mere *façon de parler*; and surely men of science should be able to understand one another in spite of variations of terminology. But the difficulty is much more serious than one of terminology only. Freud panders to every vice of popular speech and thinking; and, by doing so, effectively appeals to the lay public (in matters psychological the medical men are part of the lay public) and puts his scientific critics at a grave disadvantage. The Freudian points to undeniable evidence of some particular subconscious activity and says: Well then how can you deny *the Unconscious*? It is like the famous counsel's question: Have you left off beating your wife? I answer that the recognition of subconscious activities is of the first importance; but *the Unconscious* is a fraudulent entity that has gravely obstructed the path of progress." [McDougall 1936: 18][6]

The employment of unconscious motivations as a general explanation of accidents or illness is frequently dependent on a circular argument, for the accident or illness in itself is often regarded as prime evidence for the presence of the unconscious forces. In a footnote added in 1923 to the Dora case history Freud writes: "The motive for being ill is, of course, invariably the intention of securing some gain." [S.E. 7: 43n] Given this basic assumption he will naturally interpret *every* illness of his patients in terms which supposedly reveal an advantage. In turn, such analyses are subsequently used as evidence for the validity of this principle.

Freud's whole system is in fact pervaded by circular arguments. For example, starting with the premiss that there are certain unconscious sexual processes, he implicitly utilises this premiss in his dream interpretations. He then claims that dreams can be used to demonstrate the existence of unconscious sexual processes. Again, at a very early stage he accepted the postulate (originally proposed by Griesinger [S.E. 4: 91]) that dreams represent the fulfilment of repressed wishes. Having made this assumption he interprets all dreams in these terms—and then uses his dream interpretations as further evidence for the original postulate.

---

[6]It is interesting to note that Breuer voiced a warning concerning this very point in *Studies on Hysteria*: "It is only too easy to fall into a habit of thought which assumes that every substantive has a substance behind it—which gradually comes to regard 'consciousness' as standing for some actual thing; and when we have become accustomed to make use metaphorically of spatial relations, as in the term 'sub-consciousness', we find as time goes on that we have actually formed an idea which has lost its metaphorical nature and which we can manipulate easily as though it was real. Our mythology is then complete." [S.E. 2: 227–28]

That psychoanalytic theory is fundamentally flawed by its dependence on circular arguments is demonstrated by a passage in the
Little Hans case history. Freud tells us that in a psychoanalysis "the
physician always gives his patient . . . the conscious anticipatory
ideas by the help of which he is put in a position to recognise and to
grasp the unconscious material", and in the same section he also
writes that "the information which the physician gives his patient is
itself derived from analytic experience". [S.E. 10: 104] But of course
it is the nature of a psychoanalysis that the "analytic experience" is
strongly influenced by the subjective notions of the physician who
supplies the "anticipatory ideas". As Freud himself admitted at that
time (though on no other occasion), this ensures that "a psychoanalysis is not an impartial scientific investigation" [104]; and, since
the findings of psychoanalysis are ultimately derived from such
procedures, implies a limitation of the claims that the methodology
is a means of discovering objective knowledge.

Freud's dictum that "applications of analysis are always confirmations of it as well" illustrates the circularity inherent in his customary method of demonstrating the validity of psychoanalytic
theses. In general, the process of analysis starts with Freud endeavouring to link symptoms, dream-elements, events, etc., in an
associative chain, which, given his fertile imagination, he invariably
is able to do. He then asserts that the very fact that he has made
such associations is itself evidence for the analytic significance of
the specific associative chain he has discovered, and also justification of the procedure. This is perhaps the most persuasive of all
the arguments utilised by Freud, but it is as fallacious as the more
obviously circular ones described above.

The explanatory power of his interpretations was repeatedly
invoked by Freud as evidence of their validity: "Whenever I began
to have doubts of the correctness of my wavering conclusions, the
successful transformation of a senseless and muddled dream into a
logical and intelligible mental process in the dreamer would renew
my confidence of being on the right track." [S.E. 22: 7] This argument from coherence, rather than therapeutic effectiveness, mostly
served to corroborate his theories. It is notable that the first publication written with the express purpose of substantiating his views
on the pathogenesis of hysterical symptoms was the Dora case history, relating to a patient whose condition showed "no noticeable
alteration" during the analysis [S.E. 7: 115], and who can in no way
be regarded as a therapeutic success. That the efficacy of his
treatment was not considered by Freud to be an essential criterion
by which to judge the truth of his theories is evident from a passage
in *Introductory Lectures* in which he states that even if psycho-

analysis was totally unsuccessful in this sense "it would still remain completely justified as an irreplaceable instrument of scientific research". [S.E. 16: 255] Consistent with this sentiment is what Fisher and Greenberg describe as the "striking" fact that "Freud chose to demonstrate the utility of psychoanalysis through descriptions of largely unsuccessful cases". [1977: 285] It was to the conviction ensuing from the impression of his having revealed meaningful connections between psychical occurrences that he generally appealed, and in this, at least, he has been highly successful in the case of a great many of his readers.[7]

With regard to some of the fundamental processes and concepts which he uses, we have already noted that Freud concedes "the large extent to which psychoanalysis coincides with the philosophy of Schopenhauer" [S.E. 20: 59], and he describes Nietzsche as "another philosopher whose guesses [sic] and intuitions often agree in the most astonishing way with the laborious findings of psychoanalysis" [60]; but he argues that the unique value of his work lies in his having "confirmed by sober and painstaking detailed research" conceptions which have been "guessed" by such "bold" thinkers. [S.E. 22: 107] Now, no one can doubt the immensity of the effort with which Freud devoted himself to the task of finding psychoanalytic explanations of psychological processes already described with great clarity by Schopenhauer, Nietzsche, and others. The question to be considered, however, is whether his speculative and often far-fetched analytic explications of these processes, of which a representative sample have been presented in this chapter and elsewhere in this book, really constitute the confirmations he claims. Certainly, in the course of his expositions there occur passages which show genuine psychological insight, but the specifically psychoanalytic theses which constitute the basic elements of his theoretical explications are often at best unsubstantiated, and at worst, little short of absurd. Hence, though he has undoubtedly done more than anyone to popularise the notion of unconscious mental activity, his claim to have made a unique contribution to the understanding of the processes involved cannot be sustained.

---

[7]Of the criteria for justifying the validity of his theories the argument from coherence was the one Freud used more often and more consistently than any other throughout his career. In "The Aetiology of Hysteria" (1896) it was "the relationship of the infantile scenes to the content of the whole of the rest of the case history" which he described as furnishing the strongest "proof", the ground on which "we become absolutely certain", of the reality of the sexual seductions he was then postulating as being at the root of his patients' neuroses. [S.E. 3: 205] In his last major work, *An Outline of Psychoanalysis*, he uses the same argument to justify the "plausible inferences" made in psychoanalysis: "The relative certainty of our psychical science is based on the binding force of these inferences." [S.E. 23: 159]

Psychoanalysis Assessed

In his not unsympathetic study *The Standing of Psychoanalysis* Farrell concludes that "the impact of psychoanalysis on the West cannot be justified on the ground that it contains a body of reasonably secure or established knowledge about human nature" for it "does not contain any such body of knowledge", and the popular belief that it does is a "delusion". He poses the question of how it has happened "that the stereotypical inhabitant of Hampstead, London, N.W.3 carries around with him (or her) such a mistaken view about the nature of psychoanalysis", and, more especially, "how has America succumbed to this delusion about Freud and analysis?" [Farrell 1981: 190] Gellner [1985] has attempted an explanation from a sociological and philosophical perspective, but the answer must also be sought more directly. Part of the story is that Freud himself believed so vehemently in the same delusion, and repeated it so emphatically and persuasively on so many occasions, that others came to be equally deceived. Another part of the answer, and perhaps the most important, lies in the false claims he made on behalf of psychoanalysis. Even had he been less successful in presenting himself as a man of integrity who had been disgracefully treated by the scientific community for merely trying to reveal unpalatable truths, few people would be prepared to entertain the notion that a man of such stature might be the source of widespread deception—namely, his frequent, emphatic, but generally quite false contention that his "discoveries" had been obtained from, or verified by, direct clinical evidence or observations.

To a great extent psychoanalysis was sold by the wholesale dissemination of plausible but unsubstantiated assertions, and by extravagant claims of therapeutic efficacy that Freud and his colleagues could not actually deliver. Other than this his success in gaining widespread acceptance of his ideas appears to be largely the result of the following contingencies: an extensive and ingenious use of psychological concepts (many of which were previously posited by others) within an explanatory mode of discourse of almost indefinite adaptability; voluminous writings in which he presented his ideas persuasively to a wide public; an exceptional literary skill, which included the talents of a great propagandist; and, finally, a team of dedicated disciples who were able to promote his ideas and at the same time perpetuate the legends which arose around him (and which largely originated from his own writings and those of his friend and biographer, Ernest Jones).

Yet when all that has been said there remains the fact that he has had an immense impact in the Western world; for many people his system of ideas has become the preferred idiom for the discussion of the human personality and of human relations. In large measure this stems from the fact that the thread which runs throughout the system, the notion that the motivation for much human behaviour may not be immediately conscious to the individual concerned, is of inestimable importance. No one else has written so extensively on this theme, and in doing so Freud has caught the imagination of writers and others for whom his armoury of psychological terms has proved to be a fertile source of inspiration; and, of course, a vast amount of literature pertaining to the psychological springs of human behaviour derives, directly or indirectly, from his writings.[8] More generally, some of the processes which find wide application within psychoanalysis, such as rationalisation, projection, and ambivalence, now play an indispensable role in our understanding of human behaviour.

The reverse side of this coin is, as McDougall says, that in practice Freud panders to every vice of popular speech and thinking. At times psychoanalytic explanations come close to being a modern-day version of the primitive superstition that at the root of all adverse experiences lie the activities of malevolent spirits. Swales has drawn attention to a passage in *The Psychopathology of Everyday Life* where Freud writes that "a striking . . . feature of the behaviour of paranoiacs is that they attach the greatest significance to the minor details of other people's behaviour which we ordinarily neglect, interpret them and make them the basis of far-reaching conclusions". [S.E. 6: 255] Now of course in such cases these conclusions generally have as their basis the idea that a malevolent agent is manipulating the behaviour in question; but if "analysts" are substituted for "paranoiacs" in the above quotation we have an apt description of much psychoanalytic theorising—only in this case the agency behind the behaviour is the devious Unconscious.

Under the influence of Freud's principle that "the motive for being ill is . . . invariably the intention of securing some gain" analysts (and like-minded therapists) may find an unconscious motivation for virtually any physical symptom. How pernicious such a notion can be if used indiscriminately is apparent from the experiences of the American neurosurgeon Irving Cooper. [Cooper 1973] He has recorded the stories of a number of children suffering from a rare and debilitating neuromuscular disease whose illnesses were diagnosed as "hysterical" and who, while the symptoms pro-

---

[8]Perhaps the most enduring aspect of Freud's work is that among this wide-ranging literature are to be found writings of considerable perspicacity and insight.

gressed and their incapacity increased, were subjected to extensive psychoanalytic investigations. It was only after they had endured some harrowing experiences that their disease was correctly diagnosed and successfully treated. The psychoanalytic explanations some of them were given earlier to account for their symptoms calls to mind Wittgenstein's scathing comment: "Freud's fanciful pseudo-explanations (precisely because they are so brilliant) perform a disservice. Now any ass has these pictures available to use in 'explaining' symptoms of illness." [Wittgenstein 1984: 55][9]

Notwithstanding such aberrations, many of Freud's ideas, such as the emphasis on the significance of childhood experiences for the development of personality, have come to play a major role in a wide range of therapies.[10] However, it is far from evident that psychoanalysis in particular, and psychotherapies involving only verbal interactions between patient and therapist in general, are particularly efficacious in resolving severe neurotic disorders. Over the years there have been a number of studies of the clinical results obtained by analysis, though unfortunately they have not been without methodological defects. Extensive reviews of these by Paul Kline (1972, 1981), and Fisher and Greenberg (1977), have concluded that there is no evidence that psychoanalysis is more effective than any other form of treatment. [Kline 1981: 398, 406; Fisher and Greenberg 1977: 341] Psychoanalytic practitioners have now had something like eighty years to produce substantive evidence that their procedure is superior to other approaches, and their failure to do so invites the conclusion that there is no justification for the claim that psychoanalysis is more thoroughgoing than its rivals, resulting in more long-lasting and profound changes. In fact, Edward Erwin has recently argued from his examination of the literature that as yet there is no firm evidence

---

[9]That Freud was well aware of the dangers in his approach is apparent from a passage in *The Interpretation of Dreams* in which he mentions the issue in relation to a misdiagnosis in the case of one of his patients. [S.E. 4: 109] There are two other occasions when he reports serious misdiagnoses in relation to patients suffering from organic disease, one in a footnote added to *The Psychopathology of Everyday Life* [S.E. 6: 146n], and the other in a letter to Fliess [Masson 1985: 411–12]

[10]As Freud himself observes, the idea that childhood experiences influence a person's development was scarcely new: "poets and students of human nature had always asserted" that "the impressions of [early childhood] left ineradical traces upon the individual's growth. . . ." [S.E. 20: 33] In fact Sulloway records that by the mid-1890s a theory of psychosexual pathology, postulating that precocious childhood sexual experiences may persist in the unconscious and subsequently influence adult behaviour, had been proposed by both Jules Dallemagne and Théodule Ribot independently of Freud's work. [Sulloway 1979: 287]

that psychoanalytic therapy is more effective than a placebo [Erwin 1988: 216], and Kline has responded by agreeing that "no good evidence exists that it is effective". [Kline 1988: 225][11]

Nevertheless, many people who undergo psychoanalysis are convinced they have benefited from their experience. Why this should be so in the face of the indications that analytically-based psychotherapy rarely produces radical behavioural changes is discussed by the experienced psychiatrist Bernie Zilbergeld in his book *The Shrinking of America*. [1983: 145] Analysis provides people with the opportunity for leisurely self-exploration and the security of a long relationship with a professional healer. It is quite possible that over a period of time patients will come to view certain circumstances differently, take more responsibility for their own behaviour, or adopt attitudes which reduce the difficulties they experience in their life. All of this is of value even in the absence of more extensive behavioural or symptomatic change, though it may well be that it could have been achieved in other ways at considerably less expense.[12]

The Appeal of Psychoanalysis

There is little doubt that a great part of the appeal of psychoanalysis results from its pretension that it is able to reveal the hidden meaning behind much of human behaviour. Michael Frayn [1974: 6] has observed that we are significance-seeking organisms; one might say human beings have a strong propensity to read meanings into events. Perhaps because of this the human mind is prone to accept too uncritically explanations which apparently encompass phenomena under consideration and purport to provide underlying mean-

---

[11]Of course a considerable number of psychoanalysts no longer adhere strictly to Freud's original formulations. However, as Macmillan has demonstrated in his *Freud Evaluated*, the many partial reformulations are generally as flawed as Freud's and the clinical and observational evidence relevant to them just as weak. [Macmillan 1991: 575]

[12]In the face of the indications that psychoanalytic therapy is of limited value, sympathetic commentators are apt to at least give Freud credit for pioneering the custom of allowing patients extensive time in which to communicate their concerns in a congenial atmosphere. However, Ellenberger records that this is by no means so, Janet and Bleuler and many others before them having practised forms of psychotherapy incorporating this feature. [Ellenberger 1970: 521] In fact, it is interesting to note that at the International Congress of Medicine in 1909 Friedländer complained that psychoanalysts talked "as if, before Freud, no hysterical patient was ever cured, and no psychotherapy ever practised". [803]

ings and motivations. Psychoanalysis has prospered largely because, with its armoury of interpretive devices, it is never at a loss for such explanations, an achievement which many find impressive.

This no doubt accounts, in large measure, for the fact that Freud's forays into anthropology, social psychology, and psycho-history have been favourably received in some quarters, in spite of the occasional exposure of their inadequacies (most notably, feebly substantiated inferences and gross factual errors) by authorities in these fields. The psychoanalytic notions on which he erects the theoretical foundations of such theses are precisely those which buttress his theories of individual development, such as the Oedipus and castration complexes, with the consequence that the narratives are correspondingly highly speculative and often wildly improbable. His characteristically tendentious approach, frequently involving a cavalier disregard of inconvenient facts and the erection of analytically-inspired reconstructions on the flimsiest of evidential grounds, limits the value of Freud's enquiries in these fields.

These considerations have not materially diminished the esteem with which the essays in question are regarded by his admirers, though they have to retreat to a less vulnerable position in the face of the well-founded criticisms referred to above. Such expositions, we are told, should be judged not so much in terms of correspond-ence to truth but in terms of persuasive coherence, an approach alleged to characterise current philosophical views on the judgement of scientific paradigms. [Cocks and Crosby 1987: xii] What is important is not the literal accordance with the facts but the wealth of psychological insight which Freud brings to his discourse. This argument might have greater force were it not for the fact that these insights are essentially the same as those to be found elsewhere in his writings, most notably in the case histories, in regard to which the reader not enamoured of psychoanalytic modes of inference is more likely to be struck by Freud's misconceptions than by his perceptive-ness. That is not to say that the sociological and anthropological essays are devoid of perspicacious passages in regard to group behaviour, only that this aspect has been exaggerated in comparison to the improbable speculations which inform much of the material.

Macmillan lists among the basic deficiencies of Freud's theoreti-cal structures the use of assumptions having no empirical referents, and the reliance on uncharacterised theoretical terms. [Macmillan 1991: 199] Undoubtedly it is precisely these characteristics which in large measure account for the continuing popularity of psycho-analysis with many who work in various branches of the humanities, and most notably with writers and literary critics; as Macmillan observes, psychoanalytic explanations appeal to such groups because they already have a high tolerance for other equally indeterminate endeavours. [605] The prevalence of psychoanalytic modes of thought in certain kinds of philosophical and literary discourse owes much to its almost indefinite interpretive potential, and those proficient in endeavours of this nature are unlikely to relinquish such a versatile resource. In this context it is perhaps apposite to note the words of Fisher and Greenberg in respect to theoretical developments arising from Freud's formulations: "The diversity of the secondary elaborations of Freud's ideas is so Babel-like as to defy the derivation of sensible deductions that can be put to empirical test." [1977: ix] Psychoanalytic discourse lends itself to such an abundance of elaborations because it consists to a considerable extent of ill-defined conceptions which can be manipulated in line with the preferences and prejudices of the writer with little regard to the need to accord with a reality beyond those conceptions. This explains why so many of Freud's admirers are unfazed by demonstrations of the insubstantiality of his clinical claims, and of the inconsistencies and factual errors in his writings; their conceptual world free-floats in regions largely beyond such mundane considerations.

Storr contends that because psychoanalysis has had such an inescapable influence upon our thinking it must resonate with something deep within us. [Storr 1989: 128] But since in his recent book he takes issue with almost all of Freud's specific theories (and at one point comes close to suggesting that his major achievement was to be a fertile source of false hypotheses from which much has been learned in the process of refuting them [127]), this is not entirely convincing.[13] It is arguable that what psychoanalysis resonates with is the human propensity to rationalise and seek meaning, because it provides an all-encompassing body of concepts and formulas that, with a little practice, almost anyone can apply. Those who wish to avail themselves of psychoanalytic modes of thought have the assurance of access to an abundant source of explanations in any field of human activity. Also pertinent is the fact that, as we saw in the

---

[13]After a critical evaluation of relevant experimental studies, Kline concludes that certain of Freud's theories have received some degree of corroboration. [Kline 1972, 1981] However, the studies in question have been challenged by Erwin on one or more of the following grounds: 1. they are over-reliant on projective tests, the validity of which has not been independently established; 2. in some cases the hypotheses, though perhaps suggested by Freudian theory, were not genuinely psychoanalytic hypotheses; 3. credible rivals to the Freudian hypothesis being tested were not ruled out. [Erwin 1988: 221] Whatever the respective merits of Erwin's critique and Kline's subsequent rejoinder [Kline 1988: 225–232], claims of even limited experimental corroboration of Freud's theories remain highly contentious.

last chapter, a number of important insights, such as the notion of unconscious motivations, actually predate psychoanalysis and are consistent with views at variance with it. The assimilation of such notions (given Freud's presentation one might say "appropriation") into the Freudian schema lends some credence to Storr's contention, but perhaps more apposite is Gellner's observation in the same context: "Freud did not discover the Unconscious. What he did was to endow it with a language, a ritual, and a church." [Gellner 1985: 207]

There can be no disputing the fact that Freud was a man of extraordinary gifts who left a remarkable body of work. What is difficult to predict at this stage is what aspects of his legacy will remain part of our intellectual heritage, and how much will come to be regarded, in Peter Medawar's words, as "the most stupendous intellectual confidence trick of the twentieth century" [Medawar 1984: 140]. For the foreseeable future there is little doubt that psychoanalysis will retain its influential role in literary and artistic fields, and to a rather more limited extent in the humanities in general. Its unlimited capacity for furnishing motivations for human behaviour and explanations of symptoms is also likely to ensure its continuing popularity with many psychotherapists and counsellors, anxious to acquire insights into their clients' troubles. However, in the fields of academic psychology and psychiatry it is likely that Freud will increasingly be seen as a figure who influenced our ways of seeing ourselves, yet ultimately added little to our knowledge of the workings of the mind. More generally, while it is just to acknowledge his pioneering role in inaugurating an era of wide-ranging deliberations into the nature of the human mind, recent critical studies of his life and work indicate that a radical reassessment of his perceived stature is long overdue. It may well be that the rise of psychoanalysis to a position of prominence in the twentieth century will come to be regarded as one of the most extraordinary aberrations in the history of Western thought.

Bibliography

Abraham, Hilda C., and Freud, Ernst L. (eds.) *A Psychoanalytic Dialogue: The Letters of Sigmund Freud and Karl Abraham, 1907–1926,* trans. by Bernard Marsh and Hilda C. Abraham. London: Hogarth Press and the Institute of Psycho-Analysis, 1965.

Altshule, Mark. *Origins of Concepts in Human Behavior.* New York: Wiley, 1977.

Appiganesi, Lisa, and Forrester, John. *Freud's Women.* London: Weidenfeld and Nicholson, 1992.

Bernfeld, Siegfried. An Unknown Autobiographical Fragment by Freud. *American Imago,* Vol. 4, No. 1, pp. 3–19, 1946.

Billinsky, John M. Jung and Freud (The End of a Romance). *Andover Newton Quarterly,* Vol. 10, No. 2, pp. 39–43, 1969.

Brome, Vincent. *Freud and His Disciples.* London: Caliban, 1984.

Brunswick, Ruth Mack. A Note on the Childish Theory of Coitus A Tergo. *International Journal of Psycho-Analysis,* Vol. 10, pp. 93–95, 1929.

Bry, Ilse, and Rifkin, Alfred H. Freud and the History of Ideas: Primary Sources, 1886–1910. In *Science and Psychoanalysis,* edited by Masserman, Jules H. Vol. 5: *Psychoanalytic Education,* pp. 6–36. New York: Grune and Stratton, 1962.

Byck, Robert. *Cocaine Papers by Sigmund Freud.* Edited and with an Introduction by Robert Byck. New York: Stonehill, 1974.

Cioffi, Frank (ed.) *Freud: Modern Judgements.* London: Macmillan, 1973.

———. Was Freud a Liar? *The Listener,* 91, pp. 172–74, 7th February, 1974.

———. Freud—New Myths to Replace the Old. *New Society,* 29th November, 1979.

———. The Cradle of Neurosis. *Times Literary Supplement,* 6th July, 1984.

———. Psychoanalysis, Pseudo-Science and Testability. In G. Currie and A. Musgrave (eds.) *Popper and the Human Sciences,* pp. 13–44. Dordrecht: Nijhoff, 1985.

———. 'Exegetical Myth-Making' in Grünbaum's Indictment of Popper and Exoneration of Freud. In P. Clark and C. Wright (eds.), *Mind, Psychoanalysis, and Science,* pp. 61–87. Oxford: Blackwell, 1988.

Cocks, G., and Crosby, T.L. (eds.) *Psycho/History: Readings in the Method of Psychology, Psychoanalysis, and History.* New Haven: Yale University Press, 1987.

Clarke, Ronald W. *Freud: The Man and the Cause.* London: Jonathan Cape/Weidenfeld and Nicholson, 1980. (Paperback edition: Paladin/Granada, 1982.)

Cooper, Irving S. *The Victim is Always the Same.* New York: Harper and Row, 1973.

Crews, Frederick. *Skeptical Engagements.* New York: Oxford University Press, 1986.

Eagle, Maurice. The Epistemological Status of Recent Developments in Psychoanalysis. In R.S. Cohen and L. Laudan (eds.), *Physics, Philosophy, and Psychoanalysis,* pp. 31–55. Dordrecht: Reidel, 1983.

Edmunds, Lavinia. His Master's Choice. Johns Hopkins Magazine, Vol. xxxx, No. 2, April 1988.

Ellenberger, Henri F. *The Discovery of the Unconscious.* New York: Basic Books, 1970.

_____. The Story of 'Anna O.': A Critical Review with New Data. *Journal of the History of the Behavioral Sciences,* Vol. 8, pp. 267–279, 1972.

Elms, Alan C. Freud and Minna. *Psychology Today,* Vol. 16, No. 12, pp. 40–46, December 1982.

Erwin, Edward. Psychoanalysis: How Firm is the Evidence? *Nous,* 14, pp. 443–456, 1980.

_____. Psychoanalysis: Clinical Versus Experimental Evidence. In P. Clark and C. Wright (eds.), *Mind, Psychoanalysis, and Science,* pp. 205–223. Oxford: Blackwell, 1988.

Farrell, B. A. *The Standing of Psychoanalysis.* Oxford: Oxford University Press, 1981.

Fisher, S. and Greenberg, R. P. *The Scientific Credibility of Freud's Theory and Therapy.* New York: Basic Books, 1977.

Forrester, John. *Language and the Origins of Psychoanalysis.* London: Macmillan; New York: Columbia University Press, 1980.

Frayn, Michael. *Constructions.* London: Wildwood House, 1974.

Freud, Ernst (ed.) *Letters of Sigmund Freud, 1873–1939,* trans. by Tania and James Stern. London: Hogarth Press, 1961; New York: Basic Books, 1975.

Freud, Sigmund. *Standard Edition of the Complete Psychological Works of Sigmund Freud,* trans. by J. Strachey et al. London: Hogarth Press, 1953–1974 [S.E.].

_____. *Two Short Accounts of Psychoanalysis,* trans. by James Strachey, with a sketch of his life and ideas by J. Strachey. Harmondsworth: Penguin, 1962.

Fromm, Erich. *Greatness and Limitations of Freud's Thought.* London: Cape, 1980. (Paperback edition: Abacus/Sphere, 1982.)

Galdston, Iago. Freud and Romantic Medicine. In F. Cioffi (ed.), *Freud: Modern Judgements.* London: Macmillan, 1973.

Gardiner, Muriel M. (ed.) *The Wolf Man and Sigmund Freud.* New York: Basic Books, 1971: London: Hogarth Press, 1972.

———. Wolf Man's Last Years. *Journal of the American Psychoanalytic Association,* Vol. 31, pp. 867–897, 1983.

Gay, Peter. *Freud: A Life for Our Time.* New York: Norton, 1988.

———. *Reading Freud.* New Haven: Yale University Press, 1990.

Gellner, Ernest. *The Psychoanalytic Movement.* London: Paladin/Granada, 1985.

Glover, Edward. The Therapeutic Effect of Inexact Interpretation: A Contribution to the Theory of Suggestion. *International Journal of Psycho-Analysis,* Vol. 12, pp. 397–411, 1931.

———. Research Methods in Psychoanalysis. *International Journal of Psycho-Analysis,* Vol. 33, pp. 404–09, 1952.

Glymour, Clark. The Theory of Your Dreams. In R.S. Cohen and L. Laudan (eds.), *Physics, Philosophy, and Psychoanalysis,* pp. 57–71. Dordrecht: Reidel, 1983.

Grünbaum, Adolf. *The Foundations of Psychoanalysis.* Berkeley: University of California Press, 1984.

Hale, Nathan G., Jr. (ed.) *James Jackson Putnam and Psychoanalysis: Letters between Putnam and Sigmund Freud, Ernest Jones, William James, Sandor Ferenczi, and Morton Prince, 1877–1917,* trans. by Judith Bernays Heller. Cambridge, Mass.: Harvard University Press, 1971.

Hofstadter, Douglas R., and Dennett, Daniel C. *The Mind's I.* Hassocks: Harvester, 1981.

Jahoda, Marie. *Freud and the Dilemmas of Psychology.* London: Hogarth Press, 1977.

Johnston, William M. *The Austrian Mind: An Intellectual and Social History 1848–1938.* Berkeley: University of California Press, 1972.

Jones, Ernest. *Sigmund Freud: Life and Work.* Vol. 1, *The Young Freud, 1856–1900;* Vol. 2, *The Years of Maturity, 1901–1919;* Vol. 3, *The Last Phase, 1919–1939.* London: Hogarth Press, 1953, 1955, 1957.

Jung, Carl G. *Collected Works of C.G. Jung.* Sir Herbert Read, Michael Fordham and Gerhard Adler (eds.), trans. by R.F.C. Hull, Vol. 4, *Freud and Psychoanalysis.* London: Routledge, 1961.

———. *Memories, Dreams, Reflections.* Recorded and edited by Aniela Jaffé, trans. by Richard and Clara Winston. London: Collins and Routledge and Kegan Paul, 1963.

Kern, Stephen. Freud and the History of Child Sexuality. *History of Childhood Quarterly,* Vol. 1, pp. 117–141, 1973.

Kiell, Norman (ed.) *Freud Without Hindsight: Reviews of His Work (1893–1939).* New York: International Universities Press, 1988.

Kline, Paul. *Fact and Fantasy in Freudian Theory.* London: Methuen, 1972, 1981.

———. Psychoanalysis: Clinical versus Experimental Evidence. In P. Clark and C. Wright (eds.), *Mind, Psychoanalysis, and Science,* pp. 225–232. Oxford: Blackwell, 1988.

Krüll, Marianne. *Freud and His Father,* trans. by J. Pomerans. London: Hutchinson, 1987.

Lasch, Christopher. *The Minimal Self.* New York: Norton, 1985. (Paperback edition, London: Picador/Pan, 1985.)

McDougall, William. *An Outline of Abnormal Psychology.* London: Methuen, 1926.

———. *Psychoanalysis and Social Psychology.* London: Methuen, 1936.

McGuire, William (ed.) *The Freud/Jung Letters: The Correspondence between Sigmund Freud and C.G. Jung,* trans. by Ralph Manheim and R.C.F. Hull. London: Hogarth Press and Routledge, 1974.

Macmillan, Malcolm. *Freud Evaluated.* Amsterdam: Elsevier, 1991.

Magee, Bryan. *The Philosophy of Schopenhauer.* Oxford: Oxford University Press, 1983.

Mahony, Patrick J. *Cries of the Wolf Man.* New York: International Universities Press, 1984.

———. *Freud and the Rat Man.* New Haven and London: Yale University Press, 1986.

Malcolm, Norman. *Ludwig Wittgenstein: A Memoir.* Oxford: Oxford University Press, 1984.

Masson, Jeffrey, M. *The Assault on Truth: Freud's Suppression of the Seduction Theory.* New York: Farrar, Straus, and Giroux, 1984.

———. *The Complete Letters of Sigmund Freud to Wilhelm Fliess 1887–1904.* Cambridge Mass.: Harvard University Press, 1985.

Medawar, Peter. *Pluto's Republic.* Oxford: Oxford University Press, 1982. (Paperback edition: 1984.)

Mitchell, Juliet. *Psychoanalysis and Feminism.* London: Allen Lane, 1974. (Paperback edition: Penguin, 1975.)

Nunberg, Herman, and Federn, Ernst (eds.) *Minutes of the Vienna Psychoanalytic Society.* New York: International Universities Press, 1962–75.

Obholtzer, Karin. *The Wolf Man Sixty Years Later,* trans. by Michael Shaw. London: Routledge, 1982.

Pfeiffer, Ernst (ed.) *Sigmund Freud and Lou Andreas-Salomé Letters,* trans. by William and Elaine Robson Scott. London: Hogarth Press, 1972.

Raphael, Frederick. A Beard in the Hand. *New Statesman,* pp. 50–51, 9th July, 1976.

Rieff, Philip. *Freud: The Mind of a Moralist.* London: Gollancz, 1959.

Roazen, Paul. *Freud and His Followers.* New York: Knopf, 1975.

———. *Encountering Freud.* New Brunswick: Transaction, 1989.

Rosenzweig, Saul. *Freud and Experimental Psychology: The Emergence of Idiodynamics.* New York: McGraw-Hill, 1986.

Schatzman, Morton. Freud: Who Seduced Whom?.*New Scientist,* 21st March, 1992, pp. 34–37.

Schur, Max. Some Additional 'Day Residues' of 'The Specimen Dream of Psychoanalysis'. In R.M. Lowenstein, L.M. Newman, M. Schur and A.J. Solnit (eds.), *Psychoanalysis—A General Psychology,* pp. 45–85. New York: International Universities Press, 1966.

————. *Freud: Living and Dying.* London: Hogarth Press, 1972.

Stadlen, Anthony. Was Dora 'Ill'?. In Laurence Spurling (ed.), *Sigmund Freud: Critical Assessments,* Vol. 2, pp. 193–203. London: Routledge, 1989.

Steele, Robert S. *Freud and Jung: Conflicts of Interpretations.* London: Routledge, 1982.

Storr, Anthony. *Freud.* Oxford: Oxford University Press, 1989.

Sulloway, Frank J. *Freud: Biologist of the Mind.* New York: Basic Books, 1979.

Swales, Peter J. Freud, Minna Bernays, and the Conquest of Rome: New Light on the Origins of Psychoanalysis. *The New American Review,* Spring/Summer, 1982.

————. Freud, Cocaine, and Sexual Chemistry: The Role of Cocaine in Freud's Conception of the Libido. Privately published monograph, 1983.

Szasz, Thomas. *Karl Kraus and the Soul Doctors.* London: Routledge, 1977.

————. *The Myth of Psychotherapy.* New York: Oxford University Press, 1979.

Tannenbaum, S.A. Analyzing a Freudian Analysis. *Journal of Abnormal and Social Psychology,* Vol. 18, pp. 246–257, 1922.

Thornton, E.M., *Freud and Cocaine: The Freudian Fallacy.* London: Blond and Briggs, 1983.

Timpanaro, Sebastiano. *The Freudian Slip: Psychoanalysis and Texual Criticism,* trans. by Kate Soper. London: New Left Books, 1976. (Paperback edition: Verso, 1985.)

Trotter W. *Instincts of the Herd in Peace and War.* London: Scientific Book Club, 1916.

Veith, Ilza.*Hysteria.* Chicago: University of Chicago Press, 1965.

Wells, F.L. Critique of Impure Reason. *Journal of Abnormal Psychology,* Vol. 7, pp. 89–93, 1912.

Whyte, Lancelot Law, *The Unconscious Before Freud.* New York: Basic Books, 1960.

Wittgenstein, Ludwig. *Manuscripts.* Oxford: Oxford University Press, 1984.

Wortis, Joseph. *Fragments of an Analysis with Freud*. New York: Simon and Schuster, 1954.

Zilbergeld, Bernie. *The Shrinking of America: Myths of Psychological Change*. Boston: Little, Brown, 1983.

Index

case studies of, 53–93; persuasiveness of, 205–18; psychoanalytic concepts of, 219–39;
standards of reporting and ethical considerations of, 95–132;
theoretical revisions of, 191–
204
The Freudian Slip (Timpanaro),
98, 160
Freudian slips. *See* slips
(parapraxes)
Frink, Doris, 122–23
Frink, Dr. Horace, 121–23
"From the History of an Infantile
Neurosis", 67, 88
Fromm, Erich, 69
"Further Remarks on the Neuro–
Psychoses of Defence", 15, 16,
17, 21, 112–13

Galdston, Iago, 221
Galton, Sir Francis, 222n
Gardiner, Muriel, 67, 69–72, 81,
117, 156–57
gastralgia, 5
Gaupp, Robert, 238n
Gay, Peter, 11–12, 98n
Gellner, Ernest, 205n, 248, 254
Glover, Edward, 199–200, 227n
Glymour, Clark, 30n, 114, 190n
Greek sophists, 169, 171
Griesinger, Wilhelm, 245
Groddeck, Georg, 229
"Group Psychology", 195–96
Grünbaum, Adolf, 191
Grusha, 77–93, 107, 110. *See also*
Wolf Man case history
guilt, 122, 244n

haemorrhages, 6–8, 72
Hale, Nathan G., 79, 86
hallucinations, 2, 122
Herbart, Johann F., 159n, 221,
223–24
"Heredity and the Aetiology of
the Neurosis", 16, 17, 26n, 112n

Herr K., 37–47, 49–51
heterosexuality, 108, 242
Hirshmüller, Albrecht, 131n
Hofstadter, Douglas R., and
Dennett, Daniel C., 220
Holmes, Sherlock, 107
homosexuality, 41, 61, 73–74,
100–105, 108–9, 122–23, 192,
194, 242, 244
hostility, 57, 60, 66, 137–38, 144,
147, 155, 158, 187, 196, 214,
234
hydrotherapy, 3
hypnosis, 2–3, 75, 82, 89n, 218,
222n, 236
hysteria, 2–5, 7–8, 12–20, 22, 26–
27, 29n, 35–37, 43, 45, 50, 55,
99–100, 111, 112n, 126–27, 130,
131, 135n, 189, 209n, 211, 213,
215, 221n, 246, 249–50, 251n
Hysteria (Veith), 221n
"Hysterical Attacks", 99
hysterical paralysis, 2
"Hysterical Phantasies", 18

id, 221–22, 229–30
incest, 14–15, 28n, 30, 75, 137,
139n, 187, 195–96, 207
infantile amnesia. *See* amnesia
infantile animal phobias, 56–60,
62, 64, 68, 70–71, 155–58, 194,
231
infantile masturbation, 21, 25,
27n, 28n, 34, 42–43, 53–54, 64–
66, 140–43, 149, 192, 201n
infantile phantasies theory. *See*
unconscious phantasies theory
infantile seduction theory, x, 11–
31, 33–36, 55, 56n, 95, 110–14,
126, 133, 134n, 135n, 136, 138–
39, 145n, 146, 148, 157, 159,
170, 192, 201, 203, 209, 215,
247n
infantile sexuality, 33–34, 53, 56,
61, 91n, 111–12, 131n, 132, 133,
134n, 135–36, 137, 139, 140,
143, 153–57, 159–60, 191, 196,